On the Political Economy of Social Democracy

John Cathcart Weldon

On the Political Economy of Social Democracy: Selected Papers of J.C. Weldon

Arranged and Edited with a Preface
and Introduction
by Allen Fenichel and
Sidney H. Ingerman

McGill-Queen's University Press
Montreal & Kingston • London • Buffalo

© McGill-Queen's University Press 1991
ISBN 0-7735-0812-0

Legal deposit first quarter 1991
Bibliothèque nationale du Québec

Printed in Canada on acid-free paper

Canadian Cataloguing in Publication Data

Weldon, J.C. (John Cathcart)
On the political economy of social democracy
ISBN 0-7735-0812-0
1. Canada – Economic Policy – 1971–
2. Socialism – Canada. I. Fenichel, A.H. (Allen
Howard), 1936–   II. Ingerman, Sidney,
1928–   III. Title.
JC507.W44 1991   335.5'0971   C90-090513-1

This text was typeset in 10/12 Times by
Typo Litho composition inc.

Contents

Acknowledgments

There are a number of people to whom we owe a debt of gratitude. T.K. Rymes provided us with an evaluation of our original proposal. Lee Soderstrom had a significant role in the choice of articles to be included in the volume and in the development of the Introduction. Robin Rowley and A. Asimakopulos provided valuable comments on sections of the text. Finally, Maria Orsini-Marcheschi assisted with the typing of the manuscript.

We would also like to recognize the generous contribution made by the Douglas-Caldwell Foundation and the McGill Faculty of Arts in support of publishing costs.

Preface: John Cathcart Weldon, 1922–87

John Cathcart Weldon was a social democrat. This philosophic commitment is reflected in his writings on economic and social policy, in the role he played in the New Democratic Party, in his willingness to support and assist unions, and in his efforts to achieve social justice in Canada. Political leaders, legislators, and technicians consulted him frequently and had confidence in his technical expertise as well as in his political judgement. But it worked two ways: he never hesitated to indicate dissent when he believed public policy was going astray.

Weldon's activism was not limited to the realm of ideas. In the early 1950s, he prepared the economic analysis for the anti-combines cases in the sugar industry. During the 1960s and 1970s, he played an important role as an adviser, consultant, and conciliation board representative of Canadian railway unions. When the New Democratic Party first came to power in Manitoba, he spent two years (1970–72) as the secretary of the Planning and Priorities Committee of the Manitoba cabinet.

His professional career was centred at McGill University where, for a quarter of a century, he was the William Dow Professor of Political Economy. He made significant contributions in various areas of economic theory, including utility theory, monetary theory, and the theory of intergenerational transfers. Weldon's analysis of the role of the state in the economy is intimately related to his theoretical preoccupations. Beginning in the late 1970s, he devoted an increasing amount of his time to the history of economic thought. During the last two years of his life, he was editing the extensive teaching notes he had prepared on the history of economic thought, but this work was not completed at the time of his death.

Weldon's class lectures were carefully prepared and stimulating, and he regularly provided his students with class notes that were insightful and often original elements of economic analysis. He was the most active supervisor of graduate student theses in the McGill University Department of

Economics, and many of his students are now making important contributions in economic theory and in the development and implementation of economic policy.

Recognition of Weldon's academic achievements was marked by his election as a Fellow of the Royal Society of Canada in 1975, and by his election as President of the Canadian Economics Association for its 1975–6 term.

Weldon was often at the centre of controversy. He opposed the arbitrary use of bureacratic power and those who would use it for self-advancement. As a founder and later president of the McGill Association of University Teachers, he was a pioneer in the organization of university teachers in Canada. When that association evolved into a "company union," he became an active member and officer of the McGill Faculty Union, which seeks collective bargaining rights with the university. At McGill, there was a continual stream of academic and nonacademic employees who sought his advice and assistance in fighting bureaucratic injustice. In 1978, along with his colleague A. Asimakopulos, he began a fight against the politicalization of promotion decisions in the Department of Economics by university administrators. This is a battle which has yet to be satisfactorily resolved. In the curriculum vitae he prepared in 1986, Weldon wrote, "this battle for academic values, I hope, will have been of some use to McGill, but in any event ... [it] seems to me the chief contribution of my academic life."

Weldon was born in 1922 in Magpie Mine, Ontario, but he grew up in east-end Montreal. He received an undergraduate degree in economics and political science from McGill University in 1947 and his doctoral degree from McGill in 1952. His professional career at McGill began in 1949 and continued until his death in 1987.

Jack Weldon was our colleague for over twenty years. Intellectually and (for many of these years) administratively he guided McGill's Department of Economics. He did so democratically; all views and interests were encouraged. Jack was a man of compassion, humour, and tolerance. It was a joy and a privilege to have been associated with him all of these years.

Introduction

This book contains a collection of papers written by John Cathcart Weldon on the role of government in the economy. Two central questions run through the papers that have been chosen: To what degree should the state actively intervene in the economy? And by what means should the state intervene? The papers appear during a quarter of a century, beginning in 1961, and they reflect the approach of a Canadian social democrat to political economy during this period. However, the questions that are dealt with in these papers are of more than Canadian interest. They are now in the forefront of economic policy debates in almost all industrialized countries.

The role of the state in the economy has been at the centre of political debate in market-oriented economies since the rise of neoconservatism in the 1970s. Thatcherism and Reaganism have provided the most dramatic examples of efforts to reduce the scope of government economic intervention. Within the developing European Community, a discussion of the role of government social programs has accompanied the planned next stage of integration in 1992. This discussion concerns the steps that are needed to facilitate increased labour mobility among countries in the community while at the same time protecting workers' rights. A social charter of workers' rights is the proposed solution, but Prime Minister Thatcher has denounced such a charter as a threat to business competitiveness.

In Eastern Europe and the Soviet Union, the role of the market and the state in the economy has been a topic of discussion and experimentation for some time. But the legacy of repressed democracy and unsatisfactory economic performance has created the conditions for dramatic changes in the political economy of these countries. As they move towards different forms of governance, they are also groping for the appropriate roles for the state and the market in the economy.

Given the globalization of international economic relations, will government economic policies in developed industrial countries converge towards a variant of *laissez-faire* capitalism or towards the economic interventionism

characteristic of social democracy? And what will determine the likely course
of government economic activity in Canada, with both a "small open economy," highly integrated into the American economy, and a history of
European-style state interventions in the form of Crown corporations and
in the provision of universal social benefits?

Weldon's contributions to political economy provide the means to treat
many of these questions. His analyses of the role of the state in the economy
are from the perspective of an economist who continually draws upon the
full range of ideas available from the history of economic thought. His work
does not place him in any particular school of economics, nor was he wedded
to any particular paradigm. He understood economics as being made up of
the accumulation of accepted economic knowledge in the form of theory,
technique, and description of economic events.

The limits within which Weldon worked are captured in the following
quotation from his article "On Social Policies in the Canadian Economy,
1986":

In this essay the outside world is given. Issues in relation to the great powers, issues
in relation to the third world, these are so vast that one leaves them entirely to other
studies and better informed writers. I think that reflection on *domestic* policy (facts
and logic both) is a precondition for serious work about the outside world. (p. 110)

This is the methodology of the social scientist seeking to deal with dis-
provable propositions by limiting the number of interrelated variables in a
system. It is a means to establish clearly what exists in Canada so as to
make possible comparisons of policy with other countries. The outside world
is not ignored; its effects are relevant and accounted for, whether they be
lessons learned from the postwar planning experience in Britain and France
or international trading arrangements that affect Canadian commercial
policy.

The papers that have been selected for this book contain much of Weldon's
contribution to an understanding of the economic basis for social democratic
policy and his view of the goals to which such policy must be devoted. He
believed that government economic and social policy in Canada must have
as its central goal a full-employment economy with a more equitable distribution of income than presently exists. His principal concern was with
political will: the motivation of those who are elected to govern vigorously
to use available economic techniques to achieve social goals.

THE ECONOMICS OF SOCIAL DEMOCRACY

Weldon's early articles on political economy, originally published in the
1960s, point out that the propensity of the left to see nationalization and

public ownership as the primary tools of economic policy did not take account of the limitations of these policies. In "On the Economics of Social Democracy," published in *Social Purposes for Canada* (a collection of writings by leading intellectuals of the democratic left) he wrote:

[T]here is no reason to invest nationalization and public ownership with moral qualities, as processes that make a more than technical contribution to the good of society. They are instruments of economic control, neither good nor bad in themselves, and are to be used pragmatically and without hesitation whenever they promise advantage over other instruments of control. (p. 5)

Two decades later, he returns to this same theme in opposing the attack from the right on public ownership under the banner of "privatization."

He also warns that public ownership does not necessarily equal public control. State enterprises may be controlled by special interests and not be responsive to consumer needs or to the well-being of their employees, even when there are democratically elected governments.

Weldon's discussions of the limitations of nationalization and public ownership are coupled with explanations of the wide range of other techniques that are available to achieve social democratic goals. Most importantly, he stresses the necessity of taking advantage of the economic benefits that come from private ownership and the market, so long as economic planning takes account of activities that the private sector cannot effectively carry out or cannot carry out without regulation. It is government that has the *full responsibility* for national economic performance and it is government that must coordinate and plan in order to fulfill this responsibility.

When the neoconservative political tide and its theoretical justifications inundated economics in the 1970s, Weldon argued that these developments were an aberration from the mainstream evolution of economics.

By the end of the 1980s professional opinion and the needs of policy makers were moving the economics profession away from neoconservatism and back into the mainstream of the development of economic theory and policy. Monetarism and supply-side economics are now viewed as having been costly fads, while more recent rational expectation models, which conclude that government economic policy at best is irrelevant to economic welfare, have made their adherents irrelevant to vital areas of economic policy making. In Western Europe (excluding Britain) rational expectations models are virtually ignored by economists. In the United States, an influential group of economists is responding to the bankruptcy of the rational expectations and kindred macroeconomic models by reasserting Keynesian ideas adapted to current circumstances.[1] Weldon's discussions of Keynesian policy and the need to develop regional and local applications of these policies remain highly relevant.

In his submission to the Special Joint Committee On Canada's International Relations in 1985, Weldon was doubtful that a Canadian bilateral free trade agreement with the United States would take place. He declared that "If some radical movement towards such trade were in prospect I would be very worried indeed. We would have placed our political identity and our social programmes at risk for small economic 'gains' quite likely to prove losses."[2] As we write this introduction in early 1990, the first stage of the Mulroney–Reagan trade agreement is in force and a second stage that will deal with subsidies is next on the negotiating agenda. In these negotiations the nature of our social programs will be at issue. Debate is far from over about the future of the agreement. The initial employment and job losses caused by the agreement have been compounded by a slowdown of the economy, while benefits of the agreement are still hard to discern.

Weldon was not opposed to free trade, and his interpretation of a social democratic view on this question is pertinent to the current stage of the debate on this question. His objection to the bilateral Mulroney–Reagan proposal was in part related to the claims that were being made for the agreement by its proponents.

[A] harmful repercussion is the public search for simplistic policy that shifts the burden from democratic, interventionist governments to govern. The hopes attached to pure free trade expect market forces to be magical. They bring to mind similar hopes attached to monetarism, to nationalization of all means of production, and in earlier days to bimetallism and to single-tax panaceas.[3]

In "On the Economics of Social Democracy," he wrote that under Canadian conditions "the logic of social democracy leads to an active sponsorship of free trade, or at least trade that is much freer than it is now" (p. 18). But this support was predicated on the coexistence of economic planning.

Yet although it is a policy promising the greatest general advantage it can hardly be pursued except within the framework of the planned economy. The pace of transition must be controlled, compensation must be devised for areas and industries that are dependent on the old arrangements. Even after transition the guarantees of planning are essential. A shift to free trade lengthens the list of forces affecting the domestic economy. Their inevitable fluctuations must be offset, or else those they threaten will insist on protection, no matter what the general benefits from trade. To realize the gains from trade, economic security must be assured at home. (p. 18)

In his 1985 submission to the Special Joint Committee On Canada's International Relations, he took the same position but used the term "industrial strategy" instead of "economic planning."

In his writings on political economy, Weldon insists that government has the technical means to achieve the economic goals of social democracy, but the crucial question for him is whether or not there is the *political will* to carry out such a program in Canada.

SOCIAL DEMOCRATIC GOALS

In his defense of the economic logic of government intervention and of the welfare state Weldon attacks those elements of neoconservative ideology that masquerade as economic theory. But he also recognizes the important role of ideology in determining the goals that economic policy can make possible. His ideology is social democratic, and much of his intellectual contribution to social democracy was devoted to clarifying both its goals and the means by which a Canadian social democratic party might achieve them. In 1961, the year of the founding of the New Democratic Party, he writes in "On the Economics of Social Democracy":

A social democratic party is not simply an alternative route to agreed ends, but a party seeking a changed social order. Its character is legislative quite as much, even more than it is administrative. The recent record of the democratic left in Canada would otherwise be bleak indeed. There would be Saskatchewan and nothing else. But an ideology can be advanced from a minority position, a party can legislate at second hand by being a potential administration: the experience of the CCF has shown how many specific goals have been attained without any share in government. The tests of success are not symmetrical with those that apply to the older parties: years in office, seats won, appointments made, these have to be counted in an index that gives chief weight to social change and reform. (pp. 11–12)

Weldon gives form and rigour to the discussion of the goals of social change by relating these to their effect on net national product or national income (which he refers to as the economic surplus). It is the amount, rate of growth, and distribution of the surplus that are used as measures of the effectiveness of policy. With these criteria, recognizing their interdependence, he examines the relationship between economic policies and social goals.

In discussing decision making with respect to the complex of social democratic goals that are amenable to policy, Weldon emphasizes two overriding principles that distinguish the democratic left from the totalitarian left: concern with the welfare of persons rather than that of states and other collectives, and insistence on democratic governance and accountability; that is, insistence on democratic socialism. Wherever he proposes or evaluates policies and methods for carrying out policies, these actions are subjected to the test of their fidelity to these two principles. This is the case in this collection of articles, as it was in his activity as adviser and consultant to governments, unions, and other interest groups when actual policies were at issue.

The collected papers in this volume were written between 1961 and 1986 and touch upon virtually every important economic policy issue that affected the lives of Canadians during this period. The central problems for Weldon were the means to achieve full employment and a more equitable distribution of income. How could economic policy provide assured employment, with decent wages and working conditions, to those who wanted to work? And what policies were needed to distribute income so that those who were separated from market income for reasons beyond their control would not live in poverty?

Weldon observed that failures by successive Canadian governments to achieve full employment beginning in the 1960s created a burden not only for the unemployed but also for society as a whole. He pointed out that full employment is a public good rather than a private good in the sense that unemployment affects not only the jobless but society as a whole. By diminishing those who do not have jobs, unemployment also diminishes those who do have jobs. He maintained that the social programs of the welfare state that were introduced in Canada after World War II had yet to fully meet society's needs, and therefore that poverty is an endemic national problem. For Weldon the *sine qua non* of economic policy is its contribution to solving these two interrelated problems.

The dominant fashion in economics during the past twenty years has been to produce theories that conclude that full employment and the elimination of poverty can be best attained through reliance on free markets. Weldon rejects this proposition and explains that, although competition (including imperfect competition) and markets play an important role in the economy, reliance on these markets alone would not ensure full employment and a more desirable distribution of income. Ultimately, full employment is the responsibility of the state. His view is that attaining and maintaining full employment would increase the absolute amount of real national income. But even if this were not the case, the improvement in relative incomes associated with full employment would provide large net benefits to society by reducing both the individual and social costs associated with unemployment.

He describes the progressive retreat of Canadian governments from the full employment pledge contained in the 1945 federal White Paper on Employment and the disappearance of any employment goals in Liberal and Tory government budgets in the 1980s. He rejects the validity of the concept of a "natural unemployment rate," which has been a key element in most macroeconomic explanations of government's inability to prevent the secular growth of the unemployment rate during the last two decades. (Opinions about the magnitude of this "natural rate" vary widely, but it always seems to rise as actual unemployment rates drift higher.) He rejects the contention that changes in unemployment insurance eligibility rules and payments, social welfare programs, and collective bargaining by unions are responsible for the significant increases in unemployment rates since the early 1970s. Weldon maintains that this increase in unemployment rates reflects in large part, the failure of government economic policy to create the necessary conditions for the expansion of employment opportunities. He criticizes government attempts to use the unemployment insurance program to buy off the unemployed instead of creating the conditions for job creation.

Weldon stresses the importance of government social programs, and especially of universal programs, in achieving a more equitable distribution of income than that which emerges from a market economy. Universal programs can provide adequate benefits because they have a broad base of public support. These programs also eliminate arbitrary and demeaning means tests and the costly bureaucracy that is necessary to carry out these tests. Non-universal programs, in which benefits are limited to certain groups in society, "create two classes, those for whom society becomes a giant, impersonal charity (the workhouse and poor laws reborn) and those who administer and finance this charity, public trustees who tax themselves as lightly as the self-image of benefactor will allow" ("On Social Policies in the Canadian Economy, 1986," p. 120).

Another aspect of income distribution to which social programs are directed is individual and family concerns about maintaining their relative economic position in society. Weldon emphasizes that private markets cannot maintain relative positions that are judged to be socially acceptable. The interventionist state can do this by transforming the "market wage" into an acceptable "social wage." The "social wage" includes individuals' earnings from employment, plus benefits from social programs. The social wage, it is argued, is justified by the social nature of production in modern societies.

The role of the social wage is illustrated in his work on the theory of pensions. Private arrangements – for example, private pension plans and personal savings – cannot ensure economic security of the aged. That is, they cannot guarantee the maintenance of a person's relative position in society on retirement. Such arrangements do not provide an adequate mechanism for coping with the inherent uncertainty surrounding future economic conditions, and therefore individuals cannot determine in advance what their living standards will be when they retire. The state can cope with this uncertainty. With their power to tax and redistribute income, governments can make intergenerational transfers of income. That is, those presently working can be taxed to finance current public pensions for retirees. Public pension programs based on intergenerational transfers provide a mechanism through which today's society can ensure that the incomes of those who are presently retired are equitable in the light of current standards of living, in the sense of maintaining retirees' relative income positions. Present workers are willing to pay taxes to finance current pensions because they expect similar relative treatment from government when they retire.

Weldon's writings support government policies that facilitate the development of a strong labour movement. He sees unions as a progressive force in society because they contribute to a more equitable distribution of income, because they are a force for the establishment of a modicum of democracy in the workplace, and because of their natural tendency to provide political support for the social democratic programs of interventionist government. He opposed wage and price controls in Canada because he doubted that these government policies had much effect on price inflation, whereas they did undermine the labour movement by reducing unions' ability to defend workers' economic interests.

POLITICAL WILL

Discussions of the importance of the political will of the democratic state pervade Weldon's writing on social and economic policy. In earlier writings, he maintains that governments have the means to improve social welfare, and they need wisely to use the full range of available economic techniques for active intervention wherever and whenever the market is ill suited to do so. Many examples of active state economic intervention during the immediate postwar period supported this contention.

At the end of World War II, the memories of the harshness of the Great Depression dominated the Canadian political psyche. The Keynesian revolution provided a theoretical framework for government economic policy interventions, and in Canada federal governments accepted responsibility for employment, income, and economic growth. When the postwar prosperity faltered in 1957, government responded with pump-priming expenditures in the form of increased pension payments and improved equalization payments to the provinces, as well as special programs for regional development and winter employment. In the 1960s the Canada and Quebec Pension Plans were introduced, and the universal hospital and medical programs that had originally been introduced by Cooperative Commonwealth Federation (CCF) governments in Saskatchewan became national in scope, with the assistance of the federal government. During this period the federal government set up the Economic Council of Canada and acted in the area of economic development by establishing the Department of Industry and the Department of Forestry and Rural Development. Though on a lesser scale, there were a considerable number of examples of economic interventionism by provincial governments during this period.[4]

In 1970 the newly elected Manitoba government under Premier Ed Schreyer set up a planning commission and appointed Weldon as its secretary. The planning commission under his leadership developed a "rolling" economic plan with a six-year horizon that directly involved the cabinet in planning. The results achieved by the planning commission have been described by H.G. Thorburn.

The government developed confidence in indicative planning at the provincial level. Its approach was practical and empirical ... By involving the cabinet directly, it generated the political will to act – a unique experience in Canada.[5]

Weldon discusses the problems of combining political will and effective government in a passage in "The Attack on the Democratic Left" (1978).

Under our parliamentary forms Cabinets organize policy, in theory only. They must in these years of large public sectors organize policy in fact, becoming for most of their working life policy cabinets. But if they are policy cabinets they must have the assistance of supporting policy bureaucracies. Policy cabinets and their supporting policy bureaucracies must then have the assistance of legislation ... to make their goals attainable. And with all this the most difficult part of the social engineering remains, for policy cabinet and policy bureaucracy must have as motive a desire to govern in the interests of a civilized community ... [But] the temptation is great for the best of politicians to wish to be activist never now but after the next election. (p. 107)

Weldon was more and more preoccupied by the failure of governments in Canada to extend and improve the welfare state programs that had developed after World War II, and by the progressive abandonment of the full employment goal. He believed that the attacks on the democratic left and the interventionist state in the 1970s and 1980s were facilitated by the failure of governments, both federal and provincial, to improve pension benefits and coverage, to provide for the growing need for better hospital and medical care, and to act vigorously to wipe out persistent poverty among many groups and regions and thereby to provide a more just distribution of income. In this context, his reflections on political will are central to questions about the future of the welfare state and the prospects for social democratic government in Canada.

THE PAPERS

There are two groups of papers in this collection. The first relates to social democracy and the role of State intervention in the economy; the second to particular topics in economic policy.

Part 1: Social Democracy and the Performance of the State

The first paper, "On the Economics of Social Democracy," appeared in 1961 in a collection of essays prepared by a group of social critics who hoped to influence Canada's economic, social, and cultural policies. In this paper, Weldon presents a comprehensive discussion of the economic policy of a social democratic state. Both the methods and the goals of social democracy are discussed in the context of Canadian problems and institutions. But he is particularly concerned with goals because "Only in its choice of goals is a social democratic party fundamentally different from other political parties" (p. 3). It is in goals "that fundamental issues are found not in technique. ... A social democratic party is not simply an alternative route to agreed ends" (p. 11).

The next three papers provide a more detailed discussion of the methods of social democracy. In "What Is Planning?" three elements of social democratic planning are discussed: taking account of what the economy is capable of doing; determining what people actually want to be done; and "the deliberate, determined use of economic intervention and control to attain the goals of the Plan " (p. 35). This paper appeared as a pamphlet in 1962. It was a period in which there were many proposals for various forms of "economic planning" that Weldon believed were 'counterfeit' because their implementation would not facilitate effective state intervention in the economy.

"Notes on 'Ownership'" is the text of his speech to the national New Democratic Party convention in 1975. In this speech, Weldon discusses the role of public ownership in social democratic policy. Historically, social democracy in Canada had put considerable reliance on public ownership and regulation. Here he points out that the apparatus available to the state provides public policy makers with a wide variety of tools with which to shape the economy, of which public ownership is only one. He then turns the discussion to a theme that will take on increased urgency for him in the years to come.

My concern ... is not finally with the theology of public ownership, but with the disturbing question of whether social democracy can in fact govern. Are the instruments of government, of which public ownership is but one, are these instruments usable, are they used? That they can be, that they are, this is a far more radical claim than to claim public ownership is a principle. (p. 47)

He continues this theme a year later in "The Role of Government in the Economy," the text of his presentation to the Canadian Tax Foundation. In this text he sketches various forms of government involvement in the economy and discusses sources of public criticism of government economic activity. The problem with the state is not that is has intervened, Weldon argues, but "the lack of capacity of our governments to handle their large and vital economics domain effectively" (p. 53). He concludes that government must be strengthened, and he outlines various ways to do this. This is also one of the rare places where he mentions the problem of the relation between economic growth and environmental controls.

Since the mid-1970s, the interventionist state has been under attack. The proponents of privatization have sometimes emphasized the desirability of particular transfers of responsibility from public to private jurisdiction and sometimes a general limitation on the capacity of the state to govern. In several of these collected papers, Weldon assesses particular privatization proposals. In "A Critique of Privatization" he considers various concepts of 'privatization'. These concepts are linked to different perceptions of the role of the state.

According to Weldon, "privatization ... for Marx would not describe a policy or goals of 'bourgeois economy' ... it describes the natural tendencies of capitalism, tendencies inextricably bound to a mode of production and its derivative social history" (p. 64). In this vision, the state cannot prevent the worst excesses of competition and in the end cannot save capitalism from the suicidal forces of competition.

A second vision, not necessarily incompatible with the first, is provided by those who believe the state will (or should) eventually be supplanted by "voluntary association, cooperation or the spontaneous creativity of anarchy." Weldon uses, as examples of those holding this vision, political philosophers as diverse as John Stuart Mill, Peter Kropotkin, and V.I. Lenin. For them, "privatization" is to be viewed in the context of the inherently undesirable state: the "state-that-will-vanish." It is a view currently held by some on the left who have lost confidence in democratic interventionist government.

A third vision of the state is that provided by the proponents of *laissez-faire* capitalism. For them, the interventionist state has important, lasting, negative effects on the economy and 'privatization' is viewed as a deliberate policy which will improve social well-being.

Weldon is sceptical about the first two visions of the role of the state, but he reserves final judgement about them. He rejects the third vision, and its *laissez-faire* critique of the state, and he maintains that the nature of the modern industrial economy limits the extent to which privatization is possible.

The next paper is the previously unpublished essay, "The Unity of Economics." In this essay Weldon discusses the ideas of well-known economists of the eighteenth and nineteenth centuries. He contrasts their views of the role of the market and the state in the economy with those of the current crop of *laissez-faire* theorists. He observes, for example, that while Adam Smith saw private motivation as a key instrument in promoting public welfare, "Smith does not deny ... that public authority is a complementary instrument, and devotes hundreds of pages to legitimate interventions by the state" (p. 85).

The two final papers in Part I of this collection provide insights into economic policy and the role of the state during the 1970s and 1980s. "The Attack on the Democratic Left" was published in 1978. Its focus is on the response of government to the abrupt increase in energy prices in the early 1970s. These price changes plunged Canada into an economic crisis, Weldon argues, only because governments failed to act vigorously to offset their effects. He draws a parallel with the Great Depression when the state failed to act vigorously to offset economic collapse at the beginning of the 1930s. Abandonment of the full employment goal and failure to extend and improve the quality of welfare state programs weakened the support for interventionist government and aided the attack by the right on the institutions of the democratic left. The responsibility for these events must be borne, in part, by those on the left and others from whom more would have been expected. Weldon writes:

I suppose in some degree the [New Democratic Party] governments of British Columbia and Manitoba contributed to their own downfall. The gap between convention rhetoric and legislative performance was often too wide to prevent even the faithful from gasping. Perhaps if one had one free wish about the style of political events in Canada it would not be that the Ottawa Cabinet would be caught snuffing cocaine ... but that our social democrats would be less like tigers out of office and less like lambs in office: if they want to please everybody they might as well do it in opposition, and not waste their occasional years in government waiting for a time to govern. But this is ungrateful. The governments on the left have done a far better job than the rest, and have been in as difficult a position as anyone else from the left while doing the job. The labour movement has had its troubles too. And silence may be kind comment on academics! (p. 101)

"On Social Policies in the Canadian Economy, 1986" is Weldon's last completed paper.[6] Returning to a methodology that first appears in "On the Economics of Social Democracy" (1961), he analyzes social policies in terms of their effects on economic surplus. His analysis of surplus clearly emerges as a unifying element in his view of the relationship between economic theory and economic policy. "On Social Policies in the Canadian Economy, 1986," begins with illustrations of current attitudes towards full employment and the social wage and then presents the general principles underlying these policies. In explaining Canadian governments' abandonment first of the full employment goal and then of any employment goal, Weldon makes the following observation about the way Keynesian ideas were applied in Canada:

Any interventionist commitment from Ottawa made at the end of the war became politically more demanding as authority to govern drained from the public sector ... Planning at a microeconomic level gave way to crude manipulation of fiscal and monetary aggregates, so causing Canadian policy to mimic the only Keynesian model that could be accommodated in the United States. (p. 114)

Attempts to justify nonintervention by government in dealing with unemployment in the 1970s and 1980s rely on arguments that maintain that *less* intervention increases the amount of the surplus. Weldon doubts this, but he argues that, even if it were true that government interventions that reduce unemployment also result in lower real national income, it is far more important to society to avoid the increased poverty and increased income inequality caused by unemployment. He also emphasizes the social (as well as economic) costs of unemployment – the "public good" argument – and the advantages of having full employment in a period when public policy is committed to eliminating discriminatory job ghettos.

In discussing the social wage, Weldon contends that public policy has a role to play in moderating the influence of wealth and inheritance on income distribution:

Out of the marketplace come private wage rates (part of a pattern of privately determined distribution of surplus). Societies such as our own undoubtedly make great use of such rates as an initial reference for computing acceptable shares, and do so with widespread agreement that the reference is efficient, fair, and natural, not only for those who receive wages but for that considerable *majority* who do not. It is well understood, however, that the level of private wage rates greatly depends on the prior distribution of property, that wages earned on private account are further distributed by custom (outside the marketplace) to family members and others, and that an "initial reference" for shares in surplus has to be ratified by how successfully it is adapted to social needs. Within Canadian public policy, the centerpiece has for decades been how to transmute *private wage rates* into *social wage rates*. (p. 118)

The social wage also plays an important role in "the attempt every community makes to control its uncertain future, to plan for a *process* appropriate to unpredictable events," a function that cannot adequately be provided for by the market (p. 121). The example he uses to illustrate this is the provision of public pensions. The article ends with an all-too-fleeting commentary on the relationship between decisions about the level of public saving and the use of arguments for deficit reduction to attack social programs.

Part 2: Selected Topics in Economic Policy

The papers in Part 2 focus on particular policy issues. "Wage Controls and the Canadian Labour Movement" is an edited version of one of the two Jamieson lectures Weldon gave at the University of British Columbia in September 1982. At the time there was a great deal of interest in wage and price controls (incomes policies). Even though Canada had entered a serious recession in 1982, there was still double-digit inflation. Memories of the AIB – the Anti-inflation Board, which existed between 1975 and 1978 – were still fresh, and the federal government had just introduced its "6 and 5 policy," which was intended to keep income increases to 6% and 5% in the two following years. The American economist Sidney Weintraub was advocating an untried form of wage controls, a tax-based incomes policy (TIP), for both Canada and the United States, and University of Manitoba economists Clarence Barber and John McCallum had just published a book in which they supported the use of a Canadian incomes policy.[7]

In this paper, Weldon presents both the theoretical and administrative objections to the use of a Canadian incomes policy. He supports these objections by examining the results of the AIB experience that lowered real wages by keeping money wage increases down while having little effect on price inflation, and by a devastating critique of the latest wrinkle in proposed incomes policies: TIP. His opinion is that all Canadian incomes policies are bound to end up being essentially a form of wage controls. As such, he argues, they are an attack on a fundamental social institution, the labour movement, because they deprive unions of one of their most important functions, defense of their members' incomes. He laments that academic researchers have paid so little attention to this issue.

In recent years inflation rates in Canada have been relatively low and show no sign of accelerating. The attack on unions has mainly taken the form of attempts by employers to reduce acquired wage rates and fringe benefits, and to weaken seniority rights through "concession" bargaining in both the private and public sectors of the economy. This attack has been justified by neoconservative ideology and often supported by conservative provincial and federal governments. In this situation, incomes policies have faded into the background as a major policy issue. However, sooner or later, there will be a new bout of inflation and incomes policies will return to political and economic policy agendas.

Weldon's contribution to the theory of public pensions is contained largely in four papers: in "On the Theory of Government Pension Plans" (1968),[8] and "On Private Plans in the Theory of Pensions" (1970), both co-authored with A. Asimakopulos; in his 1976 presidential address to the Canadian Economics Association, "On the Theory of Intergenerational Transfers"[9];

and in his second 1982 Jamieson Lecture, "Pension Policy: Practice and Positive Theory." The 1970 and 1982 papers are included in this collection.

Weldon provides a formal definition of pensions that emphasizes their basis in transfers. "*Pensions* are payments in money made within a community to the aged, and originate in arrangements that exact taxes and premiums and that provide promises which directly or contingently determine the payments."[10] Payments within a community are made by intergenerational transfers, and the promises are contained in pension law. In Weldon's approach, pensions are differentiated from the efforts of individuals and groups to provide for retirement by saving, in one form or another, even though some of these efforts are called private pensions. The theory of intergenerational transfers and its role in pension policy is summarized and extended in the 1982 paper. This paper assesses various proposed pension plan reforms, among which are a higher level of pension benefits for all Canadians and pensions for housewives.[11] The 1976 presidential address, which is not included in this collection, contains the suggestion that the theory of intergenerational transfers can be applied not only to pensions but also to the public financing of education and health services.

The final paper in this collection is Weldon's preface to *Le défi du plein emploi*[12] by Diane Bellemare and Lise Poulin Simon, two of his former students. He rejoices that these two economists have reexamined and reasserted Keynes's basic proposition that involuntary unemployment can be vanquished. He uses this preface to emphasize again, as the two authors have emphasized, the social costs of unemployment, and that success in providing jobs is a public good as well as a benefit to those who are unemployed. He highlights the contribution that the authors make in recognizing that unemployment, as we have known it in recent decades, requires more than the rough-and-ready instruments of macroeconomic demand management that sufficed in the special circumstances of the immediate postwar years. It is the microeconomic interventions, initiated by the public sector and guided by consultation and cooperation from interest groups in society, that are crucial for success.

Although Weldon believes that a program such as that advocated by Bellemare and Poulin Simon could produce full employment in Canada, he ends the preface by returning to what had become a crucial question for him: does the state have the political will to carry out such a program?

I think the authors show that the basic question about "full employment" is not whether a theory exists, or a technically feasible programme, but whether the Canadian political system can put a feasible programme into operation. Do our institutions, does our history, allow our democratic State to intervene on the scale "full employment" would require? (p. 213)

NOTES AND REFERENCES

1 See, for example, Alan S. Blinder, "Economic Policy and Economic Science: The Case of Macroeconomics." Paper presented at Perspective 2000 (conference sponsored by the Economic Council of Canada), Ottawa, 30 Nov.–1 Dec. 1988; and Robert J. Shapiro, "Look Who's Making a Comeback," *U.S. News and World Report*, 1 Feb. 1988, 43–5.

2 J.C. Weldon, "A Submission to the Special Committee on Canada's International Relations." Unpublished submission to the Special Joint Committee On Canada's International Relations, Ottawa, 22 July and 7 August 1985, 2.

3 Ibid., 1.

4 See, for example, H.G. Thorburn, *Planning and the Economy: Building Federal-Provincial Consensus* (Ottawa: Canadian Institute for Economic Policy, 1984), 117–59.

5 Ibid., 133.

6 An edited version of this paper has been published as "Public Policies and Full Employment in Canada Since 1945" In Cranford Pratt and Roger Hutchinson, eds., *Christian Faith & Economic Justice: Toward a Canadian Perspective* (Burlington, Ont.: Trinity Press, 1988), 55–75.

7 Clarence Barber and John McCallum, *Controlling Inflation: Learning From Experience in Canada, Europe and Japan* (Ottawa: Canadian Institute for Economic Policy, 1982).

8 A. Asimakopulos and J.C. Weldon, "On the Theory of Government Pension Plans," *Canadian Journal of Economics* 1 (4) (Nov. 1968): 699–717.

9 J.C. Weldon, "On the Theory of Intergenerational Transfers," *Canadian Journal of Economics* 9 (Nov. 1976): 559–79.

10 This definition appears in J.C. Weldon, "On the Economic Analysis of Pensions," unpublished, July 1975, 6–7. It differs from the definitions of pensions in A. Asimakopulos and J.C. Weldon, "On Private Plans in the Theory of Pensions," *Canadian Journal of Economics* 3 (2) (May 1970): 224 (p. 159 in this volume). It is a simplified version of the definition that appears in Weldon, "On the Theory of Intergenerational Transfers," 562.

11 This paper also includes a critique of a pension proposal by Martin Feldstein, an American economist. Because of the extensive use of mathematics in this critique it has been placed in an appendix in the edited version in this book.

12 Diane Bellemare and Lise Poulin Simon, *Le defi du plein emploi: un nouveau regard économique* (Montréal: Editions Saint-Martin, 1986).

PART ONE

Social Democracy and the Performance of the State

CHAPTER ONE

On the Economics of Social Democracy*

What is the nature of the economic policy of social democracy? On what economic principles does it depend, by what methods and to what goals is it directed? I have in mind Canadian problems and Canadian institutions, for I want to discuss these questions in a familiar environment and with the facts of a specific system at hand. There is a reasonable unity to social democratic thought here and abroad, but its economic expression is dominated by the variety of circumstances that distinguishes Ottawa and London, to say nothing of the extremes that separate Ottawa and New Delhi. It is necessary to stay within a Canadian context. At the same time I want to talk about broad themes of economic policy, rather than anything so complex and immediate as the clauses of a political programme. It is policy in its simplest form that I want to consider, policy idealized to show sources and tendencies.

Only in its choice of goals is a social democratic party fundamentally different from other political parties. Because of this, what follows is mostly given to an account of economic goals, and to the economic choices that social democrats are likely to make. But there are also differences, of course, in economic technique and methodology: in particular the view that our economic affairs can be controlled in detail and with efficiency continues to distinguish the democratic left from the democratic right. The differences here are undoubtedly narrower than they were at the time the Regina Manifesto was published. Then, indeed, with other problems dwarfed by unemployment, the contrast between the newly established CCF and the older

*This began as notes for a talk to a CCF study group in 1958, was turned into a paper for a staff seminar at McGill, and after revision makes this third appearance. Revision owes a good deal to ideas borrowed from the other contributors.

Reprinted with permission from Michael Oliver, ed., *Social Purpose for Canada* (Toronto: University of Toronto Press, 1961), 171–97.

parties may well have been seen as resting primarily in methods rather than in goals. This predominance has disappeared, but the issue of methods is still very important; and since the issue is remarkably topical it is probably better treated as an introduction to a discussion of goals rather than a sequel.

Most observers would agree, I suppose, that in Canada not only has there been a narrowing of differences on the question of economic technique, but that this has been the result of changes from both sides. Seen from the right the root cause of change has simply been the great expansion in the economic role of government that was prefaced by the depression and imposed by the Second World War. Whatever one's theoretical preconceptions, economic events have in fact been reshaped by government intervention, drastically during the war but notably still in these later years. Effects have here been seen to follow causes even as they must in the rest of nature. The evidence has been plain that government can give stability and direction to the economy, and to avoid unendurable waste must choose to do so.

On the left, too, ideas have been modified by this direct experience of the creatively regulated economy, although on the left there has been an equal influence from the successes and failures of Britain's Labour Government, and from a generation's advance in technical economics. In the main the social democrat has found his expectations confirmed by events, but he has also found the methods of control advocated in the 1930s to be in some measure unwieldly and incomplete. They are methods now seen to have given an exaggerated emphasis to ownership as such, the left in a sense having accepted a fiction of the right by equating ownership with control. They are methods that did not properly distinguish between the virtues and vices of the price system, and that because of this failure gave too little weight to the use of the market place as an instrument of policy. They are methods that under-estimated the complexity, the interdependence and the administrative cost of regulatory devices conceived of in the small, and directed to control of an item-by-item kind; and although they are methods that prescribed a social democratic future for agencies such as the federal budget and the newly established central bank and the yet to be established federal housing authority, they only partly anticipated the value of control in the large, the flexibility of regulation that these massive central agencies would allow. Perhaps inevitably, until so-called big government had made its appearance, the tendency in imagining a planned economy was to overvalue fiat and specific legislation, and to undervalue operations in the open market and intervention of a general kind. It was a tendency that would have been corrected in practice by the restraints of a federal state, but it was also a tendency that had paternalistic implications at odds with the individualism of social democratic goals, and that unnecessarily alienated sympathetic opinion.

For many social democrats revision has been a troubling process. They fear that it has meant a dwindling of goals and the dilution of principle, especially where the new techniques have lessened the role seen for nationalization and direct controls. I think that in this they are, for a number of reasons, admirably but clearly mistaken.

In the first place the new techniques have made possible an extended rather than a reduced range of goals. What is economically possible to a nation is finally limited by its wealth and natural resources, by the state of its arts and by the terms on which it can deal abroad. No choice of social or economic philosophy can surmount these facts. But within such natural limits the economic pattern can appear in vastly different forms. Employment can be high or low, goods can be produced of one kind rather than another, distribution can favour this group and not that. From these manifold possibilities we can and should choose what actually happens to us. That at least is the social democratic view, and has historically distinguished the social democrat from those to his right. Since its effect is to define a wide area of governmental responsibility it goes a good deal further than simply to stipulate the existence of responsible government. Within ultimate limits economic events can be controlled, so the assertion is. From the range of events a best choice can be made, far superior to unplanned alternatives; and since this is so, responsible government must accept responsibility for the outcome of events, never pleading a lack of authority or power. It is a sweeping commitment, of course, and can never be fully satisfied. Accomplishment will inevitably fall short of the postulated responsibility. But the likely deficiency has been reduced. The new methods of economic control augment the old, and allow planning that is more efficient on the one hand and more detailed and discriminating on the other.

Nationalization and public ownership and economic planning have not been renounced. It is as irrational as it ever was to base policy on a natural superiority of private to public ownership, subordinating public interests and public enterprise whenever a choice is to be made. That principle only leads to such typically expensive absurdities as the use of the smaller Canadian Pacific Railway to measure the financial needs of the Canadian National. At the same time there is no reason to invest nationalization and public ownership with moral qualities, as processes that make a more than technical contribution to the good society. They are instruments of economic control, neither good nor bad in themselves, and are to be used pragmatically and without hesitation whenever they promise advantage over other instruments of control. More specifically, they are still the indicated remedies wherever the market mechanism is absent or impossible to regulate. Where, for example, industrialization must take place in jumps, as in the opening of a new region, or the development of a new industrial complex, the market mechanism cannot be expected to allocate resources efficiently or to protect the public against exploitation. Quebec and British Columbia may well net something from the private ventures now pushing back the frontier, but it does not follow that they will simply because the frontier is indeed pushed back; and certainly no market force exists to ensure the provinces of more than a fraction of the return available from public control of those ventures.

A strong case still exists for nationalization in the financial field, and of the insurance companies and chartered banks in particular. It is not a matter of the day-to-day and local affairs of these institutions, which nationalization need not touch, nor even of the uneconomical use they must make of the community's savings, for that can be remedied by new rules of investment and a reform of the capital market. It is the fact that more and more these institutions are the channels through which economic controls of a general kind are transmitted. The more freely they can be used in this way the less is intervention required in other parts of the economy. But one result is that their fortunes are sharply affected by the calculated accidents of policy, often to their disadvantage. They must lose or gain, for example, with any imposed change in interest rates, and lose or gain the more the larger the size of the change. Here and elsewhere their private status inevitably comes to inhibit policy, limiting the action the federal authorities would otherwise take. For once ownership as such is the crux of the matter. The situation is increasingly anomalous, rather as it would be if the Bank of Canada or the Central Mortgage and Housing Corporation were privately owned and constrained by commercial motives. To nationalize financial intermediaries is really to extend the historic evolution of central banking.

As one further case in point, nationalization remains an ultimate solution to concentrations of economic power. No doubt such problems are as much social as they are economic. Business is so interwoven with press and radio, with pension and health plans, with public and political relations, that excessive economic power entails excessive power throughout the social order. On technical grounds it may be undesirable or impossible to dissolve a given concentration of power, and no way may appear to limit its exercise to the economic sphere. Where this is so nationalization has at least the corrective virtue of bringing power that is irresponsible, and so inherently dangerous to the rest of the community, under responsible political control. It becomes a decisive resource of the democratic society.

But planning does not rely in an exclusive way upon nationalization and public ownership. Nothing, for example, can be done by nationalization to redistribute wealth and income that cannot be done more easily and equitably by taxation, by transfer payments, and by the provision of social capital. An anti-combines policy can depend on nationalization, and no doubt sometimes must; but I think that where it is directed to monopolistic conditions of an artificial kind, to the effects of the ordinary combine, say, or of equivalent "horizontal" mergers, conventional anti-trust provisions are probably all that is needed, given a heretofore unknown intention to apply them in a rigorous way. I might add that it would be a serious error to underestimate how radical such an intention is, no less radical than a *bona fide*

commitment to full employment or to low-income housing. Social democratic thinking has had to adapt itself to new problems and changed techniques, but it should not be deluded by the myth that its traditional
programme has been exhausted.

The immediate point is that regulation has its costs and is committing,
so that it is not sensible to use as strong a remedy as nationalization where
a weaker remedy will do. It is not sensible, either, to increase the number
of regulatory agencies and statutes if existing instruments can be used more
intensively to the same purpose. In making a cautious use of nationalization
the new methods of control reflect the wise theological maxim that entities
should not be unnecessarily multiplied.

In principle nationalization (and public ownership generally) might be
used to guarantee full employment, or to allocate resources, or to determine
investment and economic growth. It is possible to imagine nationalization
as the direct solution to almost any economic problem. The difficulty is that
the projected solution may easily be question-begging, a solution by definition rather than anything of real consequence. Let something be brought
under public ownership and there is no doubt the actions that can now be
enforced include whatever is closest to the public interest. But the real
problem may be, and may always have been, to find out what that best
action is and to have it performed at the smallest possible cost. It would be
pointless nowadays to base employment or investment policy on nationalization because the needed controls are much the same in the public sector
of the economy as in the private. The critical decisions – how much spending
there is to be, and in what industries, and in what regions – have the same
form after nationalization as before, and can be best implemented by methods
that have very little to do with ownership as such, by adjustments of the
budget, the licensing of investment, monetary controls, and so on.

As to the allocation of resources, public ownership is better regarded as
a regulator of the price system than a substitute for it. Undoubtedly the
system has to be regulated. It has to be regulated in the sense that a framework
is set for its operation: it is an instrument of planning, and we are free to
choose what we want it to do. It has also to be regulated within these chosen
limits, so that it operates in practice with something of the efficiency it is
conceived to possess in theory. Public ownership is essential at both levels
of regulation. The public must *own* the regulatory agencies, for whatever
their form, from planning board to exchange fund, they must respond only
to the public interests; while within the price system the public must be
prepared to use nationalization when other correctives fail to preserve efficiency. The use of the price system in allocating resources takes nothing
from the final responsibility of government. The point is, however, that
under proper conditions the price system is indisputably efficient and economical, achieving just the results that rational planning would demand.

Within a given system of goals and properly policed, it is automatic, sensitive and pervasive beyond comparison with other devices. The great bulk of economic decisions can safely be left to its care, and certainly those that are only local in their effects. Rational planning must take all major economic decisions into explicit account, but there is really no way the infinite total of minor decisions can be regulated except through the price system. Any scheme of direct controls would soon become an impossibly expensive alternative.

This has all been by way of comment on the fears some social democrats have expressed of revision. I want to add a word about revision and planning proper. Responsibility for what happens in the economy must be accepted by government, and finally by the federal government; and since responsibility is complete, *planning must also be complete*, and finally too at the federal level. The federal authorities must systematically study the state of the economy, and estimate its likely development. They must decide the range of good the economy can achieve, and plan the goals that should actually be chosen. They must determine the structure and powers of the regulatory agencies, and plan the activities of those agencies so that the chosen goals can be realized.

Critics of the planned economy charge that it predicates a moral and administrative perfection found only in the seraphim. (Some then appear to argue that the fallibility of planners proves that less planning is better than more.) There would be a good deal of truth to this criticism if the federal authorities had to undertake even a major proportion of the actions on which a planned economy depends. Undoubtedly social democratic planning would enlarge the status and responsibilities of many parts of the civil service, and undoubtedly it would seek to increase the flow of first-class minds to government work. But there would be no need for it to accept tasks that lie beyond talents and techniques as they are. As I have just observed, much can be left to the price system. In our federal system much can also be left, much must be left to the provincial authorities. The boundary is political and constitutional, and allows federal pre-eminence in times of crisis. It also allows joint activities and co-ordinated planning, since obviously such arrangements often enlarge what any level of government can accomplish. But within these not inflexible limits the decisions of the provinces must be accepted as a natural part of the total economic plan. The federal authorities must take account of provincial programmes of resource development and provincial decisions on the form of welfare benefits and social capital; they must take account of these things so that they can be treated as a predetermined part of their own planning, a part with which other aspects of the federal programme must be reconciled. Is such a reconciliation always possible? Probably it is, granted the federal financial power, and with less difficulty in the economic than in the political sphere. Basically the relation of federal planning to provincial economics is the same as it is to the price system. Economic decisions are made – collectively in the one case, individually in the other – which, because of their origin, need no testing, and can be incorporated as a self-determining, self-fulfilling part of the federal plan.

The actions which the federal authorities themselves must take are those which *complete* the general plan. They are in part actions in which the government has an entrepreneurial role, activities paralleling in principle those of the provincial governments, but sponsored at the federal level because that is the most efficient place – perhaps the only place – for them to be undertaken. I have in mind the classical illustrations from defence and commercial policy, but also the long list of modern examples, the great acts of social reconstruction and lesser changes, federal expenditures on radio and television, transfer payments in pensions and allowances, the use of taxes to redistribute real income, the provision of marketing boards and research councils, and all other actions that in their own right have an immediate place in federal planning.

The further actions required at the federal level are those that are residual or compensatory, the very important activities undertaken to bring the total achievement of the economy into conformity with federal responsibility and planning, and deliberately varied to accommodate events in the rest of the economy. Management of the national debt, and of the exchange fund, the operations of the central bank, changes in the operations of the housing agency, changes in the tax structure, even nationalization itself, these are all actions which usually belong in this second category. With some allowance for the entrepreneurial activities of government, it does not oversimplify the social democratic position to say that while responsibility and planning must be complete, action should only be, can only be, residual.

To the renewed inquiry whether this is a consistent position, I believe a "yes" can again be fairly answered, even on the basis of our experience with existing regulatory agencies. Their present practice would, of course, be very much changed under social democratic auspices, and use would be made of their extensive latent powers; there would be some nationalization; but except for effective coordinating bodies, an all-essential planning board or ministry, and a related commission to license major investments, the instruments of a planned economy are already at hand. A social democratic budget would after all be in itself a radical instrument of reform, and so would a social democratic central bank.

I have one theme more in this dicussion of methods. The social democrat contends that economic events are chosen rather than imposed, and this distinguishes him from those on the democratic right; he also contends that rational choice depends only on *individual* preferences and this distinguishes him from those on the non-democratic left. The mechanics of choice must reflect this judgment. If economic changes occur which in some sense are to the general benefit of society, then society should *compensate* persons and groups to whom the changes are substantially damaging. This is true whether the changes occur in the natural order or as the result of some deliberate action by government. Why? Because if there are advantages that can be shared so that there is disadvantage to no one, there has clearly been progress only if they are so shared. Such "compensationist" notions have been part of the labyrinth of theoretical welfare economics for a great many years. They are not complete tests of progress, and like other economic abstractions can be pressed to paradoxical results; but at the practical level they are safe and useful guides to what social democratic policy should be. Examples that come to mind include the recommendations on automation by the Canadian Labour Congress, recommendations which praise progress but properly enough only progress fully compensating those who are displaced; the single reference to compensation in the Regina Manifesto, compensation for properties taken under public control (a curious choice for the founders of the CCF to make, when one thinks of it, since it is compensation to the "right" rather than the "left" that they select); and again more recently, the response of the CCF parliamentary group to events like the cancellation of the AVRO contracts.

Social democratic goals are of an individualistic kind, but progress towards them need not depend on perverse lotteries in which a few lose heavily even when most of the community gains. It can be conceded at once that only economic changes in the large could or should be related to a principle of compensation, changes producing heavy and continuing damage to particular persons or groups, damage unlikely to be offset by benefits accruing from other changes. In the long run the random effects of economic changes are likely to balance out from person to person, and in a sense constitute a single, protracted, but generally beneficial event. This is not true of the repercussions from large and irreversible adjustments which, being uneven in their incidence, invite a perfectly rational resistance from those whose interests are harmed. Equity and progress are both served when compensation for such changes is made. It can be monetary compensation or take some other form, but it should be compensation as of right and compensation that is complete. In Canada partial compensation has usually had the appearance of a timid attempt to deflect the just severities of natural law. The costs of progress are in fact accidental, and should in reason and compassion be a first charge against the progress that is achieved.

There are endless instances against which the principle can be tested. As difficult as any in terms of public sympathies, but a very good test in logic, is the settlement a year or so ago between the railways and their diesel firemen. There is no doubt that dieselization was an enormously productive change. There may be dispute on almost any other point, but let it be agreed that the firemen were skilled workers, and that their skills were entirely lost to the new technology. Let it also be agreed that whatever its defects of form, anything offering *less* than the final settlement (which was a solution by attrition – virtually no discharges but no hirings) would not have been full compensation. Would anything less than full compensation have been just? Could the firemen have been expected to accept anything less? Society no more than the firemen foresaw dieselization, and had no better claim than the firemen to its benefits; but without compensation the firemen were to lose a great deal and society to gain. The settlement required what was reasonable, that enough be set aside from the improved product to compensate the firemen for their loss.

Take as another illustration the mines and miners at Springhill. Surely compensation in such situations is more logically applied before a crisis than after. To bring submarginal production to a halt is a gain to society, and need not be achieved by worsening the position of those who were submarginally employed. Or consider the social benefit that could accrue from a compensated increase in the mobility of the labour force, from the reduction of trade union rigidities by the use of severance allowances and transferable seniority and pension rights. The trade unions have no interest in the rigidities as such, and must make use of them as a second-best protection of the equity the members have in their jobs. Uncompensated change is almost impossible, but compensated change, initiated by government, is there to be arranged as soon as government accepts the task.

If we look to the farmer instead of the trade unionist, and ask how to overcome the rigidities in agriculture, how to adapt to a technology that needs fewer farmers, we come to the same prescription: compensated change means that progress is shared and not resisted. Or consider even such wide issues as trade and immigration. There is a strong presumption in favour of freer trade and greater immigration. Yet as every period of recession proves, it is quite unrealistic to expect particular groups to subsidize those changes. If there is to be unemployment the auto workers and the auto industry or the textile workers and the textile industry have every reason to press for protection, regardless of the case for trade and immigration. Society must determine that the costs of progress do not fall upon the individual. They are costs that are uninsurable – uncertainties rather than risks – and only society should bear them.

I come now to the economic goals of social democracy. As I said at the beginning, I think it is here that fundamental issues are found and not in technique. Social democracy is after all *ideological*. A social democratic party is not simply an alternative route to agreed ends, the purely administrative coalition that the older parties represent, but a party seeking a changed social order. Its character is legislative quite as much, even more than it is administrative. The recent record of the democratic left in Canada would otherwise be bleak indeed. There would be Saskatchewan and nothing else. But an ideology can be advanced from a minority position, a party can legislate at second hand by being a potential administration: the experience of the CCF has shown how many specific goals have been attained without any share in government. The tests of success are not symmetrical with those that apply to the older parties: years in office, seats won, appointments made, these have to be counted but they have to be counted in an index that gives chief weight to social change and reform.

There are many ways in which goals might be classified, but the most useful I can think of is to use aspects of the national income as a continuing theme. On this principle the goals of social democracy can be placed in four categories, thus, goals that determine the size of the national income, that determine the rate of growth of the national income, that determine the distribution of the national income, and that determine the quality of the national income. The categories of size, growth, distribution, and quality are not independent, of course, and goals selected under one heading will ultimately modify and be modified by goals selected under another; but they seem to me to be sufficiently independent to be useful units of thought and to allow one to reflect about goals of one kind without at every stage having to recast one's appraisal of goals already noted. A devotion to economic absolutes is not needed: the conflict of one goal with another is in any case likely to be very distant from existing practice, and it is not difficult to keep in mind the need for possibly arbitrary compromise when a conflict of goals does appear.

What are the particular issues that these four categories embrace? It is worth going into some detail (indeed into more detail than I shall use) because to put things in co-ordinate groups is itself a kind of analysis, and shows something of the values on which the categories are based. Under the first heading, the category dealing with the size of the national income, it can go without saying that income is to be maximized. The leading item is therefore employment: on the one hand the amount of employment and (voluntary) leisure – leisure deliberately chosen can be given a full place in real income; on the other, the residual of employment and leisure, the amount of involuntary unemployment, both that of the unemployable and unemployment that actually reduces the national income. Then, since the national income is determined by trade as well as by production, and includes as a critical intangible our sense of national identity, there is the nature of commercial policy and the flow of international capital. There is the regulation of monopolies and combines, listed here because the economic problem is how to enlarge the national income by forestalling "monopolistic" misdirection of resources without limiting "monopolistic" efficiencies of large-scale production. (Some would argue, I think correctly, that here the economic problem is dominated by the social and political problem of power.)

There is the issue of price stability and inflation, added not because on its merits it ranks with these other entries – under Canadian conditions it surely does not – but because again and again it has provided a rallying point about which economic conservatives have chosen to gather.

The issues relating to economic growth turn upon the rates of change in total and per capita real income. Here the leading item is the division of the national income into investment and consumption goods, since the proportion of investment goods is the simplest variable upon which growth depends; there is the further division of investment goods into growth and welfare components – it might be better to say into components affecting growth in the short run and the long, plant and equipment on the one hand and schools and houses on the other; and closely related to the welfare components of investment, there are those consumption goods that have at least a long-run effect upon growth – books, research, the services of doctors, of teachers. There are then two matters it is nowadays of considerable importance to distinguish, the size of the gross contribution to Canadian economic growth made available from abroad, presumably large and undoubtedly positive, and the size of the net contribution, inevitably smaller and conceivably negative. There is the relation of Canadian growth to growth abroad, and to the capital needs of the underdeveloped countries. These issues all arise from the single fact that if full employment is achieved, as from time to time in post-war Canada it has been, *growth and expansion are not free goods* but must be borrowed or paid for. The price in either form shares the property of all other prices that it can be excessive.

Questions dealing with the distribution of income – and of wealth – define the third category. I add "wealth" to "income" even though wealth is finally significant only because of the income that flows from it. There are difficulties of a statistical kind: wealth is sometimes part of the ordinary economic record where the corresponding income is not, and vice versa – the most important case is the failure of the usual records of income to give any account of the power that wealth confers. Statistics on wealth and statistics on income have thus an independent usefulness.

As to the category proper, economic equality is the central theme, although not equality mechanically or narrowly construed. It is equality considered in relation to families and households rather than to individuals, and then not at a particular point of time, but in relation to the full cycle of their economic history. The issue appears in the first instance at the national level, but it obviously has its specifically regional aspects; it has its specifically industrial aspects, of which an efficient road to farm parity is the most pressing example; it has its specifically ethnic aspects in the contrasting income patterns of French and English Canada; it has its specifically institutional aspects in the role of the trade union as an instrument of equality; and it has its specifically international aspects, more nearly fundamental than any of the rest, in the disparity between incomes here and in the rest of the world.

The final group of issues are those that bear on the quality of the national income, the worth of the goods and services of which the national income is composed. In one way or another the community has to decide what resources are to be set aside to produce economic growth, but once that decision has been made the investment of those resources is essentially an engineering problem; for any pattern of wants, investment should simply be embodied in whatever is technically efficient. The quality of the national income raises no issue over how the machinery of the economic process should be chosen, but only over the kinds of goods and services the machinery should be set to produce. It is finally determined only by the extent to which the wants of consumers are satisfied: wealth, investment and growth have no independent value.

What are the specific issues? I think the concept of consumers' sovereignty can be used to identify three substantial and largely separate questions. There is what might be called the "Madison Avenue" question, the extent to which consumers' sovereignty has been infringed by modern methods of marketing products, ideas, and men. Do remedies that respect individual choice exist? The question that logically follows is the proper scope of consumers' sovereignty in situations where the consumer is in fact uninformed or uninstructed. What should be done to provide a basis for rational choice? Put in this way these questions implicitly equate excellence in the national income with sovereignty rationally exercised by individual consumers. As far as it goes this equation is not only acceptable to social democratic sympathies but vital to their emphasis on the welfare of persons rather than of states and other collectives. Yet it is also true that the quality of the national income depends in many ways upon choices that can only be made collectively, and upon other choices that are much better made collectively. There is the range of choice that goes from hospitals and public architecture to town planning and national television and from there to research councils and public support for the arts. There is in brief the immensely important problem of the amount and kind of social income needed to maximize the quality of total income.

To take these categories in turn let me begin with the size of the national income, and with the flat assertion that the social democratic commitment to full employment is complete. Everyone who wants a job should either have one or be able to find one in a short space of time. As always, of course, I have in mind only the Canadian situation and no wider context. Admittedly there is nothing distinctively social democratic in the advocacy of full employment, but it is clear from the series of post-war recessions (in 1949, 1954, 1958 and again in 1961) and the growing totals of seasonal unemployment that the pledges of the older parties are of a *pro forma* kind.

Is an unqualified pledge possible to honour? I think it is. Unemployment is a more difficult problem for an open economy than a closed, more difficult on this count for Canada than for the United States; but it seems to me that such interventions as have been made – the housing expenditures of 1958, for example, or even the various programmes of winter works – have had effects direct and substantial enough to confirm that a full solution is possible. As unemployment is reduced to its chronic elements they will probably prove to be regional and structural. For efficient remedy the classical prescriptions of deficits, easy money, and the rest, will then have to be supplemented by controls of a more selective kind. But the evidence so far available is that both the classical prescriptions and the specific controls do very much what they are expected to do, and are not particularly difficult to adjust to changing requirements. The real need is determined and systematic intervention, in brief, the acceptance of economic planning.

It is not so much the technical possibility of full employment that needs discussion as the balance of social gains and losses. (In the last analysis the government could always maintain employment by operations in the open market, on the pattern of bond and exchange dealings.) The existence of some losses has to be conceded. It is inexcusable but true that no comprehensive survey has yet been made of Canadian seasonal unemployment, an expanded sampling of the labour force that would reveal who and where the seasonally unemployed are, what skills they have and what their employment history has been. But I imagine it is more than probable that in the winter months many of the unemployed are in a market sense unemployable, and in specially created jobs would add less to the statistics of real output than their jobs would cost to create, even with allowance for existing payments to the unemployed. Indeed the total elimination of seasonal unemployment would likely add little or nothing to the real statistics, and certainly an amount in negligible proportion to the man-hours now lost. But if these things are true it would still be social democratic policy to apply whatever "seasonal discrimination" is needed to provide jobs from November to April, devices such as seasonal depreciation and tax allowances to transfer work from summer to winter as efficiently as possible. The commitment would not be based upon the doubtful chance of a small gain in production, but upon the income outside the scope of the national accounts that is given in the assurance that all who want to work can find jobs. The worth of this income, like other dimensions of security, is to be conjectured rather than measured, but the social democratic estimate is that people value it very highly indeed.

The net advantage from eliminating other forms of unemployment (cyclical, structural) is even clearer, since here the same contribution to personal security is normally supplemented by impressive additions to real output. I recall a chilling computation from the 1958 recession that the steel the United

States had *not* been producing totalled more than the steel the Soviet Union had been producing. It would be easy enough to find equally picturesque consequences of recession now. And yet anyone who has read the submissions of the financial houses to the Senate's committee on inflation, and anyone who has studied the utterances of the Bank of Canada will agree that inflation, and even the prospect or anticipation of inflation, is proposed in some quarters as an equal danger with unemployment, and as requiring remedies that would nullify or reduce the prescriptions for recession whenever a rising price level is seen or expected. If employment and the price level were in fact related so that to maintain employment greatly sacrificed real output to inflation then the pledge of full employment would be unreasonable. It would be better to accept unemployment, and improve the doles to the unemployed. But it seems to me there is not the slightest evidence of such a hazard, and that attempts to place inflation in the same scale with unemployment can be confidently rejected.

It is not necessary to assert that in itself inflation is ever a good thing, although I would guess that as a lubricant and limited to a percentage point or two a year it probably is. We can agree that when inflation is rapid, ten or fifteen percentage points a year or more, as sometimes in post-war Europe it has been, its dislocative and speculative effects may become so burdensome that control is a prerequisite to economic progress of any kind. The point is that inflation in North American magnitudes has had effects that can only have been incidental in relation to the state of employment they have accompanied. In Canada wholesale prices are about where they were in the Korean War. The entire cycle of consumers' prices from the recession of 1954 through the investment boom of 1956, the further recession of 1958 and the abortive recovery of 1959, has been compressed in a range of about 10 per cent; and even in the lushest days of expansion, with investment rising from a 1954 total of $4.4 billion to a 1956 total of $7.6 billion, with inherently inflationary defence expenditures running to $1.8 billion, with a politically courageous but still modest response to those pressures by the central bank, even in those circumstances inflation amounted to only some 3 per cent a year. If a guarantee of full employment does press upwards on the price level, it is hard to imagine a result exceeding the pressures of the exceptionally buoyant days of 1956 and 1957, and in that period surely nothing intolerable or even notably onerous was experienced.

Can we price ourselves out of world markets? We may find foreign competition toughening, but not because of inflation restricted to the magnitudes of 1954–60. On the one hand it is only the differential between inflation here and inflation abroad that matters, and that has been and is likely to be negligible in comparison with other factors affecting trade; and on the other, whatever differential may appear tends to be offset by the cushioning effect of the exchange rate. We should remind ourselves that we are not world bankers, and need not imitate (or exceed!) the fears of inflation of those who are. To accept a little unemployment as a protection of trade would be the most arid kind of reaction.

But what about the impact of even mild inflation upon those least able to afford it, the pensioners, the widows, and so on? I think the social democratic answer is simple and decisive. It is absurd *not* to have pensions and the like largely fixed in real terms. Basic payments from government should be adjusted to match rising prices as a matter of course (and should be adjusted, too, to match improved national productivity, although that is a separate issue). The forms in which private savings can be stored should be regulated with the same end in view, payment in real terms for those who need that protection. Society either decides in a deliberate way the proportion of national output that pensioners and the others are to have, and modifies their incomes accordingly; or it allows that proportion to be the unplanned result of changing prices. It would be utterly fallacious to think of these things in terms of actuarial soundness or unsoundness. The payments that society makes may be high or low but unless they are borrowed from abroad they are meaningfully reckoned only on a "pay as you go" basis – their accounting basis is quite incidental.

In an erratic and discontinuous way adjustments that balance welfare payments against prices are part of the existing process, and from time to time are applied on an impressive scale. The best example is probably the political freak of the two-stage adjustment of the general pension from $40 to $55 a month. It is an example that shows, too, that a systematic policy of adjustment as contrasted with *ad hoc* changes would not constitute anything like a proportionate addition to inflationary pressure. No doubt welfare spending would increase in some measure, but an equal result would be to make rational a policy that the older parties have applied awkwardly as events have forced it upon them.

The redistributive effects of inflation are often wildly exaggerated. Within the limits of our recent experience, the limits of anything that might be attributed to full employment, I do not think the statistics show any really important problem except for the welfare payments we have just discussed. The expropriation of the savings of bondholders and similar repercussions are not real possibilities. Reference to the surveys of liquid assets conducted by the Dominion Bureau of Statistics shows that the inflationary redistribution of wealth must be almost nil for the majority of families, and of slight consequence for most of the rest. In 1956, for example, the average family (non-farm and with "unattached individuals" counted) had only $1,525 in liquid assets and an additional $476 in mortgages and personal loans, while the median family had corresponding totals of only $234 and $28. To find a *total* of monetary savings various insurance and pension funds would have to be added in, but judging by the experience of the United

States these would certainly fall short of doubling the sums already counted. Even without an allowance for the offsetting effects of debt, real losses to inflation can only have been small, not more than a few dollars a year for most families. Persistent mild inflation might eventually induce people to *transform* their savings – hence the bankers' fears? – but since the change would favour equity investment it might even improve the capital market. As for redistribution via salaries and wages, again it is only differentials that matter, and again inflation on the Canadian scale can hardly have produced important differentials. Moreover, there are few groups whose bargaining position is weakened by moderate inflation in the way it is checked by the smallest touch of unemployment.

In setting out questions bearing on the size of the national income I listed other issues than employment and inflation, and suggested that inflation really had more importance as a political than an economic theme. But since I am not going to try to give equal treatment to equal themes, except to declare their equality, I shall let these further topics pass with a few dogmatic sentences apiece.

There is the choice of commercial policy. Under Canadian conditions I think the logic of social democracy leads to an active sponsorship of free trade, or at least of trade much freer than trade now is. The theoretical credentials of free or freer trade are not so impressive that we have to accept its value misty-eyed; but at the practical level there is really no better peg on which to tie international co-operation. It is an instrument of rational economic planning, just as the price system is in the domestic economy. Its role goes much further, though, because in the international economy so little else can be used. In such terms the Canadian case for freer trade has been a strong one for many years. With the emergence of the new trading blocs, and the danger of our economic isolation, it has become urgent. Our clear interest now is to free our trade with Europe, with the Commonwealth, with the United States, to press for the exchange of markets with any of these and with other trading areas as well. Yet although it is a policy promising the greatest general advantage it can hardly be pursued except within the framework of the planned economy. The pace of transition must be controlled, compensation must be devised for areas and industries that are dependent on the old arrangements. Even after transition the guarantees of planning are essential. A shift to free trade lengthens the list of forces affecting the domestic economy. Their inevitable fluctuations must be offset, or else those they threaten will insist on protection, no matter what the general benefit from trade. To realize the gains from trade, economic security must be assured at home. As I said before, it would be quite unrealistic to expect any industry willingly to subsidize trade by unemployment. But if there is such an assurance of security, if disruptive changes are cushioned and employment maintained despite the vagaries of events abroad, I think the persuasive part of protectionist arguments largely disappears.

Acceptance of the controlled economy also allows a coherent attitude to the inflow of capital from the United States. If we agree that it is desirable to regulate the total and distribution of investment financed at home, we are bound to agree that investment financed from abroad must also be regulated, and by the same test of national interest. But we are then freed from the appeals to economic nationalism that have come to be a crude substitute for planning. In this area national identity can be preserved by a general control of capital markets without the dangerous adjuncts of discrimination and anti-American sentiment.

One further brief subheading: there is the social democratic approach to monopoly and anti-trust problems. I am afraid that this is an issue of the first importance on which agreement can be reached on final goals of policy, but for which the known machinery of policy must be regarded with meagre faith in its efficiency and purpose. In the light of recent jurisprudence – beer and sugar – it is tempting to say that only those who believe in planning have any real confidence in the price system. One object of social democratic policy is certainly to reduce the wide difference between promise and performance in the conventional anti-trust programme. Partly this is a matter of adding to the resources of the enforcement agencies; but to a greater extent I think it depends on substituting administrative for juridical procedures in testing business behaviour. Rules of mechanical application, so-called *per se* rules, are not much use, for example, in examining a complex merger, for though they may be predictable and objective, they still fail to distinguish the good merger from the bad. The defect is fatal and so "rules of reason" are required; but then the ordinary court cannot be expected to provide them in so specialized a field. The need is for an administrative court or commission as specialized in its processes as the problem itself. It might be empowered, say, to review all mergers above a certain size and to act as a kind of licensing agency, accepting some as being in the public interest and rejecting others. This would not bar either appeals to or enforcement in the ordinary courts, but it would allow an economically meaningful determination of the facts. Such an administrative emphasis is normal enough in social democratic thinking, in a context where economic controls do not have to be regarded as either reproof or punishment.

I want to turn now to the second major issue, the rate at which the national income is to grow. With due allowance for leisure the size of the national income should be as large as possible. There is no correspondingly simple presumption about growth. A buoyant and fully employed economy may show a very low rate of growth, while a depressed and stagnant economy may, with less likelihood, show a high rate. The ideas are easily confused, and often produce unwarranted hymns to growth.

There is no reason to accept either the rate of investment or the rate of growth that the market grinds out as having a natural claim to superiority in even the sense that ordinary market prices have over non-market prices.

The *repercussions* of growth are often large, and may greatly modify and even reverse its immediate effects upon welfare. For example, the unregulated inflow of United States capital in the past decade has undoubtedly been of immense benefit to particular regions of the economy, but at the same time it has conditioned our economic development for many years to come, limiting the routes we can follow in the future. The restraint is likely to prove costly, not because of its American origin or a considered subordination of Canadian interests, but simply because its effects are haphazard and unforeseen.

But more nearly fundamental than the external cost of growth is what can be called the "horizon" problem. Growth is good or bad, depending almost entirely on the persons whose welfare is taken into account. The great-grandchildren of those in the Chinese communes may gain from the misery of this generation and the next, but no comparison of rates of growth can say much about the worth of the substitution. Growth generated in the market is less harsh in its results, but it is equally arbitrary in its valuation of persons. There is no natural boundary within which growth is to come to fruition.

Since the market can give no guidance it follows that the best rate of growth has to be determined by society. It certainly cannot be taken for granted (as it was in the Bank of Canada's *Report* for 1956 – there have been afterthoughts) that the object of economic policy in the world of today is "to facilitate economic growth at the highest rate that can be sustained for years at a time without endangering the stability of the currency. ..." On that severe principle we would at once abolish pensions. It seems to me that the typically social democratic view of how this determination should be made is that all persons must count, and all must count equally; and that the estimate of people's wants that follows from this view is that they prefer welfare to expansion, that they value many of the things growth displaces more highly than growth itself and are prepared to accept a low rate of growth – in per capita terms – because of its concomitant benefits in consumption and social capital.

I will have to qualify this in a moment because it would be unrealistic in an open economy to press for goals that might be ideal in a closed one. In practical terms the qualification is important. I would emphasize, too, that this estimate of wants presupposes a technically advanced economy where living standards are already tolerable and where the individual who wants to save can always do so. In the underdeveloped countries I suppose the social democratic estimate would join the rest in judging that hope is to be found only in a high rate of growth, although high even then by New Delhi's standards and not those of Peiping.

Let me be quite clear that there is nothing deliberately ascetic in this view of growth. Other things being equal, of course the more growth the better.

Where growth is a free good, as it is in a recession of any depth, it should always be accepted and encouraged. When equipment is to be replaced or reinvestment undertaken, there is no reason to choose less than the most profitable and efficient of techniques. Innovation is at least as welcome as it is under any other choice of programme, and though the emphasis on welfare expenditures is directed to the present good of those affected, there is no hint of austere regret that spending on health and housing will in the long run also enhance growth.

Growth for its own sake, or solely for the welfare of those yet to be born, or for the fame of the state as something apart from its people, is an essentially totalitarian goal. If all persons are to count, and to count equally, and if the claims of posterity are not in some mystical way to be ranked above our own, it is a necessary consequence that a high standard of living in the present should not be sacrificed to a still higher standard in the future. The alternative is a kind of regressive tax paid by one generation to the next. The logic of the social democratic position, I think, is that expenditures for *per capita growth* in an economy like our own should be a residual of other expenditures, a slack variable that ensures the full use of our resources but that is not applied until current needs have been satisfied. I have never been able to imagine future benefits that most people are likely to rank above the value of good housing *now*, of first-class and easily available medical services *now*, of free education *now*, and of the other entries in the catalogue of the welfare state.

With some reluctance I must come to the qualification I spoke of, the limit to our choice of growth that is set by Canada's role in the world economy. It is unlikely that we can insulate ourselves from the pattern of growth in the United States, unlikely that we can insulate ourselves from the competitive growth of the totalitarian economies, unlikely that we can, or should choose to, insulate ourselves from the capital needs of the under-developed countries. Each of these forces operates to require investment rather than welfare expenditures. Growth in the *open* economy cannot be left as a mere residual, but must include a calculated defence against external pressures. In response to American needs and Soviet growth, social democratic planning must accept whatever rate of development is necessary to preserve national identity, so that to this extent at least it must accept growth as an autonomous object of policy. In addition to this necessity, in addition to adapting to growth in the advanced economies, social democratic planning must offset such transfers of wealth as *are* made to the underdeveloped areas, thus narrowing further the range from which growth can be chosen, in the long run perhaps more decisively than anything else.

Does it make any practical difference to emphasize welfare rather than expansion if expansion must nevertheless be accepted and even encouraged? I think it does. If we think of expansion that is pressed upon us by external forces rather than deliberately chosen, if we think of such expansion in the same way we think of spending on defence, as something to be reduced and minimized when circumstances allow, then our policies have a different and more rational direction than if we indulge in an endless eulogy of growth. To admit that *some* response has to be made to external pressures does not prevent a systematic effort to enlarge consumption and social capital even when those pressures are greatest. Given such a view of growth, it would not be necessary to think of the federal housing expenditures of the past few years as an emergency programme required only to compensate for an unfortunate lapse in normal spending, inherently wasteful policies to be eliminated from the accounts as soon as normality returns, but as social contributions of great value in their own right that should have been expanded to exclude any element of slack, and then continued for many years to come without a sense of shame.

At the practical level how are the benefits of the welfare state to be paid for? At the practical level I think the social democratic answer to that durable question from the right is to turn first to the slack in the home economy and to the funds that can be diverted from the more wasteful follies of our military budget. When there are idle resources, the limits to policy, of course, are again internal to the home economy, and welfare becomes just as much of a free good as expansion. Only when those limits have been reached is it necessary to determine a margin between welfare and expansion, a margin as I say that is to be determined as a balance to external pressures.

The practical result would be a fully employed economy, a rationally employed economy. In all probability it would also be an economy in which the rate of growth is low. I think this consequence would follow not so much because of the substitution of welfare for growth – there *is* slack to be taken up, the military waste exists – but because of the one external pressure that would be difficult indeed to balance, the call upon our resources to support development in the new economies. That transfer is bound to take place, whether it is volunteered or enforced, for it would be naïve to imagine that expansion in the advanced economies can continue to have priority over the pyramiding claims of the rest of the world. Our choice is the basis of the transfer. I would guess the great majority of persons are ready to support large-scale assistance to the underdeveloped countries as a matter of right. If that is so, it would be disastrous to reduce its quality by sponsoring the transfer as national defence cleverly disguised.

I want to add only a comment or two under the subheadings of this category of growth. One very specific point is the social democratic attitude to the division between work and leisure. Unless the economy is regarded as a factory or a barracks, leisure is as much a component of the national income as any other consumption good. The difficulty is that both the total of leisure and its annual distribution – in daily leisure, statutory holidays, and summer vacations – are determined even more by convention and statute than they are by individual preferences, inevitably enough in view of industry's dependence on standard patterns of leisure for the efficiency of its operations. As a result industrial arrangements for leisure have to be recognized as being as much an object of policy as the level of employment. Where individual preferences can be expected to have had a determining effect, as in the collective bargaining of the "pattern-setting" industries, the role of policy is clearly to be guided rather than to guide. But this is not the general rule. It simply is not known, for example, whether most people prefer a shorter workday to longer vacations, or the extent to which they may prefer a shorter workday to the goods for which leisure has been traded. There is no presumption in favour of any given arrangement, and nothing in market forces that would automatically produce a best selection. The role of policy in such circumstances is to investigate what individual preferences actually are. It is an exercise in democratic planning. The conventions and statutes controlling leisure can then be changed as the facts suggest, quite possibly producing a notable improvement in welfare at almost invisible cost.

A more general point is the fact that goals with respect to growth obviously depend on a much finer classification of goods than a simple division into investment and consumption, although that is a useful first reference. The social democratic stress on welfare gives a very high rank to social spending, to the provision of goods that are used collectively. But that is a category that overlaps the division between investment and consumption, and that in each has markedly uneven effects upon growth. It is probably true that in the short run very little public spending makes a contribution to growth, whether the spending is on capital or current account. On the other hand, it is at least arguable that in the long run nothing would assist growth as much as extra spending, capital or current, on education and research. Discussion in these terms becomes increasingly tenuous as attention is turned to public spending on transportation, from there to spending on communication, to spending on health, on entertainment, on the arts. No doubt in every case there are long-run effects upon growth, but as one goes through the list these effects become more and more complex and remote, and less and less likely to deserve much weight in deciding policy.

Does this blurring of lines as specific goods are examined much affect the assertion that welfare is to be preferred to expansion? Not really. It would if welfare generally assisted expansion, but that fortunate case is exceptional. Social democracy must regularly make choices in which welfare is *substituted* for expansion in a quite deliberate way. As I have just observed, there is no bleak presumption against leisure, the consumers' good *par excellence*. Its total is to be whatever the bulk of individual preferences want it to be. Subject to external pressures there is no presumption either against light industry, against consumers' durables, no presumption that saving is

to be encouraged or is of special merit. There is no presumption that consumers' credit is of less social worth than commercial credit. This is all in
contrast with the existing puritanical presumption in favour of investment.
But I think the most important (domestic) substitution of welfare for expansion contemplated in social democratic thought is the diversion of resources to those leaving the work force, to those pensioned or retired. The
substitution offers a choice of earlier retirement, it increases the income of
those who have retired, and it extends the opportunities and services society
makes available to them. It is an enlargement of the *unenforceable* but basic
contract between the productive and no longer productive members of society. To the charge that it is sentimentality to widen the contract I suppose
the social democratic reply is that it is one further act of civilization. In any
case, it is as clear a test as there is of the competing claims of welfare and
growth. The planned transfer to welfare spending is very large, and at the
same time is a transfer that can contribute nothing whatever to growth.

The third of the major themes that I set out earlier was the distribution
of the national income. There is no reason to expect that social democrats
will depart from the traditional goals of equalization and equality. Admittedly, faith in equality must have some other source than economic doctrine,
if we set aside the assistance fo faith that lack of support for a counter-faith
provides. There is nothing within the compass of theoretical economies that
passes an accepted judgment on the worth or efficiency of comparative
patterns of distribution. No doubt the social democratic position rests directly
on the same value that affirms the political equality of men, a belief in the
equal worth of human beings and a disbelief that any overwhelming advantage flows from an uneven pattern of social benefits. I must be content
to leave deeper explanations to the political scientists.

It is not the article of faith as such that I want to discuss but the sense
in which it is to be interpreted, and the qualifications that are to be attached
to its practical implementation. One sense in which it is *not* to be interpreted
is as mere equality of opportunity. I think that variant appears because a
mechanical interpretation of equality, conceived in terms of individual income tax returns or some similar measure, would be obvious folly. To have
a conceptually consistent basis the idea of equality of income must admit a
great many varieties of purely monetary inequality. The considerable
variation in the cost by which individual incomes are attained must be
recognized, the time given to acquiring skills, the particular risks and uncertainties attached to specific occupations, even the rate at which given
money incomes have increased or decreased. (Even in the redistribution of
income a compensationist approach has its value.) Similarly, the variation
in non-monetary components of income must also be recognized, the availability of leisure, the pleasure to be found in particular kinds of work, the
elements of status and authority. Of the same importance, equality cannot

reasonably be sought in terms of individuals but in relation to families and households, and then only in relation to families and households considered by size and age distribution and other distinguishing features of the needs that income is equally to satisfy.

To clarify the concept not unexpectedly reveals that there are insurmountable difficulties in the way of its unqualified attainment. If equality were set as an absolute goal, the repercussions on the size of the national income would be fabulously expensive simply because of the energies that would have to be applied to equalization as such. "Equality of opportunity" instead of "equality" avoids most of these difficulties, the conceptual as well as the practical, but it is really a quite different principle and leads to a different choice of goals. A parent may hope equally for the welfare of his children, the dull as well as the clever, but if he does, it is the attainment and not the opportunity of their equal welfare that concerns him. Although the difference is obscured in a society where there is a great deal of inequality by either test, it may already be a matter of critical importance for at least one decision, the resources to be set aside for education. Education on the principle of equality is directed to the needs of the individual and only then to society's interest in those who are educated. It is mass education, education as a free good and to the limit of individual capacity, and not education for an élite, however meritorious and productive and self-sacrificing that élite may be.

The difficulties with "equality" as a goal of policy are inherent, and cannot be defined out of existence. Equality is complex to measure, and it interacts with other goals. But despite this, I do not think we have to retreat very far from absolutes before we come to systems of equalization that would be administratively feasible in a closed economy. Larger transfer payments, to persons, regions, and industries, a wider system of social services, the subsidization of housing and other "necessities," these like other items of spending represent reasonably cost-free methods of equalization, while widened tax exemptions for low-income groups are probably an even more economical device. As for taxation, although the expense of income tax collection undoubtedly accelerates as rates are raised, it would be surprising to find that it has yet reached a limiting level, the more so if rates are raised by discontinuing exemptions of a typically "high-income" kind. If equalization does have to depend more on increased spending than on increased taxation, then balance can be restored by monetary controls and other restraints on investment. The social democratic concern for equality is in harmony with its attitude to economic growth.

In practical terms equalization must stop well short of equality. But note that the compromises with pure principle so far accepted do not depend on disadvantages in equality itself, supposing equality to be attained, but on the prohibitive cost of equalizing processes used in an unlimited way, on the cost of *administering* unqualified equality. Indeed I am not ready to agree that within a closed economy there *are* net disadvantages to equality as such, in the sense of repercussions that would clearly subtract from the size of the national income. The usual marginal arguments – a high income tax dulls incentive and limits effort, welfare payments dull incentive and limit effort – must meet the objection that at some levels these things sharpen incentive rather than dull it, and the further objection that many occupations cannot be entered on marginal terms but must be accepted or rejected as they stand without any variation of their requirements. Admittedly the force of this second objection is less clear cut in respect of entrepreneurship than for less "dynamic" factors, but I think even there it has some weight; and I am certainly not convinced that entrepreneurship is encouraged or rewarded by anything as much as it is by power and responsibility. There is the point, too, that equality presumably diminishes wasteful, emulative effects of a Veblenesque kind.

Statistical evidence on either side of these issues is, of course, very thin. The range of our experience is too narrow and spread over too long a time to decide such effects as the impact of tax rates on incentives. But whatever the worth of speculative argument on these points there is one qualification to goals of equality that makes much of the discussion academic. Pretty clearly the easily crossed frontier a few miles to the south and the distribution of incomes found beyond that frontier are determining factors in the extent to which equalization can be pressed within our own economy. Extensive measures to equalize income can be sponsored even though the much wider United States market is generally open to Canadian factors of production; but the predictable result of such measures, seen in the movement of factors across the border, is the index of what it is reasonable to propose and what it is not.

There is a considerable simplification of policy in this outcome. As with the choice between welfare and expansion, so here the governing fact of policy is the situation abroad. Most of what I said under that earlier heading could be repeated here without change. It is important once again to establish that departures from ideal conditions are enforced rather than chosen. This at least allows policy to be redirected in an automatic way when changes in the controlling conditions occur. Social democratic policy, I would judge, is to move as far as possible towards an equal distribution of incomes. How far is that, and what in fact limits policy? Evidently the effective limit is set by the influence of the United States economy. Equalization can be pursued up to the point where American arrangements have become unduly disruptive of our own, a limit that has to be set pragmatically and tested politically.

The one subheading under which I have a comment to make is the role of the trade union in redistribution. The trade union has a certain function in redistributing money incomes in the market place, but it also contributes other elements to its members' incomes, thus, independence, security, a share in the power structure of the nation. Many would even argue that these latter functions exceed the first in importance. They are functions that are remarkably sensitive to the institutional framework within which they operate, to trade union structure itself, to the laws limiting or encouraging trade union activity, to the boards and agencies the laws establish. Historically, both the bursts of energy the movement sometimes shows and its long periods of stagnation have been closely related with the question of whether or not outmoded institutions have been reformed. On this view the trade union movement needs nothing today so much as institutional change. The basis of the favour with which social democracy regards the union movement is partly the movement's narrowly economic role, but much more its role in giving its members an equal place in society. In that respect the movement has gradually but undoubtedly lost much of its vigour. Remedial policy is simple enough to state, if decidedly less simple to implement. It is to assist the movement to make institutional changes, and in particular, to help it follow its members as they advance in the new technology from blue collar to white collar and semi-professional status. One element of reform is to have laws that regard unionism as beneficial to society, as something to be encouraged rather than merely permitted wherever it can be instituted.

Let me be very brief in dealing with the last of the four main categories with which I began, the quality of the national income. I want to be brief to bring an overly long paper to a close, and because the tests of quality have already been suggested by the discussion of other goals. I do *not* want, though, to subordinate the issue of quality itself for if the categories must be ranked it may be that correct choices here are vital to a degree they are nowhere else.

I suggested earlier that discussion in this area could be made to turn on the concept of consumers' sovereignty. As item one of a short enumeration: social democracy is obviously prepared to restrict attempts to make consumers' choice less rational. Policy goals include selective and much heavier taxes upon advertising, much more stringent rules about labelling and advertising copy, perhaps devices in the BBC fashion which separate advertising from communication proper. The needed qualification is always that the rules by which the consumer is defended do not themselves intrude on his freedom.

Social democracy, I think, is also prepared to commit itself to measures intended not only to preserve but to widen the rationality of consumers' choice. Education as a free good is the obviously predominant example, but at a more humble level there is the provision of public funds to consumers' associations and research agencies. Social democracy is also prepared to accept the responsibility of multiplying the flow of social income, of implementing collective choices in the many areas where individual choice cannot be effectively realized. In this its position is taken not in order to override consumers' sovereignty, as though it were entitled to provide a paternal authority, but to extend consumers' sovereignty to decisions from which the consumer would otherwise be barred. In both aspects – the increased flow of social income, the deference to the authority of the consumer – this endorsement of collective choice is basic to the social democratic position.

Social democracy, that is to say, looks for its economic values to consumer opinion that as far as may be is undistorted, that as far as may be is informed and instructed, and that often seeks expression in social choices – in all of which the essential thing is that it looks to consumer opinion. I speak of "economic values" and "consumer opinion" because this paper has been limited to economic issues, and more honorific terms are therefore not available. But I imagine that if social democracy is to command sizeable support it must be as ready on wider issues to accept the values of the consumer-as-citizen as it is to accept his values as mere consumer on purely economic questions. I suppose this amounts to saying that social democracy must above all else be democratic in its socialism.

CHAPTER TWO

What Is Planning?

Only yesterday it was just one more example of leftist folly to call for a planned economy. Along with the rest of the program of the Co-operative Commonwealth Federation, it was labelled impractical and visionary and revolutionary and wicked. And now today almost everyone is saying that planning is a good thing and there should be more of it. The Quebec Liberals claim they are already indulging in something called democratic planning. The federal Liberals confess that they too will plan if they are allowed a further chance in office. And as if there were no end to wonders, even the British Tories have let the world know they intend to use the language of planning. To find planning spoken of in the good old fashioned way as a term of anathema and vile reproach, it is necessary to go to the pure rare air of Arizona and the four-square doctrines of Senator Goldwater.

This sort of thing is an old experience for the democratic left. The CCF knew only too well what it was to present ideas for years on end, and then have them borrowed or copied by the older parties. Hospital schemes and the like would be fought until it was political suicide to fight them any more, and then the right wing parties would calmly reverse themselves. They would present social progress as their own idea, taking care to dilute it as much as they dared. Obviously at the level of practical politics the device worked very well indeed. It blocked progress as much as progress could be blocked, and it prevented CCF politicians from winning elections. Imitation was a flattering fact but a decided political handicap.

In this area of planning, however, the imitations we hear about give no reason for comfort on any basis. Very little about them is real. They are bogus imitations. They are fakes. They do not represent sick-bed conversion,

Reprinted with permission from *Democratic Planning: A Symposium* (Toronto: Ontario Woodsworth Memorial Foundation, 1962), 1–13.

but the use of the language of repentance to deceive. These imitations of planning belong to the same species as "right to work laws" (which are there to break unions and have nothing to do with guaranteeing work) and codes of "fair trade" (which are there to help monopolies exploit consumers, and have nothing to do with fair trade).

Social democratic planning has to be distinguished from its counterfeits. Let me begin by saying a few words about a number of things that planning is NOT.

PLANNING IS NOT FORECASTING

Planning is not the mere announcement of what will happen to the economy this year or next year or in years to come. It is not the mere announcement of what is expected to happen, even if the announcement is very detailed and gives information about what will happen to specific industries and to specific regions. It is not forecasting the unemployment rate this year, or the rate of recovery next year, or the investment in primary iron and steel in the year after that. All of this is simply economic prediction, and depending on whether it is done well or badly stands somewhere between prophecy and magic.

There is nothing wrong with economic forecasting in itself, of course. It is a basic tool of planning, and in that task is steadily becoming more efficient and reliable. But to substitute it for planning amounts to accepting the free enterprise myth that whatever happens to the economy is inevitable and good. In effect we would be saying that we can predict what is going to happen to the economy, but cannot – or should not – do anything about it.

Even within its own narrow sphere, economic forecasting is much less accurate without planning than with it. It is like the problem of predicting where a motor car will go. Keep your hands on the wheel and you can predict where the car will head pretty accurately. Take them off the wheel and you can make only the roughest guess just where in the ditch you will land.

This bears on a curious argument opponents of planning sometimes use. They will point to some gross error they have made in prediction, such as promising that the year 1960 would take the economy back to boom conditions. They will then say with modest candour, "Look at that really remarkable error we made. We are only human and we admit it. Clearly nobody can make reliable economic forecasts. How can the New Democratic Party or anyone else be so irresponsible as to call for a fully planned economy when prediction is so difficult?" One answer is certainly that to confess incompetence does not prove someone else is incompetent. But I think a more restrained reply is just this fact that prediction without planning cannot be compared to prediction with planning. We can tell where we are going with planning, and cannot without it.

PLANNING IS NOT SUMMING UP

So planning is not simply forecasting. Nor is planning the mere lumping together of the separate programs of government departments. Whether it takes place at the federal or the provincial level, that lumping together of separate programs is part of the uncoordinated system we already have. Planning begins with a general estimate of what the federal or the provincial economy can do. It deals next with the major components of the total, with the amount of consumption and investment, with the main kinds of investment, with the varieties of consumption, and so on. Planning works its way down from totals to particulars. It does not begin with the particulars which only by chance might add up to anything sensible.

At the centre of planning must be the economic plan itself, a program for both the short run and the long. It is the economic plan that eventually says what the economic activities of government departments should be, and not the other way around. Full employment is an achievable goal of the planned economy because we begin with that goal and work our way through to the things government agencies need to do to attain it. We do not begin with the programs of the government agencies, regretfully announcing that when we add them up it will leave half a million or three-quarters of a million persons out of work.

THE ROLE OF INVESTMENT

The same point appears in another way when we look at the investment plans of private business. There can be no economic planning that means anything unless the investment decisions of large private businesses are regulated. Nothing else touches the progress of the economy as much as those decisions do. They determine employment, they account for expansion and growth. But notice why it is vital to regulate them. It is not at all for the kind of reason which the opponents of planning suggest – that planners in Ottawa or Quebec City believe they know more about making steel or newsprint than the managers who have spent their lives in those businesses. Sensible planners would never imagine themselves as being expert in every technical field, nor would they seek a general authority over people at the practical end of industry.

It is vital to regulate the big investment decisions, first, because these decisions are often made under monopolistic conditions and, secondly, because they are uncoordinated. They are made by this firm and by that, by this industry and by that, and in general are not going to add up to anything that is economically correct either for a province or Canada as a whole. One by one these investments may be planned, are almost certain to be planned; but taken together they are inevitably unplanned and wasteful. Look back to the investment boom of 1956 and 1957, and see a very clear example. Look at investment totals jumping by about 75% over a two-year period for no reason that could possibly make economic sense. It is no wonder the federal Liberals begin to speak respectfully of planning, having allowed such absurdities to happen.

PLANNING IS NOT SETTING ECONOMIC GOALS

To come back to things that planning is not, it is certainly not a mere statement of economic goals, even if that statement is a refined and elaborate catalogue of the things people want from the economy. When such statements are passed off as planning they are at best wishful thinking and they are more likely to be greater or less of a hoax. The hoax is especially crude and blatant where the supposed plans are logically or physically impossible to attain. I suppose the monetary cure-alls of the Social Crediters are still as good an example as any of these gross oddities. But the hoax is still there even if the supposed plans are possible to attain: the hoax is there because plans are not self-fulfilling, and without determined intervention in the economy, are never likely to be fulfilled.

The hoax is at its most subtle and misleading when the supposed plans represent real possibilities closely related to real needs. Everything is there except the real intention to make what is promised happen. And that amounts to saying that there is really nothing there at all. This is the pseudo-planning which the Liberals offer us – planning that has all the solid usefulness of a mirage.

Planning should be democratic, planning should be based on consultation, planning should be based on individual wants; but anything that presents itself as planning in those terms and nothing more is just a conjuring trick. Planning without some economic control and intervention is utterly meaningless. It is political sleight of hand, like the Progressive Conservative plans for full employment or their plans to divert trade from the USA to the United Kingdom. The Conservatives apparently thought, when making those plans, that they might be desirable things to happen just so long as no one had to do anything to make them happen. And in the outcome, of course, nothing did happen, and things went on exactly as before. No doubt in the more remote areas the Diefenbaker people report to each other: "You know this planning business really doesn't work. We tried it ourselves. The unemployment is still there, and the trade hasn't been diverted. We were right in the old days when we were frankly and simply planless."

PLANNING IS NOT TOTALITARIAN

What I have been saying applies mostly to the varieties of ersatz planning we get from the "free enterprise" parties. But social democratic planning is also very different from communist and other totalitarian notions of planning. Social democratic planning does not merely consist in proposing goals for five years or twenty years or a lifetime away – even when such goals are attainable and in themselves good and desirable. Planning is distorted and degraded when it proposes over and over again to sacrifice the present to the future, when it repeatedly promises Utopia later for the acceptance of misery and hardship now. I am no authority on the real situation on the Chinese mainland, but if conditions are as they are reported, if in fact life is being held at the margin of subsistence to enhance expansion, if in fact it is to be held at that margin for years to come, there is a horror to the program that only modern totalitarians can produce.

Such programs regard present human happiness and comfort as raw materials of progress, to be used up as authority may decree just as steel and coal are to be used up. Certainly there is the possibility of sacrificing one generation for the possible benefit of the next, or the next again if the sacrificial process is continued. Certainly it is possible to sacrifice the well being of the people who constitute the Republic of China to the strengthening of the abstraction called the Republic of China. It may even be that in fifty or a hundred years there will be people in the Republic of China who will benefit from the calculated misery of today. They may even look back to the present leaders of China as benefactors, forgetting the faceless millions from whom progress was pressed. But these ruthless programs of the totalitarians have nothing to do with planning in a social democratic sense. Our view of planning knows no needs of the state that are not the needs of the persons who make up the state. It knows no benefits a generation away that call for misery today. We affirm the old humanist theme: planning is made for man and not man for planning.

Let me mention one further contrast with totalitarian programs: planning is not the substitution of the values and tastes of the planners for the values and tastes of the rest of the community. Even when totalitarian programs attempt to pursue human values instead of the mystical lunacies of the state, even then they impose values and choices on the community instead of being an instrument by which people attain what they themselves want.

Examples abound in the remote heaven promised the Russians by Mr. Khrushchev in 1961. In twenty years, so the Communist Revelation maintains, there is to be apartment space for everyone, comfortable and free. This is at least a human response to a human want. But if free apartment space is provided for everyone, then living space in other forms and other goods that people want will not have been provided for those who may have preferred them. Obviously there is nothing wrong and everything right with apartment space in itself, but to decide from on high that precisely this is wanted by everyone is inevitably wasteful, and in less happy examples than apartment space, may well be inhumanly wasteful. As the old gag line puts it: "Comes the revolution and you'll eat strawberries and cream and like it." Social democratic planning, in contrast, is just what its name implies. It is basically and entirely democratic. Like political democracy, it is an instrument that allows people to make their own choices, and to make them on a basis of equality. It has no higher purpose, but that is a very high purpose indeed, and we can take full pride in it.

DEMOCRATIC PLANNING

So much for the counterfeits from which social democratic planning has to be distinguished. What then is democratic planning? It has three major stages.

1 *It is an account of the possibilities*. It is an estimate of what the economy can do, of what it can do this year, and next year, and in all the years of the foreseeable future. The range of choice is enormous. Even in the short run the list of possibilities is very long, and for lengthier periods it is virtually endless. The choices made today affect the choices that can be made to-morrow. How much education today? How much northern development? What combinations of these things are possible? How does education today or northern development today affect the possibilities five years from now?

In the unplanned society there is a feeling of inevitability about what happens. Only this could have taken place, these things that actually happened. But a planned society shows how wide and rich the possibilities are from which we can choose. Certainly to have one thing is to forego another, to follow one route is to leave other routes unused. Economic planning recognizes that these alternatives exist, and makes it the first order of business to find out what they are.

2 *Democratic planning is the discovery of what people actually want*. It is the discovery of the route people want the economy to take among the multitude of possible routes. Amongst other things it is the use of the political process to present people with choices. It is the use of politics to let people know that such and such choices are possible. It is the use of the administrative process to let people reveal their wants. I have in mind the various advisory councils that appear in the New Democratic program, the channels of communication with consumer groups, with labour, with farmers, with industry. I have also in mind the use of the market place to let people make their own choices, in that area of individual choice where the market place

is efficient, and given that the market place is properly policed and in good working order.

Planning is also the use of government to allow people to make choices they cannot possibly make in the market place, or can only make there in a most difficult and inefficient way. I have in mind the choices that can only be implemented collectively, the social choices people make, the choices people make in groups. This indeed is one of the basic ways in which the New Democratic Party seeks social democracy – it lays great emphasis on the use of planning to allow people to make collective choices barred to them in a purely market society. Planning allows slums to be cleared and cities to be reshaped; it allows transportation to be organized on rational lines; it allows a collective choice of medical and welfare plans. These are all things that people almost certainly will be found to want; but they are not things that can be efficiently attained without planning. The market place knows no means of providing them, and so where it is left to itself, must deny some part of democratic choice – usually without any sinister intent. It is worth underlining: the market place cannot of itself be anything but undemocratic in these areas.

Planning thus produces a Plan, not simply an annual budget or one of those granite-like five year plans, but a systematic program of the goals people want for the short run and the long. The Plan is the product of what is possible and what is wanted. The Plan is not inflexible. Its long run goals are always uncertain and conditional; they have always to be revised as technology changes and as tastes change and as errors are found and corrected. And at the same time the short run goals on the Plan have to be rewritten as they become the facts of the day and are accomplished and done with. The Plan is always changing, but at any given time it is the best evidence there is of the things people want from their economy.

3 *Social democratic planning is the deliberate, determined use of economic intervention and control to attain the goals of the Plan.* As I have already said, without intervention and control democratic choice is ended. Things the community wants and could have will not be gained. In what other aspect of human affairs would so obvious a proposition need debate? Yet in discussing the economy of Canada it certainly has to be debated. Nowhere else in our human arrangements does anyone seriously contend that nature should generally be left to look after itself. Here alone is the effort to control our affairs denounced.

Now of course intervention and control are of no value in themselves; it would be preposterous to want to control or regulate anything in the economy simply to admire the beauty of control. It is also true that little if any intervention in the economy is costless. The Bank of Canada is a necessary instrument of control, and even in these sorry recent years has probably

paid for its costs many times over. But costs it does have. Planners may
not live like railway presidents, but still they live and have to be paid. But
planning does not make the vulgar blunder of imagining that it is without
costs. To talk of the things the economy can achieve with planning is only
meaningful if full allowance is made for all the costs of planning. And it
is only in such terms that social democratic planning presents itself.

In brief, then, planning involves three things: finding what the economic
possibilities are; choosing what people want done; and controlling events
to make what is chosen happen. Why plan? Because these three things, if
all of them are done, are likely to be marvellously productive of human
well-being.

ASSESSING THE POSSIBILITIES

I now want to turn to some of the specific ways in which these three aspects
of planning are carried out. As I said earlier, the first stage of planning
begins with estimating those facts that finally limit economic choice. Canada
has such and such natural resources, it has a given stock of capital, it has
a population with certain skills. Canada is further limited by the given state
of its technology, and by the intentions of foreign governments in matters
of foreign trade and investment. These are the ultimate economic facts of
life. Planning begins with knowing as precisely as possible what these facts
are, for these facts set the outer limit to what Canada can do. In planning
for the long run, of course, all of these can be seen as flexible. Skills can
be improved, technology will change, relations with foreign governments
will alter. But even the later flexibility is finally governed by the state of
things as they now are. And so planning begins with taking inventory of
these basic facts.

And then these basic facts give rise to questions like these: What patterns
of national income are available to us over the next several years? What
patterns of income are available to the various provinces? Even in the short
run there are many choices. We might, for example, have a shorter work
week and a smaller national income, or a longer week and more income.
In the long run an infinitude of patterns are possible, for our choice of goods
today will greatly affect the income that can be produced tomorrow. Other
questions which must be answered are: What use of foreign capital, of
foreign resources is open to us? What gains and losses are involved? What
kinds of foreign trade are possible? What happens if more free trade is
chosen or more protection? What choices are possible between consumer
goods and capital goods, and between one class of consumer or capital goods
and another? What choice do we have between factories and housing, between public and private capital? In brief, what is the menu from which the
Canadian economy is to dine?

There are more questions in other areas: What distribution of goods is possible from one income group to the next, or from one region to another? What contribution to underdeveloped countries is possible? The list goes on indefinitely. All of these questions eventually involve every imaginable political complication, but at the first level of enquiry there is really nothing at all political in them. They are technical questions, to be answered as well as may be so that not only will democratic choice be possible, but democratic choice that is instructed and informed. In a planned economy answers to them must be continuously worked out and revised.

The answers to these questions must come from experts in all parts of the community. Trends in a given industry, trends in its output, its markets and its technology, will usually come from experts within the industry itself. Inventories of natural resources come from wherever the experts in those things happen to be – in government, university or elsewhere. No one person or groups of persons even begins to be a universal authority in this complex age. The ultimate planning authority at the federal or provincial level is, of course, the federal or provincial cabinet. But it would be naive to think that cabinet ministers, however well qualified, would or could occupy themselves with the technical problems of planning.

Even the federal and provincial agencies of planning – the planning and investment boards or whatever they may finally be called – need only be and will only be expert in a comparatively narrow technical range. They will know, as well as these things can be known, how to handle and condense and report on the information that other experts provide. Sometimes, no doubt, they will acquire and process information directly. But the constant review of what is possible does not depend on any foolish assumption that somewhere there will be an omniscient body capable of being a kind of oracle of planning. A planned economy will need more trained minds in government than there are now; but it does not presuppose or need some drastic reshuffling of the present sources of technical knowledge.[1]

MAKING THE CHOICES

After exploring the range of possible choice, planning continues by making choices. I want to make a special point about the way in which this process

---

[1] I might add a word about planning in the comparatively narrow perspective of the official technical agencies. As a purely logical problem this matter of listing possibilities for the economy depends on two things: first, the various basic limits on the economy found in its natural resources, population, etc., and secondly, the technology of the economy and its likely development. The facts of these things generally come to the technical agencies from outside experts. But the official technical agencies would use these facts to make models and projections of the economy, sometimes very complex, often very simple; and from these models reasonable estimates of what is possible emerge.

is democratic. The program of the New Democratic Party, for example, contains certain choices which were selected by the Party Convention. But since the Party asserts that it has no intention of trying to impose its values – nothing could be more contradictory of the Party's nature – the economic program of the Party becomes the economic Plan of society only when society has chosen that Plan. The Party wants a full employment act, and vested pensions, and heavy spending on social capital, because it thinks these things are essential parts of a good society. The program exists before the political majorities are known. But if the program becomes the Plan then it is only because it has been democratically endorsed, only because society has chosen to have the full employment act and the vested pensions and the social capital.

A political program, however, can only fix the main framework of an economic Plan. Admittedly that main framework is the most important feature of the Plan, but there has to be a great deal of planning of a specific kind that cannot possibly appear in a general program. Planning at all times has to consult public opinion on day to day choices. No forum is better for this than Parliament itself. In Parliament and its committees the people's representatives of all parties can scrutinize proposed programs as they can nowhere else. They can scrutinize the Plan, they can amend or reject it in part or in whole, they can adapt it and accept it in response to the popular will and their own judgment.

A further device for finding out the public's wishes is an Economic Advisory Council such as is proposed in the program of the New Democratic Party. Through a council of this type it is possible to keep in close touch with the views of agriculture, commerce, labour and other groups. The consumer's point of view must also be considered. The New Democratic Party program suggests that a member of the federal cabinet be charged with the responsibility of representing the consumer point of view on all isues, and that a specific research organization be created to assist him. The planning body also needs to consult public opinion in ways that are not quite so direct. By its own research it must keep track of the large proportion of opinion that will not be expressed through formal channels. It must consult public opinion in the market place, taking as its principal task here the duty of keeping the market place representative. It must oppose itself to monopolistic practices on the one hand, and to the distortion of communication and information on the other.

Planning at this second stage is planning at its most fundamental. It is at this stage that the Plan is formed. It is at this stage that planning invokes the political process. Both before and after this stage planning is on the whole a technical business, at any rate in most of its details. But here choice is exercised, and planning becomes a decisive agency of the democratic process.

IMPLEMENTING THE CHOICES

What of the third and final stage of planning? Planning is concluded by applying the techniques and agencies of economic control. What has been planned must be made to happen, as nearly as may be in this imperfect and naughty world. Perfection is not possible but neither is it required or expected. Near achievement is far better than no achievement.

As I have already said, controls are neither good nor bad in themselves. They have value only as they help to achieve goals of real worth. Nationalization, for example, remains an important instrument of control for the New Democratic Party, but it has no higher virtue than that. It is to be used without qualms when it makes goals easier to attain, and when still better instruments are not available; but it is not to be pressed for its own sake as though it were itself a goal. In fact the former emphasis on nationalization was largely a result of there being very few other effective controls around. Nowadays the range of useful controls has been very much widened, so that we are free to examine a great many alternatives before we decide on one choice or another.

The examples are obvious, so I shall spend only a moment in commenting on them. Most important of all nowadays are the spending and taxing powers of the federal and provincial governments. These ar exceedingly versatile instruments, and can be used in countless variations. I would also say that if no other controls were available, these alone would be sufficient to allow smooth and effective planning. But in any case they are far from the only instruments available. Many other agencies already exist. To take examples, one can list the Bank of Canada, the Central Mortgage and Housing Corporation, the Board of Transport Commissioners, the Wheat Board, the Restrictive Trade Practices Commission, the Tariff Board, and a very large total of provincial agencies. Such agencies can be strengthened (or reduced, for that matter) as need suggests, and new agencies can be created; but like nationalization, all of these are means to an end and nothing more.

DO WE NEED CONTROLS?

On this issue of controls, I want to add two brief technical comments and one general comment. One of the technical comments is to point out why a number of instruments of control have to be used and not just one. Why not make one instrument (e.g. the Bank of Canada) very powerful, and leave it at that? The difficulty is that while one powerful agency might be able to assure the attainment of almost any one economic goal, it could not attain a wide range of goals. If a variety of goals is to be attained, then a corresponding variety of action is needed, and probably action by several agencies.

The second of the technical comments is to remark that the agencies of control have been vastly improved in recent years by the dramatic changes that have taken place in the gathering and processing of economic data. Democratic planning is likely to be much the more efficient for that. There is no comparison between the statistical sources we have now and those of a generation past. The improvement will continue and perhaps accelerate. The most notable thing in this picture is the almost revolutionary changes made possible by the immense speeds of the modern computer.

The general comment is one that I think is of absolutely basic importance. Let me emphasize it with all the care I can. Those who believe in planning are misrepresented over and over again on this point by every right wing commentator and student of affairs from Donald Fleming to Little Orphan Annie.

To control an economy does not mean supervising every economic action that takes place in the economy. It does not mean directing or regulating every act, or even any very large number of acts. In a democratic society no one could or would want to undertake such a pattern of intervention. It is wholly unnecessary. It is wholly undesirable. To control an economy means taking only those extra actions that turn what would happen anyway without control into what is desired. In general those extra actions are only a minute fraction of the total activity of the economy. A controlled economy on social democratic terms has nothing in common with the detailed inter-ventions of a totalitarian economy: it controls to allow choice, and not to impose it.

Let me give you one or two examples. Take a policy to produce full employment. Even without planning, even under the most muddled activities of the present government, 90% of the population will find satisfactory jobs. Simply with the efficient use of existing agencies I suppose the 90% could easily be raised two or three points – one would only need to eliminate such comedies as having no communication between the Minister of Finance and the Governor of the Bank of Canada. Control involves the extra actions that offer employment to the final percentage of those willing and able to work. Planning involves the total picture, it involves providing the opportunity for work to everyone. But the intervention to achieve the plan is marginal, it is residual, it adds to what is going to happen anyway the pieces missing from the total. Mind you, to change 90% or 95% employment to full em-ployment adds much more than that proportion to welfare, because the change provides security to everyone. But the action itself is marginal.

Take one further case. A well known device of planning is to use a so-called exchange fund account to affect the value of Canadian money in international markets. It involves very few people and practically no equip-ment. Our money is traded as a matter of policy in the world's money markets. No one looks over the shoulders of our exporters and importers.

The handful of people looking after the exchange account see nothing of specific trade transactions, attend in no way to the details of a specific business. And yet these very simple extra actions have a marked influence over the whole range of foreign trade, affecting the totals of every export and every import. In this case I suppose planning directly accounts for less than one-tenth of one-tenth of one percent of the activity in the economic sector it affects. And yet in some circumstances this simple marginal operation is enough to change a most unsatisfactory unplanned result to a greatly improved planned output. Planning is complete, but control to make what is planned happen is residual. It has to be determined and purposeful, of course, but it has no remote resemblance to the tangle of red tape and bureaucracy opponents of planning describe.

PLANNING IN A FEDERAL STATE

To bring this to a close I want to say a few things about the interpretation of planning in a federal state. From time to time I have conscientiously spoken of federal planning and then followed it up by a courteous extra reference to provincial planning; but the relation of these two areas of planning is obviously no casual problem and the importance of the relationship was recognized in the New Democratic Party program.

There is nothing in principle that says planning must be centralized or that it is only feasible in a unitary state. Indeed the economic question is practically on a par with the political question. Neither a unitary nor a federal constitution has general political superiority, nor does either have general economic superiority. Superiority depends on the facts. For Canada there is no doubt at all about the essential value of a federal political scheme. Nothing else is imaginable. And on the economic side, even if something else could be contemplated, which I find very unlikely, there is little doubt either about the essential superiority of decentralized planning. Decentralized planning is vital for Canada at the second stages I have just described, the stage in which choices are made from the things that are technically possible, the stage of democratic choice. In our highly regional economy and in our bi-cultural state we are far more likely to achieve democratic choice when planning is shared between federal and provincial authorities than when it is not. We must regard these federal arrangements as advantages that make planning more efficient, and not as handicaps that have to be endured and overcome.

What lines of division are there between federal and provincial planning? I suppose at a practical level the lines of economic division will follow from the lines of political and constitutional division. Those lines clearly are in a specially flexible state at the moment and are no doubt never going to be rigidly fixed. In principle, though, I think at least the following can be said.

With both federal and provincial planning to be taken into account, there is always a problem of coordination to be worked out. But just as there are no political gaps in our constitutional structure, so there can be no economic gaps: responsibility always lies somewhere for any given aspect of planning. Clearly economic planning must be co-extensive with political jurisdiction. This means that there are very important ways in which federal planning must embrace the whole economy, and so must also embrace the results of provincial planning.

Does this respect provincial jurisdiction and does it lead to efficient programs? I think it does. The federal authorities must plan with the whole economy in mind. But in those areas that belong to the provinces the federal planners must take as given whatever the provincial authorities decide to do. The federal planners must respect and welcome the democratic choice the provincial authorities represent. The federal authorities have the power and the duty to see that national economic totals make sense. Their taxing, spending and monetary powers are, I think, an ample and even lavish basis for this responsibility. The federal authorities have a special duty to encourage co-ordinated planning in the many areas where decisions for one region interact with decisions for another. In the last analysis, I suppose, the federal authorities have responsibility for reconciling positions where there is a sharp conflict of interest in provincial programs. And in the same way I think the federal authorities have a final responsibility to act wherever there is a long continued vacuum in policy.

I do not see a New Democratic federal government seeking to overturn a political choice made by a provincial government of some other political background. But where it is constitutionally possible I see no reason why a federal government should feel compelled to leave some important area of policy as an eternal desert if provincial authorities simply ignore their responsibilities.

All of this may suggest a complete pre-eminence for the federal authorities. It is not intended to. Provincial planning is also very wide ranging, and is also in its own jurisdiction a final authority. No doubt it is reckless for me to stray still further into constitutional matters, but I might offer one rough economic test of what provincial jurisdiction should be. It goes without saying that it must cover those fundamental cultural guarantees on which the very existence of the country rests. But then at a more materialistic level I think it might be said that provincial jurisdiction can and should extend to all questions affecting the kind and quality of provincial income. It can extend to all aspects of the exploitation of natural resources, certainly without limit until provincial geographic boundaries are reached. It can extend in general to the form public spending takes within the province, to the particular provincial patterns imposed on such spending. Why? Apart from constitutional rules, because the most direct test of what people want in those areas is found at the provincial level. There is no reason for the federal authorities to try to assume tasks better performed elsewhere. This is the essence of co-operative federalism, the term invented by the Founding Convention of the New Democratic Party to describe the federal-provincial relationship.

CHAPTER THREE

Social Democracy: Notes on "Ownership"

Democracy is at the same time means and end. It is the means of the struggle for Socialism, and it is the form Socialism will take once it has been realized.   E. Bernstein

Social democracy has objects of policy and means of policy. Its objects of policy are well known throughout the party, and become obscure only as means are confused with ends. I submit that the objects of policy are *three*: as in Bernstein's view, that the method of acquiring policy is itself a policy and that this method must be democratic; that waste – as, say, from unemployment – should not be tolerated; and that equality (not mere equality of opportunity, but *equality* simple) must be pursued. I submit further that the means of policy is *one*, the determined, unrestricted use of the democratic state to achieve the goals of policy. Each of these items, is, of course, a code word for a complex scheme of ideas, but I think within the party (and within the ranks of its implacable enemies) the code words are well understood.

What are the particulars of confusion? Let me pick three illustrations from discussions at this convention. A choice between private and public ownership cannot involve an issue of principle. The principle is the detachment with which the social democratic state regards either form of ownership, ready to use one or the other for its true policies as cold-bloodedly as it might, for example, change the tariff on treacle. I come back to this, as the theme of these notes, in a moment, but recite the other examples. There is the no-growth theme. But growth as such is not an object of policy, whether negative, zero or positive. It emerges from policy, but does not determine policy. True, there are many important questions of a technical kind about how growth should be correctly measured – pollution costs, for example,

Unpublished notes for a presentation to the Winnipeg Convention of the New Democratic Party, February 1975.

should be subtracted from the usual measures of output. Fair enough, but that is a very different thing from deciding that correctly measured growth should be zero. Equality is the guide to a correct rate of growth, equality considered in worldwide terms and with respect to the inheritance one generation bequeaths to the next. A simplistic choice of no-growth must disturb us by the number of fellow travellers it brings from the far right, for to them, no-growth may be the cover for preserving gross inequality and privilege. And then there is the appeal the great advances made in Cuba and China must have for any sensitive observer. The genius of Chairman Mao is beyond dispute, the possibility that he has done more for humankind than almost anyone in history a real possibility. But this is not a reason for becoming Maoists. An extremely primitive and unjust society has been advanced in a generation or two by a stage that without Mao might have taken a century or more. The achievement, though, brings China that much closer to the vision presented by social democracy. It does not displace the vision or provide a higher vision. Chinese society, as all visitors report, contains democratic attributes it has never displayed before. Those attributes, however, are contained within the attributes of a true social democracy. Can we learn from Mao? Of course, as we can still learn from Woodsworth or the Webbs. The reality of our social democracies is flawed and human, not the vision without defect.

The practical question for social democracies is whether their governments can govern. Within the range of instruments at their disposal most of their local programs can be easily achieved – global programs are of a quite different dimension, so vast as to make all instruments available to the national state look puny. I am reminded of the foolish exercises in constitutional revision that have so occupied our eleven governments. None of those governments has come close to the constraints its existing constitutional structure would impose. What stops us from getting rid of capital punishment? from creating employers of last resort? from implementing equality for women (a theme I no longer add *pro forma*, as the injustice – obvious but not seen – is now made plain)? Constitutions? No, a lack of will. The lack of will is of no concern to the Liberal/Conservative party, for that party is chosen to administer and to abjure government. To social democracy, on the other hand, the capacity and will to govern is everything. The statements of policy are otherwise vain and sentimental posturing. If social democracy claims that universal public ownership is a matter of principle it can only be because either it judges that hostile power cannot otherwise be democratically controlled – which would be a consistent position theoretically but contradicted, in my view, by experience – or because it has elected a showy slogan that will condemn it to political impotence.

Public ownership is a powerful instrument of the state. It should be freely used, widely used, used without apology since the right to use it has been democratically obtained. But it should not be used where it contributes nothing to policy proper, or where it is inferior to simpler methods of government. To be wasteful of a capacity to govern that is itself always limited, and on which pointless exercises in public ownership can make a heavy drain – this is to subvert social democracy.

Let our governments govern. Condemn them when and if they do not carry out their program or walk away from their promises. Reject the excuse that their instruments of policy are too fragile. What has been promised within our provincial governments can be implemented if those governments set up an apparatus to govern and use the apparatus. A high unemployment rate in a social democracy condemns those who have office. Lack of housing condemns them, as does persistent poverty or persistent regional inequality or persistent discrimination amongst groups within the community. The condemnation, naturally, has to be measured in units we could accept when applied to our own failings. We are judges judging ourselves, so [we] had best be moderate and be patient, though not infinitely so, with the argument that change takes time.

Where are some of the situations in which public ownership is, as the doctors say, a likely specific? I list a few.

1 Where it is needed to maintain democratic sovereignty. This is the classical theme. I accept its power, and reject only the notion that its use may be universally required, or even very frequently. One can, after all, prohibit this foreign acquisition or that, or require this foreign corporation to sell to Cuba, or that domestic corporation to pay the social costs a sudden reduction in employment would impose. When such milder measures to defend sovereignty have been tried and have (unexpectedly) failed, then by all means use the stronger medicine.

2 Where it provides desired redistribution in kind. The well-intentioned liberal might say that housing and medical and educational needs can be handled by simple transfers in money. But that is nonsense. Without public housing, large sections of the population will not be adequately housed. Without nationalized medicine (on which only part of what is needed has been applied) large sections of the population will suffer from illness that could be prevented or cured.

3 Where it is needed to reclaim – to repatriate, usually – the "rents" from our resources. Let this be done in reality and it will dwarf in significance all the slogans crying for universal ownership of the means of production. The slogans are solutions by definition, are geometrical exercises. They amount to describing the good society, and are no guide at all to steps to its achievement.

4 Where it assists with antimarket policies like the "Stay Option" – for the

"Stay Option" deliberately rejects the forced migrations the market would compel. On what grounds? That the market, by more tests of efficiency, cannot capture the true costs of forced migrations. And what the market, faced with a social choice in equity, can only ignore that choice.

5 Where public enterprise has natural advantages, as with Auto-Pac, and the still unfinished business of organizing that most natural of state activities, the provision of insurance.

These are examples, only, and in addition, bypass the many difficult questions of the variety of forms public ownership may take, of the problem of ensuring that public ownership means public control, and of linking public control to its democratic mandate. They bypass, too, the matter of whether this or that alternative instrument would assist public ownership taken by itself. I would argue, though, that they do not represent an attempt to erase public ownership from the list of tools the social democratic state can use, but instead recognize its high rank in that list.

My concern, in brief, is not finally with the theology of public ownership, but with the disturbing question of whether social democracy (alone in its *wish* to govern *democratically*) can in fact govern. Are the instruments of government, of which public ownership is but one, are these instruments usable, are they used? That they can be, that they are, this is a far more radical claim than to claim public ownership is a principle.

Cooperative ownership has been left to the end. This in a way is very odd, given our origins in the Cooperative Commonwealth Federation. But it too represents a reality: tribute is paid to cooperative activity whenever social democrats gather, but little is then said of what basis these tributes have, or what role social democracy sees for cooperatives with its benign state. My view is that we may be allowing a very valuable conception to vanish because of a failure to do our homework, thinking through again what actions might turn a little-used form of enterprise, but one that has impressive credentials on the face of things, into a flourishing partner in the new society. Only a few points come to mind, but they may as well be listed to close this commentary.

1 The cooperative seems to differ from the ordinary firm, (a) by being composed of households that operate as a firm but retain their individual identities, and (b) by being their own customers, at least in some large degree.

2 These qualities would seem to make cooperative ownership different in kind from either private or public ownership, for it would be (at its best) more than a mere instrument, something imbedded in the objects of policy (especially "equality").

3 The structure is handicapped in relation to private enterprise because of the lack of access to funds and technological and managerial resources that give firms economies of scale.

4 These handicaps are not, however, inherent, if the "holding company" (so to speak) of the cooperatives – that is, the social democratic state assists in filling the gaps. Nor would this be a mere handout; it is the completion of a naturally efficient structure.

5 Because they are part of a policy object, cooperatives have a claim to be nurtured by the social democratic state. That nurture, too, may also be an instrument of policy, for the existence of the cooperatives helps the state in dissolving concentrations of economic and hostile political power.

CHAPTER FOUR

The Role of Government
in the Economy

The attainment of the common good is the sole reason for the existence of State rulers.

INTRODUCTION AND THEME

You will know that a speaker who comes before you in November to talk on something like the "role of government in the economy" must have accepted his invitation in June or earlier. It is like talking on the role of God in the universe. It is even like talking on what the role of God should be in the universe. Still, the easy commitment in June is what leads to the heavy November harangue.

My theme is this: most of the attack on the role of governments in the economy is dangerous nonsense. Our governments in Canada are not too strong for the economic tasks they must inevitably perform but too weak. The question we need to be asking ourselves is whether our government *can in fact govern, not whether they should.*

The attack, of course, is fashionable and undiscriminating, popular wisdom too obvious to debate. Even those on the political left are apologetic and defensive. All parties compete in promising a proper discipline of the public sector. Look what government spending has done to promote inflation, so they say. Look at the waste in welfare programs. Look at the mismanagement of public enterprises. What an easy target the governmental apparatus has become!

The basic confusion in all of this is the muddling together of the *scope* of government activity with the *efficiency* of government activity. Let me subdivide my theme into (a) a recital of what roles government has taken in the economy, (b) how this has happened, and (c) what repairs are needed or at least should be sought.

Unpublished notes for presentation to the Conference of the Canadian Tax Foundation, November 1976.

WHAT GOVERNMENTS DO, ESPECIALLY IN THE
PROVISION OF PUBLIC GOODS

Government, I believe, has various duties to perform that by now have largely frozen the minimum scope of its activity. Let me not sail under false colours. I rejoice in the fact. But the fact is by now not a matter of ideological dispute. For better or worse we have experienced a largely inevitable evolution of our society. One might wish the world different than it is, but the world will roll on nonetheless, in this case requiring government to look after such and such a large fraction of our economic affairs, no matter what. It is not just that, say, the Bank of Canada is here to stay, but that so are government pension schemes, government responsibility for medical care, government responsibility for all levels of education – and much else. Medicare, for instance, came that much earlier because of Saskatchewan, but medicare certainly would have come to Canada by now anyway, as it presumably will come to the United States before long. The political left and the political right must surely agree that medicare and the rest should be vigorously and strongly controlled once they exist. And how else is this to be accomplished without a strengthening of government?

Without debating, then, how wide government should extend, we might consider what principles to appeal to in such a debate. The obvious can be stated and then set to one side: there is presumably no such thing as an economy that can function without a state and government to enforce various ground rules about things like ownership and the execution of contracts. But what else?

If we are going to have to resort to the impersonal efficiency that market forces can provide – for some sizeable part of our needs, certainly – then we would in theory appeal to government to defend the market system where it can function well. What civic-minded businessmen would ever search for the comfort of a wasteful tariff? What virtuous professionals would ever seek to bar entry for the sake of keeping their profession small and prosperous? Where are the workers or the employers who would combine or conspire against the price system? Alas, pretty well everywhere: so one might hope, at least on behalf of everyone else, for the state to give the market system some chance "to do its thing," although to say this with a straight face clearly takes some doing in these years of the great freeze.

We can go on to more contentious aspects of government activity. Government naturally will not leave the distribution of economic output to the market place, but will involve itself according to the political forces in the country with redistribution through taxes, transfers, and a thousand particular devices.* Just what redistribution should be attempted seems to me a wholly normative question, fundamental but not technical. The technicians, true,

---

* For a second but final observation about not sailing under false colours: let redistribution flourish!

can offer advice on the wide differences there often are between what a policy is expected to accomplish and what in fact it may actually accomplish and may point to many possible consequences that have not even been considered when this scheme or that is proposed. To clutter up every act of public policy with some trivial redistributive clause is hostile to true redistribution and efficiency both. As everyone knows, too, the *nominal*, *planned*, and *actual incidence* of redistributive schemes are three very different things, as the egalitarian has discovered over and over again to his sorrow.

So government goes this far with the economy at the very least. How much further must it go? *It cannot sensibly avoid trying to determine the production and distribution of those goods the market cannot handle.* The very reasons that make the provision of some goods a natural function of the marketplace ensure that for other goods the market cannot meet society's needs. There is a large class of *public goods* that confer gains or losses on third parties and so cannot be left to the market, and another large class of *public goods* that for *technological reasons* cannot be effectively supplied through the market place. If things were left to the market, such needed goods would not be provided at all, or would be provided in the wrong amounts – usually too little, but sometimes too much – and in the wrong places. No modern society (and I would guess, not really any substantial society from antiquity) could imagine government adopting a *laissez-faire* attitude to the provision of such goods. Examples? There is always the textbook's favoured case of national defence, but I would offer the great social programs in health and education as supplying better illustrations for discussion in our own day.

Here is where the role of government in the economy begins to provoke unkind adjectives, where we look at each other as bleeding hearts or neanderthals (and sometimes as both, for I think our uncle neanderthal was rather a simple soul, no match for our crafty fathers). Some large total of public goods there must be, though, everyone must agree. And if those goods are to be provided, they have to be provided under "handicap," as it were, for the simple effective market mechanism by the nature of the situation cannot be used. Government in this domain faces always an intrinsically difficult task, one in which waste could be avoided entirely only by chance – and one in which the measure of waste even after the fact is difficult.

The sources of friction about this most characteristic role of modern government are all around us. If something is provided by government, it may be that it is provided without a price or without a fee. That in fact may be the correct way to put the good to our service. But the absence of the fee does not mean the good had no costs; and beneficiaries of the good may then be careless of the existence of the cost. Thank God – to voice a personal opinion – that we have medicare. Would to God – to voice a personal judgement – that our governments could bring more efficiency into that health industry which uses resources on so mammoth a scale. Another example: we have all respect for the good intentions of many of the "slow growth" people, for those who wish to preserve the ecology for the future and preserve our buildings and folkways from the past. We accept that in many areas they are forcing government to do good things within the economy. Yet their projects, too, can pass from the well-intended to the absurdly wasteful if every desirable end is measured as though it were costless. The heart of the matter is that there are goods the market cannot provide and that form a large portion of our needs in the affluent, urbanized society of postwar Canada. We must have *public goods* in enormous amounts. We have big government because we must have big government; it is not simply chosen but inescapable. Of course big government can be wasteful and never more wasteful than when it undertakes activities that have no natural place in the public sector. Big government is necessary, but by no means is everything within big government necessary. The democratic left neglects this guideline at its peril.

There is at least one other major activity that the state is expected to undertake in this general context. In one sense it is merely a subdivision of its redistributive function, but it is a subdivision so consequential and so little noticed that it deserves a special heading. There are massive transfers to be arranged across the generations, from those in the working force to those yet to enter the working force and those who have left it. These transfers are complicated to identify because they are interwoven with the saving and dissaving that people undertake (and with the income that arises not from work but from one's ownership of "capital" and other things).

Even the vocabulary of these giant transfers is a complete jumble. We have savings plans, money-purchase pension plans, formula-based private pension plans, a veritable bazaar of governmental plans, incredibly complex patterns of subsidization for various levels of education and for various groups who are selected to be educated. There are puzzles within puzzles. Consider the lilies of Ottawa. They toil not, neither do they spin, or so their slanderers say. Solomon in all his glory did not retire more comfortably than one of these!

We might sum up. What has government to do with the economy?

- It polices the ground rules that make an economic system possible.
- It intervenes to make the market system work smoothly where the market system in principle is effective.
- It redistributes income.
- It organizes the supply of public goods.
- It looks after intergenerational transfers.

Looking at things from the political left, I would also say government from time to time should also provide private goods, partly because occasions will arise when government sees itself as an efficient "private" supplier, but chiefly because effective demand is notoriously erratic. Government in principle can provide compensating demand – which is all that can be said of this vast Keynesian prescription here.* Other activities of government are on the list by implication. Commercial policy is a complicated extension of the item on "smoothing the market." Monetary policy is part of the public goods business (since money is the quintessential public good).

WHERE THE CRISIS OF CONFIDENCE HAS ARISEN

So much for description. What about diagnosis? What basis is there for saying that these tasks of government, required within the economy on *some* substantial scale, are customarily handled by an apparatus that is too weak, too amateurish for its duties? This goes against the diagnosis by public opinion now being routinely expressed from both the political right *and* the political left. Government has made a mess of things: it is a cliché.

Nonetheless, I repeat that the realities have not been thought through. Take the revolutionary reforms of the welfare state. I make no bones about this laudatory language, nor would many whose family recollections of the Great Depression are not wholly forgotten. For the ordinary person, hosts of disasters have been made remote and uncommon. It is as certain as any social projection can be that those changes are irreversible. But those programs are nowadays not being compared with the barren world without such programs but with worlds – hypothetical worlds – where the waste has been cleaned from the programs, where the administrative absurdities have been cancelled. Medicare is a triumph compared to no medicare. It takes on aspects of fiasco, though, compared to the polished programs most of us can imagine. We can see a medical industry virtually unchanged from its form when medicare was being born. Elsewhere we have watched the commitment to full employment degenerate into a sloppy, inefficient assurance that the jobless will not have too much trouble getting make-do funds. In a sense when the great reforms were made the clock was stopped. Government is in disgrace for the inefficiencies, the flagrant follies, that it so routinely allows.

But this produces the fatal *non sequitur*. The fault that needs remedy is not the existence of government intervention. That is irreversible, rightly, so one thinks, but irreversible anyway. The fault is in the lack of capacity of our governments to handle their large and vital economic domain effectively. Let me agree that the government bureaucracies do many things

---

One either mentions this item and says nothing more, or goes into great detail. This is not the place for a full account. The same thing is true of the decision about effective demand that government must determine as between consumption and saving, the choice of the rate of economic growth.

badly. They intervene in all sorts of things they should not touch. They commit in particular cases all the particular sins with which they are charged. To make fun of the bureaucracies is good sport. They often do comical things. Heaven knows they would have to do very comical things, though, to outperform our university bureaucracies, or even (one guesses) the bureaucracies of the great private corporations. Their tasks are immensely difficult. Their organizational forms are not much adapted to an astounding growth in responsibilities.

One does not strengthen those bureaucracies by trying to destroy them! Equally *one does not confuse mere size with strength*. To those close to government who complain of civil servants doing useless jobs, who complain of bloated payrolls and ridiculously expensive expansion of office space, who complain of idiotic questionnaires to be filled in according to the old maxim that paper work done by someone else is costless – to all such who complain of too frequent silliness and arrogance one would again plead for discrimination. The pruning of the bureaucracies is one thing, often desirable, often needed; but to give our governments *and* their bureaucracies "muscle" is even more desirable and even more urgent.

WHAT REFORMS MIGHT BE SOUGHT

This is not recantation about what our governments have accomplished. The security of life, the reasonable prospect of employment, the appearance of decent minimum standards throughout Canada – these events have been in their own way the signs of a civilized revolution, thirty years or more in the making. But the governmental apparatus has not kept pace. That failure is provoking disenchantment, and causing people to turn to reaction, destructive reaction rather than reform.

And as to remedy? To sketch a few ideas, of which the first is the critical conception:

1 Whether our governments should be larger or smaller, they should certainly be stronger.
2 The scope of economic activity that should be undertaken by our governments is inherently wide, and so should *not be pointlessly enlarged*. Redistribution, employment policy, the provision of essential public goods, intergenerational transfers – to get these things even roughly right stretches to the limit the capacities of any apparatus to govern we may devise. Government for the sake of government should be smothered in infancy – we need no son of AIB when the dismal adventure with AIB itself is over. This is a plea from the left!
3 The proportion of policy making to managerial activity within government should be considerably raised. We need to know how in principle to

rationalize health costs, for example, much more than we need to capture the financial records of the system as it stands.

4 The feudal structure of Canadian governments should make way for cabinet planning. Baronial systems in which departments are the focus of policy, or even presidential systems in which premiers and prime ministers inspire such policy as there may be, are wholly insufficient. Policy today is complex and interwoven from area to area as never before. A fragmented or casual basis is no basis at all.

5 Planning cabinets must have planning bureaucracies loyal to and integrated with the general policy-making processes of government. Seconded bureaucracies will not work, for primary loyalty belongs to the primary home. Planning in this large sense should be directed to the large unified themes of particular governments. Derivative, operational planning should proceed at the departmental level much as it already does. A corollary of the needed close relationship of the cabinet and the cabinet's bureaucracy is that planning agencies correct in form except for this *direct* relationship will be ineffective. Even cabinets – no, *especially* cabinets – need a staff that serves no other masters, for coherence of policy is not possible otherwise.

6 The senior bureaucracy should, as necessary, be overtly political, coming and going (if government wishes) with government itself. Whether the mandarins are neutral, who can tell? But neutrality is not good enough, not if *elected* governments are to govern.

7 Decentralization of policy should be a chief goal, not on sentimental grounds, but on hard technical principles. The maximizing rules that so assist the private sector are hard to parallel in the public sector. Decentralization produces maximizing agents. The central authority has to control global totals in the great social programs. It adds to theoretical efficiency and husbands scarce political strength to let local authority handle things within the global totals.

I say all of these things dogmatically, as though I thought that most of these horrendously difficult problems required only a little commonsense for their solution. This is far beyond one's hopes or competence. I am pretty confident about the main theme. The mood of resentment and disappointment with government has to be resisted. For better or worse our governments will have to supervise a large part of the economy. So we may speculate on things that might make it "for better" rather than "for worse". We invite speculation from others.

A final point: I believe that there is some freedom within governments themselves to improve their relations with the public at large. It is hard, no doubt, for them to swim against this particular tide. But governments do not have to waste their all too slight administrative capital on, say, failed or failing experiments with price and wage control, against virtually all expert opinion. Governments do not have to let go of full employment as a goal, substituting analgesic solutions. Governments, in brief, can fight on better ground than they have so far chosen. Can the game be won? Who can tell about an unprecedented situation? But there is little sense in proclaiming defeat while the issues are undecided.

CHAPTER FIVE

A Critique of Privatization

With few exceptions, privatization advances steadily.

> Review of the Thatcher program, Toronto *Globe and Mail*, 3 May 1983

To be under the power of some one, instead of being as formerly the sole condition of safety, is now ... the only situation which exposes to grievous wrong ... Modern nations will have to learn the lesson that the well being of a people must exist by means of the justice and self-government of the individual citizens.   John Stuart Mill, *Principles of Political Economy*

In fact, nearly all the programs that are advocated by economists to promote equality and combat poverty – and are often rationalized in terms of stimulating consumption – in actuality reduce demand by undermining the production from which all real demand derives ... "Give and you will be given unto." This is the secret not only of riches but also of growth.

> George Gilder, *Wealth and Poverty*

A PREAMBLE

In the federal budget of late June [1982], there was an open attack upon three of the principal supports of the society reconstructed from World War II and the Great Depression. The direct pursuit of full employment was abandoned. The practices of the welfare state were reduced. The trade union movement was subverted.

None of the three supports had escaped earlier attacks, of course. Even by the beginning of the 1960s the notion had gained ground that compensation for unemployment would substitute very well for actual employment, and during the 1970s it became increasingly fashionable to propose any measures by which the State would create missing jobs. As to the welfare state, while undermining of its practices has been both more delayed and more theoretical, that undermining now has visible successes. The principle

Reprinted with permission from G. Mason, ed., *Macroeconomics: Theory, Policy and Evidence* (Winnipeg: University of Manitoba Institute for Social and Economic Research, 1983), 25–49.

of universality has been the focus of debate, with the propositions often being advanced, first, that in this much wealthier society it has become too expensive to provide what a poorer society could afford, and second, that by retreating from universality to selective charity much more can be provided. And third, while the trade union movement was a principal support of the reconstructed society it was granted reciprocal support by that society for only a few years. At the best it has been approvingly tolerated, and more often only just tolerated. It now often finds its purposes again placed outside the law in some areas, and the spirit of the law in almost all.

Considered item by item the budget of late June did not *invent* reactions against the interventionist State, reactions that were without precedent. The crispness and self-confidence, however, with which the great social programmes were reduced *en bloc* may make June 28th a day to remember. On *full employment* the budget spoke sufficiently in three sentences. "The onslaught of recession has triggered demands for a fundamental reappraisal of our economic policies ... . Any departure from our broad policy approach has been rejected ... . We have rejected massive fiscal stimulus and the abandonment of monetary restraint because this would only worsen inflation and aggravate unemployment."[1] On *the progress of the welfare state*, the budget limited "the indexing factor applicable to Family Allowances and Old Age Security"[2], and then with respect to Old Age Security not only expropriated a substantial sum from the real incomes of pensioners but moved the system away from universality and did damage to the all-important factor of trust. The welfare state functions or fails as those taxed today believe in the continuity of the rules: the compensatory transfers belong to an often distant future. In this same way, as well known, medicare has also been under siege. Then, on *the commitment to trade unionism*, the budget declared "pay restraint in the federal public sector," and set wage increases well below expected inflation for unionists – and all others – in the federal service. Other unionists have since been pressed into this unpredictable programme, recruited under successive improvisations. Where federal writ now runs unions are *free*, rather as in Poland, except to act as unions; and if this troubles workers, they can at least take comfort that a new experiment in "incomes policy" so long demanded is in place to substitute for their leaders' stubborn resistance to the higher wisdom.

This does not hint at admiration for the budget or its inspiration, but that is not the point. A review of its merits and those of its distinguished predecessors belongs to a different occasion. In the context of "privatization" the budget should be taken as a datum, as a phenomenon representative of the times. Thirty years ago, twenty years ago, such a statement of economic and social policy as that of June 28th would have been unthinkable. Public policy in Canada has certainly been "privatized" in its appearance and may have been "privatized" in its reality. At least three large questions are worth reflection.

Item, has there in fact been a substantial change in the actualities of policy? It may be, for example, that the supposedly interventionist State of the 'fifties was largely illusion, with the rhetoric of the times being descriptive of a collection of accidental events. If that is so, it may also be that in the large "privatization" affects nothing: the privatized State and the interventionist State are one. *Item*, if there has been a substantial change in the actualities of policy, has it been the result of calculated "privatization" or merely of novelties in policy associated with the vocabulary of "privatization"? It may be, that for short periods bursts of intervention by the State are *possible*, but that effective intervention is *impossible* in a systematic way. *Item*, if there has been a substantial change, and if it has been a change politically chosen or politically imposed, has it enhanced welfare (in comparison, of course, with the welfare available from the interventionist State, or from some practical alternative)? The question requires some agreed test of enhanced welfare. It may be, with such a test accepted, that some clear superiority can be shown for "privatization," or for the interventionist State, or for some other social structure (of which forms of voluntary association seem to have the most durable credentials). I think we might move on from preamble to definition.

"PRIVATIZATION" AS A CONCEPT

Admittedly "privatization" is an extraordinarily ugly neologism, but it has become an important slogan, and a summary of an ambitious technocratic programme.

In the technocratic aspect it proposes that the economic and social structures of, say, Canada be speedily "privatized," changed in one direction and prevented from change of an opposite kind. I should define variables. "Privatization" in Canada would have much the same forms as it would have in any other economically advanced nation-state in which businessmen, capitalists and markets have a large place in determining events. The programme becomes more vague and hypothetical in settings further from the industrialized "Canadian" model, but seems to me recognizable in the debates about policy of almost any society. As to the desired direction of change, this consists of transferring authority, decision and power from the State to private organizations and especially (but *not* exclusively) to the apparatus of the marketplace. The State is always to be reduced in its economic and social influence, although privatization sometimes emphasizes a general limitation of the capacity of the State to govern, and sometimes particular transfers of responsibility from public to private jurisdiction. Reduction of State authority within the programme is to proceed more or less rapidly, more or less voluntarily, and more or less completely: at the asymptote State authority may have vanished but may also be a basic authority of a subsistence kind, a State authority that supports everything but modifies nothing.

Those who would privatize, as each sees the others, must live with strange company (as is no doubt true of those who regard the programme as barbaric or empty or both). When Friedrich Engels[3] writes, of a redeemed future, that "state interference in social relations becomes in one domain after another, superfluous, and then withers away of itself", he sees a society at the end of time only what Peter Kropotkin[4] affirmed (in his essay on the historic role of the State) has recently existed and can soon be reconstructed for an anarchic and by no means distant future. Milton Friedman[5] describes in *Capitalism and Freedom* (and many other writings) the methods and advantages of taking almost every allocative and distributive function the State may possess and relocating them in markets adorned by equal opportunity. George Gilder[6] speaks above in his inimitably Promethean style and does so in association with John Stuart Mill[7]. Even in Canada, and without David Stockman to write his reviews, Donald Johnston[8] – as this is being prepared, the president of the Treasury Board – adds an audible voice to this diversified choir: in his still quoted "Fiscalimity" he decides that Canada could be a great country "were it not for too much taxation, too strong a bureaucracy, too much government, too much welfare, too many politicians and too few statesmen." Probably if those who would privatize were divided into two groups, according as their State is to give way to private co-operation or to private self-interest, computed from within each group, kinship would thereby be much improved.

SOME CONJECTURES BY MARX ON PRIVATIZATION

Karl Marx certainly had no high regard for the economic and social structures of the capitalism he experienced or the capitalism he foresaw. The "Canadian" model that I have used as the reference for privatization would of course be merely a reasonably well defined stage in the evolution of his "bourgeois economy." Marx's appraisal of that evolution is a useful beginning here, for privatization can be seen as a test of some basic Marxian conjectures.

I have in mind the arguments concerning crises. "Bourgeois economy," claims Marx, develops in a contradictory way, in the fundamental sense that its development must generate forces that will be fatal to the system. Capitalism was not seen as unique in this life history. Self-terminating evolution was built into precursor systems and would characterize successor systems (at least until class, like time had ceased). Still, capitalism has been the system of the here-and-now, so that its self-termination was the natural focus of Marx's analysis. I do not think there is any doubt about the general description Marx used for the death of "bourgeois economy." Eventually there would be an economic and social *crisis* that could not be contained or resolved within capitalism. Capitalism would inevitably create crises. They would vary in intensity but would tend to *deepen*. Capitalism would recover from all of them save one.

Against the general description there are the specifics. It seems to me there are three logical distinct explanations given for the ultimate collapse. Although they do not exclude each other, any of the three is a sufficient cause, and each of the three is at one point or other the single cause that Marx invokes. The obvious question is whether the three explanations have as a matter of *fact* a shared origin – not that clearly stated – in some still more basic feature of "bourgeois economy".

The most conventional of the explanations, I suppose, is that which is a composite of reasons to expect *cycles* in trade and business. "The ultimate reason for all real crises always remains the poverty and restricted consumption of the masses as opposed to the drive of capitalist production to develop the productive forces as though only the absolute consuming power of society constituted their limit."[9] On the face of it Marx has chosen a simple underconsumptionist theory. That must be a misreading, though, because he has already complained that it "is sheer tautology to say that crises are caused by the scarcity of effective consumption, or of effective consumers."[10] There is not space here to chase down texts scattered through so lengthy a primary source, but in rough terms the essential argument seems to be this. Repeatedly Marx points out (much as Malthus had done)[11] that in the complex circular flows of "bourgeois economy" the likelihood of demands matching supplies is vanishingly small. The system is competitive and so in a fundamental way uncoordinated and fragmented. At all times those capitalists who supply commodities are driven to reduce costs so that they may remain capitalists, and in reducing costs most use the complementary methods of consolidation and concentration.[12] Accumulation is thereby accelerated, and fixed capital becomes more durable. Obsolescence is accordingly always an inescapable threat to the outcome of decisions about production: *supplies* are generated under a notably *different regime* than are *demands*.

Once some external shock or internal miscalculation has been experienced, there is nothing mysterious about how a cycle can be generated. Luxury goods will be sacrificed by capitalists who have failed to "realize"[13] well produced products – very often massive and long-lived fixed capital – in prices that have an equilibrium relationship to values. The lost surplus value erases aggregate demand where it is most easily erased. Unproductive labourers[14] are dismissed, and like all labourers who lose employment, take with them from the markets their demand for necessaries. From a sizeable shock or miscalculation there appears crisis, and from crisis proper there follows collapse and stagnation. The circular flow is interrupted not only by the immediate mismatching of demands and supplies but also by hoarding in the face of uncertainty, planned hoarding of money and unplanned hoarding of ordinary inventories. This explains the paradox of underconsumption. In every period of collapse, consumption *ex post* will be low just as the reserve army will be large. A door is opened for recovery because of the exceptional depreciation of previous accumulations that stagnation produces. In general demand eventually revives and crisis gives birth to counter crisis.

At a culminating stage, though, there is no recovery. Accumulation piled upon accumulation, and manifested in a falling rate of profit, allows for a wider amplitude for cycles: and by a mixture of chance and this widening of dangers a collapse is experienced too shattering to allow "bourgeois economy" to recover.

The capitalists are unable to organize a State in which collective action has much effect on ordinary cycles or is able to forestall the culminating cycle. So recovery owes nothing to economic policy. There is one open question that has to be posed, the question of how periodicity is controlled. "One may assume," says Marx, "that in the essential branches of modern industry this life-cycle [of industrial capital] now averages ten years ... [though] we are not concerned here with the exact figure ... This much is evident, the cycle [embraces] a number of years in which capital is held fast by its fixed constituent part." [15] Such then is the first explanation.

The second explanation can be described more briefly although it benefits from some of the most memorable of Marx's dicta. As consolidation and concentration proceed (for so far things are unchanged) "that which is now to be expropriated is ... the capitalist exploiting many labourers ... One capitalist kills many." [16] The enforced competition amongst capitalists is revealed by success or failure in reducing costs. For those who fail there is bankruptcy or forced sale, and the transfer of assets to those who succeed. Capitalism grows as measured by output, by productivity, by the number of employed workers, by the size of the reserve army, but it contains all the same a "constantly diminishing number of the magnates of capital" and a working class "disciplined, united, organized by the very mechanism of the process of capitalist production itself." [17] In brief, within the boundaries of a capitalistic nation-state the ranks of the capitalists are thinned by virtue of market forces, and the coherence of workers is steadily increased. "Bourgeois economy" becomes a system that is capitalistic only in name, for competition has virtually disappeared and the organization of a socialist state is already in place.

Under this explanation of collapse, centralization of capital and socialization of labour "become incompatible with their capitalist integument. This integument is burst asunder. The knoll of capitalist private property sounds. The expropriators are expropriated."[18] The capitalists again are unable to organize a State in which collective action is able to sustain capitalism.

Finally, as to the third explanation of why its own growth stifles capitalism, there is Marx's judgement about the ever growing domain in which capitalists compete. One should keep in mind that for Marx capitalism is always a system of production, that the many "capitals" the observer will note *never* coalesce into a single "capital," and that any single capital may at one time exist well *inside* the boundaries of a State, may sometime later be dominant throughout a State, and may later still cross State boundaries in a wide variety of international forms. There will be international trade, the export of capital, colonial ventures, and overtly political growths in the style of Lenin's "imperialism".[19]

The process is unchanged in its simple, primary cause. Within a single "capital" each single capitalist must compete in the contest for survival, and perforce must use any method of cutting costs that comes to hand. Elaborate systems of credit were invented because they may provide advantages in costs, and then must be used by all who remain capitalists as the condition for their status. Colonies are used as markets and then as suppliers of cheap labour and cheap materials, for no better reason but no worse than that in competition each capitalist must use any device another capitalist may use. Eventually the contest, the *enforced* contest in its institutional and political dimensions, intensifies to such an extent that one "capital" or many "capitals" are violently overthrown. Marx did not get much outside the domestic, private economic system in *Capital*, but where he did, was faithful to the far more ambitious review of capitalism projected in the *Grundrisse*. This third explanation of collapse therefore has a less focussed origin than the other two have, but it seems to me to come directly enough from Marx without having need of the complete but secondary support of Lenin.

I think the recital of the three explanations is clear enough evidence of what their shared origin in Marx's "bourgeois economy" must be. As a mode of production capitalism is inherently and finally competitive. As a consequence of this technological datum, capitalistic society is always competitive and fragmented. Workers compete with workers, and capitalists of one kind compete with capitalists of another, the industrial capitalist with the money capitalist and the money capitalist with the landlord. The most familiar form of competition is that between workers of all kinds and capitalists of all kinds, but "most familiar" though it is, it is also the focus of – in Marx's usage – contradiction. This central competition creates a class of workers, a class of capitalists, a class struggle, and so social arrangements that tend to produce collective activity embodied in unions on the one side and State apparatus on the other. Marx finds, however, that while "bourgeois economy" survives, the tendencies to collective behaviour are insufficient responses to the *dissolving* powers of competition.

Under any of the explanations of final crisis, *competition amongst capitalists* has persisted as both cause of the crisis and as the final, *mortal* impediment to cure. Collectivist intervention might repair imbalances between the demands and supplies of the system. An effective State apparatus might forestall the concentration and consolidation by which capitalists expropriate each other. The "many capitals" of the international sphere might find it possible to establish *modus vivendi* and become a single "capital." In no case does Marx think it possible that the suicidal forces of competition can be overcome. Collective action would preserve capitalism but collective action is not possible to capitalism. Marx conceives of the invisible hand as possessing Midas' touch. Where Smith saw competition as a feature of his society that needed to be nurtured, as a regime that called for a *policy* of natural liberty, Marx saw competition as inescapable in "bourgeois economy," both as to its influence in increasing productivity now and as to its inhibition of current welfare and future stability; and of all forms of competition, ironically that which is fatal will be the competition amongst capitalists.

"Privatization," in brief, for Marx would no more describe a *policy* or goals of "bourgeois economy" than would "natural liberty" or *laissez-faire*. It describes the natural tendencies of capitalism, tendencies inextricably bound to a mode of production and its derivative social history.

PRIVATIZATION AND THE PURPOSELESS STATE

When our Canadian children are first given Marx's *Capital* to study, as many of us must recall, I think they agree with their school teachers that is is the mindlessness of the capitalistic State that Marx indicts rather than its purposes or an overbalance of evil amongst individual capitalists. Competition creates a rate of exploitation, and then requires *industrial* capitalists to invest the surplus of society not so much to improve their situation as to maintain it. There is for Marx the great paradox that the contemporary mode of production is marvellously capable of supplying commodities but has astonishingly little capacity to improve the lot of either the exploiters or the exploited. So far as there is a State apparatus it is *dominated* by capitalists, but it is not thereby converted into a purposeful apparatus, or into a collective expression of class interests. Since at all times there is a struggle amongst the classes (a distributive struggle in the main) it is reasonable to think of the State as *jointly* but ineffectually controlled. Out of the dynamics of "bourgeois economy," the economic actors will construct monopolies and cartels, will create trade unions, will organize colonial enterprise and will take their places in the affairs of a capitalistic State; but it is always from the pressure of competition that these *shared* activities result, and it is always to renewed competition that they tend. The capitalistic State might have much to do were it an integrated entity, but it is in fact mindless.[20] Thus Marx describes his State.

My own ideological preferences are social democratic, so that I am well aware that to concur in Marx's judgements on the abilities of the "bourgeois economy" to provide itself with a State, is to confess to unreal expectations about the scope of economic policy. One need not accept those judgements, however, in order to believe that the questions Marx has posed are as basic as they are topical. The "privatization" that so many economists have come to recommend and that so many politicians seek to apply is a prescription Marx would not deny them: for Marx it would be a prescription they will gain whether they search for it or not, and that will signify the chronic and desperate ills of their system. Where the means of production in an industrial society are privately owned, there "privatization" is of the nature of things and hopes and fears of a rational State will be equally silly. I have no intention, of course, of speculating about Marx's eschatology, and am ready to accept decidedly narrower boundaries than Marx uses in assessing the contest between State policy and privatization. During the period since the end of the Second World War the contest has in any event been sufficiently intense in Canada to make recent and local evidence well worth study. The tides have changed more than one since 1945. Possibly the Canadian State administers but cannot govern, and should not govern if it could. These are no longer propositions dismissed out of hand in the political economy of Canada.

SOME DISTINCTIONS

Whether the degree of privatization is endogenous, or *chosen*, I leave aside for the moment. It may seem, though, that since privatization reduces the authority of the State it is a recipe to diminish the extent of the State, to contrive or at least applaud a smaller State. Certainly the evangelists from our immediate neighbour use language that conveys such sentiments, and not least the evangelist-in-chief who speaks so often about getting government off the backs of the people, of not looking to the State for help in tasks the industrious should perform for themselves, and similar formulae for lessening the State. Size, however, is not purpose, and in itself seems to have very little to do with privatization. Undoubtedly the size of the State is a very difficult thing to measure, for its boundaries are vague and its structure is heterogeneous. Quantification has many and arbitrary dimensions. Even in simple societies, though, as K. Polanyi has convincingly evidenced,[21] a multitude of resources are absorbed merely to keep the State in being, a first charge more demanding than the claims of the market. I know of no data to show any solid correlation between the size of the State (measured perhaps by some count of real costs required for its existence) and whether it is mature or primitive, purposeful or mindless, dynamic or immutable, egalitarian or greatly hierarchic. The State that President Reagan or Prime Minister Thatcher bequeaths may be different in its functioning than the State over which President Mitterand presides, but this difference will not be exhibited by changes in size in the various apparatuses of State. Even in States the mind occupies very little space. Parenthetically, one might note how confused and important the programmes are which seek to decentralize the State and assign public tasks to collective bodies as close to local, individual decision as possible. He or she who seeks purpose and rationality in the democratic State looks to decentralization as *strengthening* this kind of State in all of these dimensions. He or she who wishes privatization looks to decentralization from an opposite view, as euthanasia of purpose and intervention. From area to area, of course, either may be right or either may be wrong. Opponents find themselves at times joining in programmes where they really shared only slogans. The farce of the propaganda for the negative income tax is a fine example. Decentralization does not so much discriminate amongst alternatives as conflate them.

Against the abstraction of the purposeless or mindless State a critic can oppose more than one alternative, for at the least either the adjective *or* the noun can be disputed. Still deferring the vital question of causation (that is, whether privatization is a policy or an event), I observe that contemporary economists routinely invoke the notion of a rational and purposeful State whenever they wish to add to the pure theory of markets the pure theory of welfare. They have found the idea indispensable in every use of social welfare functions, in all discussions of public choice, and in the construction of many varieties of collective demand. This totally rational society constitutes as much of a polar case for society collectively, as does economic man in reasoning about private markets, and is equally a formal construction to assist analysis when behaviour and causation have been discovered. The economically rational State is collectivized precisely as economic man is privatized. The critic of privatisation, all the same, must know there are a myriad of economically rational States – as against the unique, *perfectly* privatized system – and will have to classify them farther according to other qualities, perhaps along the dimension from the *oligarchic* State to the *democratic* State as the leading variable.

It has often been that the critic objects to the noun rather than the adjective, and proclaims the society that abjures the State entirely. Competition is not a force that can safely be exploited within the confines of a State, purposeful or not. Voluntary association, co-operation, the spontaneous creativity of anarchy, this is an alternative that must (or should, or will – for causation continues to be undecided) free humankind from motivations that are ignoble and from coercion that is unnecessary and oppressive. If an invisible hand mediates our affairs it is through our social sense it operates rather than our selfishness. The State is *the* enemy. In more modest abstractions the State is an unhappy refuge while co-operation slowly displaces other forms of organization, or when voluntary association fails or is shattered.

Hear a little more from Peter Kropotkin and his bitter indictment. "The role of the nascent state in the sixteenth and seventeenth centuries in relation to the urban centres was to destroy the independence of the cities ... to pillage the rich guilds [and] by taking over the local militias and the whole municipal administration, crushing the weak in the interest of the strong by taxation, and ruining the country by wars." He closes without ambiguity: "*Either* the state forever, crushing individual and local life, taking over in all fields of human activity ... or, the destruction of the state, and new life starting again in thousands of centres on the principle of the lively initiative of the individual and that of free agreement. The choice lies with you!" (Here there *is* causation.) Earlier Kropotkin has observed explicitly the error of "confusing state with society," and the subtler error of confusing state with "government," and he has also noted that "so far as Europe is concerned, the state is of recent origin – it barely goes back to the sixteenth century ... [The] most glorious periods in man's history are those in which civil liberties and communal life had not yet been destroyed by the state, and in which large numbers of people lived in communes and free federations."[22]

For John Stuart Mill the guidelines to a co-operative future are on the one side pragmatic and on the other as visionary as anything in Engels. In his extensive reflections on the "Probable Future of the Labouring Classes"[23] he looks to a European experience he regards as already promising a new future.

The civilizing and improving influence of association, and the efficiency and economy of production on a large scale may be obtained without dividing the producers into two parties ... The speculations and discussions of the last fifty years, and the events of the last thirty, are abundantly conclusive ... The relation of masters and work people will be gradually superseded by partnership ... in some cases, association of the labourers with the capitalist, in others, perhaps finally in all association of labourers among themselves.

This is a modest if incorrect projection. Mill has also ventured the glowing projection on the co-operative world of the stationary state.[24]

The density of population necessary to enable mankind to obtain, in the greatest degree, all the advantages both of co-operation and of social intercourse, has, in all the most populous countries been attained ... Hitherto it is questionable if all the mechanical inventions yet made have lightened the day's toil of any human being ... They have increased the comforts of the middle classes. But they have not yet begun to effect those great changes in human destiny, which it is in their nature ... to accomplish. Only when, in addition to just institutions, the increase of mankind shall be under the deliberate guidance of judicious foresight, can the conquests made from the powers of nature by the intellect and energy of scientific discoverers become the common property of the species.

The vision of Mill overlaps that of the princely anarchist, but it also sees at the end very much what V. Lenin claims to see. In his *State and Revolution*[25] Lenin draws upon Marx and Engels to conceive of a society where "it will become possible for the state to wither away completely ... when people have become so accustomed to observing the fundamental rules of social intercourse and when their labour becomes so productive that they will voluntarily work *according to their ability* ... There will then be no need for society to regulate the quantity of products to be received by each: each will take freely 'according to his needs'." This world will be remarkably productive, it will have learnt voluntary association because of the disappearance of private property and of classes, and it will be a society without a State. It will, however, be the sequel not only to the capitalistic economy but to the society that manages collectively owned property under a transitional socialistic State. It will come into existence as history unfolds, an event "which no one has ever promised or even thought to 'introduce' because it generally cannot be 'introduced'." Something very, very different from the interventionist State will develop from "bourgeois economy," but it will develop according to its own historical dynamics.

Despite the spectacular differences in how such authors and their works have been perceived, it is not at all artificial, I believe, to join the authors and to ascribe a strong pattern to their conceptions. Authors and conceptions alike are agreed that now or ultimately both State and competition must be expelled from renewed societies. Nor is it artificial to regard Mill as a leading intermediary in transmitting and improving on a theme that was continuously prominent from the one great European revolution to the next. The abstractions that Mill selected from his precursors were visibly influential in most of the meditations still to come. In his famous *What Is To Be Done?* Nikolai Chernyshevski[26] wrote of his appalling new men and women in language that might make one swear off reform forever; but if his novel is oppressively didactic it also communicated the abstractions from Mill to many – including Lenin – who had a certain knack for practical affairs. Here the pathbreaking husbands and wives set up co-operative workshops on the best examples from Mill. They are materialists, and as remorselessly utilitarian in word and honest in deed as Mill himself could hope. The new men and women lead all to a happy equality under voluntary association, and expect this marvel by applying the same faith in education that Mill had. "And so history will begin again in a new phase. And that will last until men say: 'Now we are good', and then there will be no longer any special type, for all men will be of this type, and it will be difficult for anyone to understand that there ever was a time when it was regarded as special and not as the common nature of all mankind."[27] It is true that this progress will be cyclical, and that successions of new men and women will be needed before the co-operative ideal is realized, but as against Marx the cycles create good men in a good society instead of bringing a flawed society to an end. To build or hope for a good society containing only men who are not good but ordinary, this would have been to defer too far to reality.

From Mill to Chernyshevski to Lenin of the State-that-will-vanish seems no great distance, and measured in conceptual units rather than historical units is perhaps no distance at all. Chernyshevski translated Mill,[28] wrote the *What Is To Be Done* that was the favorite work of Alexander Ulyanov, and that was then read intently by the brother the Czar overlooked to hang. "It is the kind of book that influences you for your whole life," says that Lenin who also wrote a prominent *What Is To Be Done*. *Pace* Marx, there is some continuity here!

In all these co-operative societies, so different from "bourgeois economy," humankind will have been able by education and instruction to change the natures of its members, and will be able to free itself first of the oppressive and then of the interventionist State. Education – there *must* be teachers and those who are taught – is indeed the elixir, for it transmutes the old materialism without disturbing its essence. Canadian illustrations can hardly compete in a Canadian university with these glorious inventions from abroad. Still, they exist. The Co-operative Commonwealth Federation of the depression and post-depression years is usually thought of as the certain parent of the New Democratic Party and as parent-like to social democracy throughout Canada. In a practical way it was of a mind to do much more violence to Canadian "bourgeois economy" than its softer successors have ever contemplated. Its chosen name and its logical base, however, *combine* objections to the mindless State that have been sketched above, and are by no means merely the interventionist opposite of a privatized society. "Commonwealth" is strictly contradictory of private wealth, and envisages social modes of both production and of distribution. "Co-operative" is contradictory of competitive, and is plainly applied in the style of Mill and according to the considerable experience with co-operatives gained since Mill's evidence was compiled. As "Co-operative Commonwealth Federation" was being compressed into "CCF" its complete name was forgotten by all but the most faithful; and although this compression represented distaste for a cumbersome name, it seems also to have marked decline and failure in the "co-operative" principle.

More topical, but perhaps not as much noticed, is the invocation by Canadian governments, in these last dozen years, of voluntary association over the whole domain of prices and wages. At the beginning of the seventies there appeared "the institutionalized exercise in the co-operative determination of absolute prices (and the freezing of relative prices) under the auspices of the Prices and Incomes Commission. There have been *ad hoc* repetitions ever since until the revival of the idea in the federal budget of June 28th last".[29] The Minister of Finance then announced that he was "urging Canadians to lower their demands for income increases ... calling on everyone to help Canada make the difficult transition from the 12 percent world that has mired us in recession to the 6 percent world that will bring recovery ... Solidarity and sharing built Canada ... . I count on the willingness of all Canadians to bear their share of the collective effort." Voluntary association is not admittedly to displace "bourgeois economy" entirely, for there is to be that conscript army of federal public servants to stiffen the ranks, and a general use of genteel blackmail to help the skeptical to believe. If this lessens the connection with Mill a little, the official contention that "solidarity and sharing" were building the Canada of 1867, even as Mill wrote, more than compensates for that slippage. The immediate task, too, of affecting prices and wages in every sector could hardly be more ambitious vis-a-vis privatization: not only is the goal at the centre of the privatized economy, but to reach it by universal self-denial needs a route unknown to "bourgeois economy." Prices and wages would be determined twice over.

PRIVATIZATION AND THE INSTRUMENTS OF PUBLIC CHOICE

Of the alternatives available to the privatized society, therefore, it is only the purposeful, interventionist, democratic State that I shall consider in the remainder of this text. The discussion, again despite Marx, will be kept within the framework of "bourgeois economy", although in making this choice I am highly sceptical still of Marx and Mill rather than persuaded beyond recall of their views of future realities.

Within "bourgeois economy" privatization is expressed in a political programme, just as its social democratic antagonist is expressed in a political programme; and since this is so, it begins with a preferred myth, the picture of a system never part of human experience but well known all the same by catch-phrases. For privatization the mottos are "*laissez-faire*," or "free enterprise," or the "market system," and have incorporated in them overtones of property rights, of maximum personal and social welfare, and of a blessed rate of growth. Such matters invite confusion with the works of Adam Smith and his predecessors, those dynamic and turbulent works so eminently practical in their conception. They belong much better with the abstractions of a hundred and twenty years later. Vilfredo Pareto[30] has a far stronger claim to be the patron saint of the intermediate text-books than any of the classicists: here is the "community" that is totally individualistic, that denies social purpose, that is wholly competitive in its basic logic, and that is a set of deductions extracted from the presumption of equilibrium for all demands and supplies.[31] Privatization is there given its idealized form.

In the political expression of privatization I suppose one strategic consideration is bound to be an effort to freeze public policy, to make the democratic State apparatus less able to function creatively, to dismantle instruments of collective choice. There are now quite spectacular examples in the constitutional domain. The ability to legislate day-by-day is to be taken from the State and subordinated to the management of pre-existing law. Constraints upon policy are imbedded into revised constitutions. The fact of California's "Proposition 13" was extreme and rare. The prospect of a constitutional requirement in the United States that Washington's budget be balanced has a different dimension. "The next amendment to the U.S. Constitution will very likely be the Republican right's perennial dream of forcing Congress to balance the Federal budget ... . Codified as Senate Joint Resolution 58, the ... amendment seems a cinch to be approved by the full Senate" – so *Newsweek* reports how matters stood this July 26th. Here in Canada the months devoted to patriating the British North America Act and adding warranties about ancient rights were notable for the silence about the mechanics of maintaining the economic interventions of the welfare State, let alone about how any further advances could be made. Undoubtedly the motivations for decentralizing economic authority were many-sided, but it is arguable that in part (and even in Ottawa) a diminished capacity for *any* authority to be exercised was regarded with equanimity.

A less direct but probably more effective dismantling of instruments of public choice has been the exclusion of the trade union movement from the centre of society. In North America the union movement has almost always been resisted rather than assisted, hardly a favoured institution even under the protection of social democratic governments. For purposes of the interventionist State, I suggest, the unions have not been too strong but too weak and fragmented, diverted from their primary purposes at times to mere exercises in survival, and made vulnerable at other times to imposed and tainted leadership, of fumbling tactics industrially and politically. For better or for worse – it is not the value judgement that is being discussed – the trade union movement in Canada has allied itself with the interventionist, democratic State on almost every political issue one can think of, from support of the authority of that State as such, to support of the attempts of that State to intervene on everything from full employment and medicare to metric conversion and statutory holidays, and to exhortation of that State

to pursue actively goals still left to the visionary corners of political programmes (those resolutions on the Third World and the ecology and nuclear
disarmament that might seem daunting even to the hopes of a Chernyshevsky). To weaken such an ally would seem inevitably to weaken the interventionist State and to speed privatization. Privatizers have had no doubts
about this relationship, but it has been surprisingly obscure to others. The
"eighty" come particularly to mind.

It would seem that the purposeful, democratic State would surely realize
that the attack upon its ally was an attack upon itself, and would accordingly
have made it impossible to resist unionization wherever in industry it was
wanted and in whatever degree. The reality, of course, is that in white collar
occupations, in occupations where employment is transient and always at
risk, in occupations where the doors to managerial positions are not closed,
any individual's wish to join a union may be lawful but is prudent to suppress.
The purposeful State could protest and insist on unionization but it does not;
and such a durable spokesman for privatization as Ian Sinclair[32] can express
some confidence of "the movement from the shop floor, from the working
people overriding the union leadership," a phenomenon "in Great Britain
... apparent to everybody. Maybe it's coming here. And it's needed; some
realistic attitudes are needed by everybody, business too." Mr. Sinclair is
especially worth listening to on the point, for he speaks in the context of
having just been "picked by Prime Minister Pierre Trudeau and Finance
Minister Allan MacEachen to sell the Federal Government's new 6-and-5
percent wage-and-price constraint programme to the nation's corporate leaders." Even though other advocates of such programmes look longingly to
the assistance they might gain from social contracts, and so from much
strengthened trade unions, they join in the crunch with Mr. Sinclair and
accept the programmes *without* the social contracts and *without* the trade
unions.

That the opponents of the purposeful State would act against trade unions,
I re-emphasize, is as certain as the failure of support for trade unions by
the democratic State is surprising. In logic *that* State should supply support.
In logic so should those who benefit from both trade unions and *that* State.
In logic those who admire trade unions should not admire an AIB or a TIP.
In logic these things are so if the idea of the purposeful, democratic State
has much strength. The failure of support for trade unions perhaps points
not to a victory for privatization but to unreal expectations about the capacity
of the State to organize any sustained purpose.

A third route to the neutralization of the State is followed from the opposite
direction. The domain of "bourgeois economy" is enlarged so that its control
of economic and social events is taken, *ipso facto*, to be correct and complete,
in this way denying the political process the right to function in affairs
already satisfactorily decided. Under such rules the interventions of the State

are said to be at the best redundant but more often mischievous or destructive. It will be remembered that in his classic "Contribution to a New Theory of Just Taxation"[33] Wicksell had seen the engrafting of the democratic political process as essential to the tolerable functioning of an industrial society, and *this even after* institutional questions had been settled to allow markets to function efficiently, to determine original endowments, and to determine the consequent pattern of distribution. (I might interpolate that Wicksell made a much greater demand on "bourgeois economy" than this, for in the indispensable interventions needed to provide monetary policy and population control the purposeful State had to be a strong federation of nation-states. He offered as required solutions for the difficulties of "bourgeois economy" prescriptions that Marx would presumably have happily taken as proof positive of the impossibility of solutions.) Countless examples of the doctrine of privatization by exclusion are published every month, and if practice follows that doctrine with a lag, yet follow that doctrine it does. "But the fact is, the squandering and laziness routine in government simply would not be tolerated in the real world." So says K. Spicer (Montreal *Gazette*, June 23 1982) as though reporting an axiom rather than developing an argument; and as speaks Spicer so does "commonsense" throughout the land. There is a "real world" constituted of markets in which the State is on the whole unnecessary machinery and a burden.

The part of this thesis (and its day-to-day applications) that is concerned with the peculiar delinquency of those outside the "real world" seems to me improbable and in any case beside the point. Where the thesis bites is in the privatized nature of this reality, for if the State has only unreality to add to bourgeois economy, then one or other of the messages of privatization has been confirmed. Perhaps the interventions of the State need not be repeated because the political process has added to the markets few effects that are not illusory (subject to the usual qualification, that bourgeois economy requires a State-in-being so that its markets are protected). If on the other hand the interventions affect events they can and should be checked. In case of ties the markets win and the State loses; and there are few ties.

Finally, in this matter of rendering the State ineffectual, there is the almost automatic attempt in systems on the Canadian style to separate large actors in the public economy from the State itself. One surely does not want politics to colour the behaviour of monopolies merely because, say, they *are* monopolies and have been nationalized. Privatization, as far as I can see, has no stauncher friends than our mammoth chartered banks and nation-wide railroad companies. It is taken for granted, even or especially when a social democratic government has a turn at office, that whatever is important to the economy and has come into the possession of the State, that such an asset should be insulated from State control as much as possible. Hydro-electric companies, housing corporations, banks, Central banks, railways, caisses des depôts, crown corporations of every other kind, all of these enterprises that might arm the State in its economic and social purposes are to be surrendered. For once the privatizer can correctly invoke the *works* of Adam Smith as well as the *name*. One thinks back to the struggle within the New Democratic Party of a dozen years back (of which ripples remain), the struggle about whether any danger to Canadian purpose could be imagined that was as great as the flow of direct investment from the United States. Experience since has revealed no intense interest by Canadian governments in controlling enterprises of any kind: the expropriating foreigner may have been at the gates, but that hardly seems to have mattered. For many members of Parliament and of the provincial legislatures, I think it is fair to say that in their perception, economic and social policies have become specialized activities that must be sub-contracted to independent agencies. For them it would be a nightmarish responsibility to bring the Bank of Canada or Hydro Quebec under full political direction: let there be states within the State, perhaps, but that must be the outer limit of public responsibility. For the privatizer it would be supererogatory (or at least prideful) to attempt to remove from State control enterprises already so safely separated from interventionist use.

PRIVATIZATION AND THE WELFARE STATE

Let me turn from the effectiveness of the instruments of public choice (successfully attacked, successfully defended, or whatever) to the purposes of this State we are discussing, the interventionist, democratic State operating within the boundaries of "bourgeois economy." Without investing much thought in categories, I shall comment first on arrangements directed to taxes and transfers, whether in money or kind, then on arrangements affecting the composition and total product of the society (devices to affect the level of employment, the rate of growth, the volume of public goods and so on), and finally and *pro forma* on residual arrangements (in which items not so mechanically economic can find a place).

Social democracy is probably identified with the "welfare State" more closely than with anything else. Privatization would return this construction to the bits and pieces of the market-place.

Take as a first example the facts of hospital and medical care. Few whose memory carries back to the days before public care in hospitals and public medical care were embedded in Canadian life are likely to dispute what a splendid achievement that use of taxes and transfers represented. Few who look to the ghetto medicine on which our neighbours to the South rely are likely to overlook how retrograde a return to such crudities would be. No one, however, who reads of privatization by means of deterrent fees,[34] by means of the "opting-out" of professionals, by means of extra billing, can be certain that the achievement is permanent. In some measure the advances of the sixties are already curtailed and for all that can confidently be predicted may be reversed entirely.

It has been especially important that, from the time the reforms were instituted it was well known that they had been *roughed in*, and on purely technocratic grounds, would require successive stages of improvement. In unfinished form they were very likely to prove unstable, as has indeed been testified to by experience. The State all the same did not – or was inherently unable to – deal with the danger. It was folly to leave unsettled how to deal rationally with the claims of the professionals, as though the programme could be conceived of eternally as only a defense against selfish privilege; and it was equal folly to do so little about the archaic institutional constraints on efficient medical care. It was "folly" (in these and other instances) to do nothing if it is accepted that there were required needs unaccomplished. It may be, though, that the purposeful State was incapable of developing this particular purpose any further. It may even be – as in this context has always to be considered – that the "splendid achievement" was pretty much of an accident into which we have chosen to see purpose, a splendid, transitory happening neither chosen "then" discarded "now."

Medical care gives a first example and a very important one. There are others of comparable importance, however, each with its differentiated features of fact and theory. From the earliest days of "bourgeois economy" there were many aspects of the welfare State that had at least a shadowy existence-in-the-small, and some aspects (financing the expenses of the sovereign, national defense, the State-in-being) that existed in-the-large. It has been well known from physiocratic times to the present that it is not possible, it is indeed meaningless, to say of this person or that in an interdependent society (epitomized by "bourgeois economy") that he or she produced such and such goods. It should be pointless then, *a fortiori*, to pose the further question of whether producing such and such goods would convey property rights in those goods, and to ask whether under various moral hypotheses those rights would be well-founded. In any event, distribution cannot take place in "bourgeois economy" without social decision of some kind about taxes and transfers. A centrepiece in the debate about taxes and transfers, I think, has been the obvious arbitrariness of solutions pressed against the obvious necessity for solutions. Competition is of the nature of things, but so is the State-in-being and the defense of the State-in-being, as Carl Menger[35] was careful to emphasize before axiomatizing pure market behaviour. A social consensus emerges to permit taxes to be paid and transfers to be collected, but it rests upon individual interests that are always in conflict. Popular notions on how the consensus should form have two predictable versions. There is the kind of second-best privatization borrowed from Adam Smith (the transfers support the State-in-being, and the taxation is as near as may be neutral vis-a-vis the market), and there is the more or less complete egalitarianism (an idea with many variants) taken as the economic corollary of political democracy.

I have already remarked on the primacy of education in the logic of the societies-without-a-State. For the welfare State, too, education has ranked almost as high, but of course as something that would flow from State purpose rather than substitute for it. Almost every issue one can think of touching privatization can be illustrated from the immense variety of experience Canadian society has had with primary education first, and then with education of all levels more recently. Some truly basic questions, however, may be more sharply posed in considering parallel experience with the old rather than the young, that is, Canadian experience with pensions. Here let me take notice of privatization *ex definition*, the affection for private schools. Inheritances through private schooling, I suspect, are nowadays easier to pass on than are inheritances in land. One sometimes wonders, although it is an unworthy thought, whether there is any simpler gauge of how progressive one's friends are than how exclusive the schools are to which they send their children. Privatization directs society to elite schooling because it takes inherited status as a datum and knows no mechanism for interfering with the bequest of those kinds of wealth the market can transmit. Here, the instrument of privatization is not direct suppression in the budgets of universal schooling, but acceptance of the separatist schools. Where the separatist schools are of high quality, academically or as a door to status, then parents indeed face a dilemma however egalitarian their views in general may be. They will be reluctant to wait while schooling in general is constructed or reconstructed to high and equalized standards. Waiting will pass their children by, and in any case, however high general standards may be, selective shools – all those "difficult" left behind – will have higher standards still. In education the suspicion becomes harder to dismiss that the disputes about privatization are in the main disputes about original endowments.

The principal example I would give, however, is the contest about the leading basis of pensions in the country. It perhaps deserves a place because it so clearly illustrates the contending possibilities, that on the one hand there is a largely empty debate in which privatization is cheered or deplored, but in which the course of pensions will be largely independent of calculated, deliberate choices of policy, and that on the other hand, there is a normative debate under way in which the wish to privatize or to defeat privatization will have great practical consequences. My view, argued at length elsewhere,[36] is that *here* the welfare state is not so much protected by positive economics – the language is then inconsistently normative – as it is the necessary consequence of the system. It was striking that in the wide ranging schemes of privatization in the early days of the Reagan regime an abrupt and unexpected check was experienced when the privatizers to the South attempted to tamper with the social security system. Further the positive economics revealed in this portion of the welfare state seems *prima facie* to have some force elsewhere, in logic wherever the population at large benefits from protection against incalculable contingencies. If this view is supported by events in Canada, the reduction in Old Age Security protection will prove an aberration, within a strongly evolutionary process towards continuity in living standards throughout retirement.

If privatization is *sometimes* a sham battle, in which our wishes interfere with our reason, it certainly does not follow that it is always so. In touching on the welfare state, I should report fascination with a favoured example by Friedman of why some touch of the welfare state must be retained: there are indeed madmen abroad even in the most privatized of societies, and for these exceptional people the market is not well equipped to provide remedy. One might almost say, those lucky madmen for whom a society will still exist, and for whom the State will have a human face. Where privatization may well not be a sham battle is where it touches the scope of the welfare state and the principle of universality: distribution and redistribution are normative surely in their ultimate origins and ultimate results.

A Word on Property Rights: Privatization would give new force to property rights, and would make legal ownership and rights over what is owned more nearly co-extensive. I cannot think of a classical economist from Turgot to Marx for whom the mechanics of the alienation of property, the relation of the state apparatus to property, the technical and moral rationale of property rights, are not seen as fundamental to the scope of economic science, perhaps able to be described without hyperbole as the economic question of all economic questions. Friedman's justification, incidentally, for strengthened property rights, runs in terms of economic efficiency. I doubt there is much belief in any society that one's individual fortunes are more affected in any degree by efficiency that by where one begins with original endowments. A few thousand acres amply compensates for the marginal equalities.

A Word on Employment: Privatization would also inhibit the State from intervening to correct the ills of the *laissez faire* economy, at least in any degree that might impair the structure of power in the economy. In April, 1945, the Minister of Reconstruction published the sparkling assurance that the "central act of reconstruction was to maintain a high and stable level of employment and income ... a primary object of policy ... [not thereby selecting] a lower target than full employment." The assurance has failed, for reasons that certainly go beyond a retreat to (or the fact of) privatization. Few would dispute that the complexity of what was promised was underestimated, and the growing, accelerating interdependence of *this* promise with competing promises was only partly understood.

I believe all the same that the heart of the matter is that the assurance *was* repudiated as a retreat to (or as an aspect of inescapable) privatization. The critical event was the election (chosen or forced) of tolerated, compensated unemployment as a satisfactory substitute for direct employment. The substitution belonged to the family of "cures" of which, say, negative income taxes are a prime example.

A Word on Wage Controls: Since I have only recently written at length[37] on the use of wage controls in this past dozen years I shall be brief here. The union movement in Canada was certainly greatly nurtured by evolution in the late thirties in the United States, and then again by the non-privatized economy of the war years at home. Whatever else wage-controls may be, their compulsory enactment by the State seems logically to be the creation of an anti-union, designed to do what unions intend to do, only replacing positive numbers with negative.

SOME CONCLUSIONS

Examples on all sides of these questions are abundant, and in any particular case should certainly be investigated as to their particulars as something much more detailed than mere chapter headings. All the same, it is time to come to some conclusions, even though in the context of the limitations of a sketch of so wide a domain conclusions cannot pretend to be more than tentative and explanatory. I return to the questions that Marx raised, for *ex post* they seem to me to point to fundamentals.

Item, on the great question of the ultimate fate of bourgeois economy, I see nothing in local experience that tells us much. One would guess the answer lies in two sequences, one of which was largely foreseen in Marx and the other of which, I fear, neither Marx foresaw nor none of us here *can* foresee. There is the matter of third-world economies, and the connections amongst bourgeois economics, the floating States of multi-national corporations, and the social tensions in the hinterlands of bourgeois economy: on that evolution as a *cause* of instability Marx has much to say, though from within Canadian experience I find the effects wholly unpredictable. There is the matter – the second of the sequences – of nuclear armaments. Bourgeois economy might explain catastrophe if it comes, and were there explainers left alive for the needed analysis; but I judge *ex ante* explanation via Marx or any other economist to be of negligible value.

Item, on the lesser questions that suppose the economic and social system as we see now is for better or worse all that we shall see, the questions that appraise what may happen or be made to happen within bourgeois economy, I conclude first that some substantial matters debated in the name of such language as privatization are in fact endogenous, part of the positive properties of the system. This does not require that the form or degree of these matters become fixed points in the system, but only that they are reasonably predictable consequences of the system. In terms of the world that we can examine and deal with I suppose that in relation to Marx's questions they constitute a stabilizing factor that mindlessness of the State does not negate public pensions, perhaps, are a consequence of the system from the simple fact of its existence, and are not much affected by political choice.

Item, if this is accepted, it leaves over the matter of privatization in a practical form. The residual question is whether governments can govern, whether a democratic, purposeful State is an actor for whom a role has been written, and so whether the privatizers in fact have an opponent. It seems to me this is so. Governments can choose universality or selectivity in their social programmes, for example. Governments can intervene or reject intervention in the allocation of investment. Governments can foster trade unions or impede trade unions – and so on, and so on. Governments, alas, in the jargon of the trade have always two social welfare functions before them, that of the society and that of the government: that government must face elections, must deal with durable problems in short intervals of time, and must create an apparatus commensurable with the problems. The requirements are not necessarily compatible. Even in the residual areas of policy Marx's questions therefore carry a certain sting.

NOTES AND REFERENCES

1 Budget Speech, 28 June 1982, 3.

2 Ibid., 5.

3 F. Engels, *Anti-Duehring*, a translation from pp. 301–03 of the third German edition. I am making use of V. Lenin on the *State and Revolution* where some the pithier citations on the withering away of the State are gathered.

4 P.A. Kropotkin, "The State and Its Historic Rule", *Selected Writings on Anarchism and Revolution*, MIT Press, Cambridge, Mass.; p. 212 et seqq.

5 Popular versions of these influential theses are to be found in Friedman's regular contributions to *Newsweek*.

6 The introductory citation (page 57 of this text) seems to me no more or less striking than this assessment on the dust-jacket of *Wealth and Poverty* from David Stockman of the administration currently enjoyed by our neighbour.

7 The introductory citation is from Mill's *Principles of Political Economy*, p. 755 of Ashley's edition.

8 I have the citation without yet being able to find the book itself, in a search that has been languid but will continue.

9 K. Marx, *Capital*, Volume III, Chapter 30, p. 484. The edition used is that published in English by Progress Publishers, Moscow, beginning in 1954.

10 Ibid., Volume II, Chapter 20, p. 414.

11 Marx had a harsh view of Malthus, but if he did not borrow from Part II of the *Principles* certainly repeats points that were well made by his predecessor. *Inter al.* Malthus pointed to the vanishingly small probability that time consuming production would be closely matched by current demands, and was skeptical that convergence to equilibrium would be either speedy or assured – and was ready to praise unproductive consumption as a partial solution to failures in demand.

12 "Concentration" and "consolidation" are not consistently used in the Marxian literature (nor does it much matter that the usages vary). For Marx, though, "concentration" is the growth of an enterprise by accumulation and "consolidation", its growth by combination and merger. See, for example, *Capital*, Volume I, Chapter 13.

13 Ibid., Vol. II, Chapter 20, Section V.

14 Ibid.

15 Ibid., Chapter IX, p. 189.

16 Ibid., Vol. I, Chapter 32.

17 Ibid.

18 Ibid.

19 For Marx see the early argumentation, e.g., in the *Communist Manifesto*. "National differences ... are daily more and more vanishing: owing to the development of the bourgeoisie, to freedom of commerce, to the world market ..." For Lenin see the continuing themes of *Imperialism, The Highest Stage of Capitalism*.

20 Marx frequently allows his indignation on his political purposes to transfer the focus to iniquitous behaviour by individuals. He frequently allows himself to speak of the capitalist State as a co-ordinator of capitalistic purposes. Nonetheless the system he described is not seriously affected by private motivation, for good or bad, and his State seems rarely to deal with problems deeper than the length of the working day.

21 This judgement is based principally upon the Polyani-inspired researches of M. Mendell, who is completing a doctoral thesis with me. The evidence seems overwhelming that as one looks at societies in general, first, there is a very large fraction of resources required (often absorbed "in kind") to allow any State to sustain itself, second, that the fraction is not monotonically connected to the complexity of the society, and third, that the manifestation of the apparatus is of a hierarchical kind.

22 P. A. Kropotkin, op. cit., p. 264.

23 J. S. Mill, op. cit., p. 763.

24 Ibid., pp. 746–51.

25 V. I. Lenin, collection cited in footnote (3), pp. 111 et seq.

26 N. Chernyshevsky, 'What Is To Be Done?' originally published in St. Petersburg, 1863, cited here from B.T. Tucker's translation of 1883, printed with

an introduction by E.H. Carr under Vintage Books of Random House, 1961. The title is the parent, naturally, of V.I. Lenin's programmatic but far from independent *What Is To Be Done?* which, with Lenin's correction, appears on 1 April 1902.

27 N. Chernyshevsky, op. cit., p. 175. Since this was written I have had the message of the Prime Minister of Canada from three talks in a similar vein. We are to become new men and women. In the nineteenth century it was perhaps not pure romanticism to imagine that example and education could create new men and women. Experience has made plain that it is with men and women as they are that society must fashion its programmes, and that new men and women are elitist phantasies.

28 "The question of morality seemed to him to have been solved once for all by the English Utilitarians, known to him principally through John Stuart Mill, whom he translated." Chernyshevsky, op. cit., Carr's "Introduction", p. xii. I think Carr understates. The *programme* of Mill is borrowed (the Mill of second thoughts), and not simply the *calculus* of motive. On the transmission of this influence to V.I. Lenin, I have in mind such strong, direct evidence as that cited by L.H. Haimson, *The Russian Marxists and the Origins of Bolshevism*, Harvard University Press, 1955, circa p. 98.

29 See the beginning of this piece again, and recall the content of the addresses by the Prime Minister looking to voluntarism strengthened by conscripts. This does double duty, as an introductory citation and as part of the text proper. The notion that a spontaneous outburst of goodness can direct economic affairs as a substitute government seems to lie somewhere between the comic and the tragic.

30 See the text and the mathematical appendix of V. Pareto's *Manual of Political Economy*, (originally 1903–06) in the translation by A.S. Schwier and A.N. Page (1971). For this reader the translation at times seemed inconsistent with the flow of the argument. In any case the device of reasoning back from assumed equilibrium to process rather than from process to possible equilibrium is Paretian, not Walrasian.

31 Ibid., Appendix. The sequence of argument is perfectly plain when the structure is formalized.

32 The quotation comes from a variously reported interview on Mr. Sinclair's new tasks. I confess to a certain regret. Can it be that only social democrats are left to defend some part of the marketplace for the Canadian Pacific Railway?

33 It dates from 1896, and is found (e.g.) in *Classics in the Theory of Public Finance*, R. Musgrave and A. Peacock, 1958.

34 For an interesting account of this aspect of medicare, and of other aspects discussed in the next few sentences – particularly the matter of leaving the programme half-finished and of pointing to the physician as scape-goat – see L. Soderstrom, *Health Policy At A Crossroad*, forthcoming from the Canadian

Centre For Policy Alternatives, and initiated by the Douglas-Coldwell Foundation.

35 Perhaps it is widely known, but it was news to me that the second version of Menger's *Principles* appeared in 1923 posthumously and was not translated. As with the information of footnote 21 the advice comes to me from M. Mendell's Polanyi-inspired researches. In 1933 when an edition was republished in English it was the first version accompanied by very unkind suggestions from F. Hayek about the inexplicable addition to the second version. The principal oddity seems to me an excellent and far reaching point thesis, namely, that economies widely conceived have a technocratic problem but not necessarily a scarcity problem: a State is always needed. Economies that experience scarcity (in relation to things that are known to exist!) constitute a narrower set, but necessarily also rely on a State-in-being.

36 In the Jamieson lecture at the University of British Columbia, dated 30 September 1982.

37 In the Jamieson lecture dated 1 October 1982.

CHAPTER SIX

The Unity of Economics

Economics is the social science that analyses how *surplus* is produced in a community and distributed among its members. The terms of the definition are strong enough to give the science unity, and flexible enough to account for its evolution and the considerable variation in its expression.

This fundamental conception of surplus is easiest to understand in a stylized example. An agricultural community, say, produces grain and sets aside certain amounts for seed. After a period of production new totals of grain are available, sufficiently large to replace both the seed and all other depreciation entailed by the productive process, and then additionally to provide a *surplus* of so much grain available for any other purpose the community may choose (for example, investment in an enlarged total of seed grain for the next harvest or further consumption made possible by the newly produced excess). Part of this decision will involve the *distribution* of the surplus in preferred proportions from one group to another, i.e., the sharing of the surplus. A contemporary version of surplus is the familiar (net) *national product*, a statistic reported in Canada nowadays not as bushels of grain but as dollars, about $350 billion.

How such a surplus is identified is in many ways arbitrary, and so is a fertile source of technical misunderstandings or political debate. Membership in the community that receives the surplus needs to be defined, the things to be counted in the surplus have to be chosen, the method of calculating the surplus has to be decided (for there are many ways to homogenize physically distinct objects), and rules for computing depreciation have to be agreed upon (whether to include human depreciation, for example, or the costs of maintaining state institutions and the social fabric).

Preface to "A History of Economic Thought," 3d ed. (unpublished), iii – xv. This text contains lecture notes that Weldon was preparing for publication at the time of his death. Copies are in private circulation.

As a social *science* economics is no more than four centuries old. This does not deny that economic events are as old as our knowledge, or that economic institutions of great complexity have a history that goes back as far as the Middle Kingdom of Pharoanic Egypt. In the great societies of antiquity, economic surplus often required immense acts of public enterprise – to harness anything like the Nile left no alternative – and so required corresponding systems of banking and public finance, organized on quite modern lines. In those great societies, surplus tended not only to be created in the public domain, but also to be publicly distributed in supporting a stable society. Theory may be recent, but economic practice is rich and ancient.

SMITH AND THE REGIME OF NATURAL LIBERTY

In his *Wealth of Nations* (1776), Adam Smith dealt with surplus as it would develop under his "regime of natural liberty." There are earlier treatments that require attention, and many later treatments, but Smith's celebrated model is an indispensable reference for the work of precursors and successors alike. Smith saw surplus as something to be *managed* by the community with the primary purpose of providing workers, the bulk of the population, with as many consumption goods per head as possible. The purpose would be frustrated, however, if the growth of surplus did not run well ahead of the growth of population, or if levels of investment and saving were too low to sustain needed growth. It would also be frustrated if the accumulation of capital goods did not create markets large enough for the division of labour and other sources of technological progress.

Since such obstacles were only too characteristic of the Europe of his day, Smith judged that surplus would best be managed by instituting at a controlled pace the regime of "natural liberty," and, specifically, by allowing nature to take its course in economic events and by giving individual capitalists great freedom in choosing the form and allocation of their capitals. This would result in a comparatively *efficient* use of these capitals (a still fundamental if often challenged theme in economics). It would also generate levels of investment and saving not only much higher than earlier levels, but "best" in relation to the fundamental contest between population and consumption. Here he supplied little supporting argument, except perhaps to appeal to the confidence his "natural liberty" might inspire in those who invest and those who save, a not easily tested proposition that politicians have usually found congenial.

Smith required a theory of exchange to explain why natural liberty could be efficient in producing surplus, and borrowed (and improved upon) the idea that goods are traded according to the toil and trouble with which they are fashioned. Those who purchase are guided by *cheapness*, a proposition that points to efficiency without distinguishing between domestic and international trade. Under "natural liberty," private motivation is accordingly a most powerful instrument of the public weal. Smith does not deny, however, that public authority is a complementary instrument, and devotes hundreds of pages to a catalogue of legitimate interventions by the State.

MERCANTILISM AND PHYSIOCRACY

The *Wealth of Nations* takes as its index of errors the nationalistic writings scattered over many years and many pamphleteers that Smith summarized as "mercantilism." In its political expression, the thesis of mercantilism was that *merchants* who sell abroad are the mainspring of national prosperity and deserve every protection the State can provide. The state was called upon to restrict imports and to encourage exports, a policy that obviously contradicts the test of cheapness Smith would advocate.

At the theoretical level, in such a sophisticated study as Thomas Mun's *England's Treasure by Forraign Trade* (1630), the nascent dispute is seen to be far from trivial. Surplus in mercantilist theory encompasses only activities outside the domestic economy and must be measured by the accumulation of wealth arising from the excess of exports over imports. Mun applies an analogy between the vast household of England and any ordinary household: accumulation takes place in both cases by selling more to the stranger than one buys. It was the *boundary* of surplus that essentially distinguished Mun from Smith. Few societies have consistently rejected mercantilist advice about how to maximise mercantilist surplus, or the mercantilist portrayal of trading surplus as blessed.

Adam Smith was impressed in a quite different way by the first economists who thought of themselves as creators of a new science, the physiocrats, who in the middle of the eighteenth century established a considerable position in French intellectual and political life. Within physiocracy, pride of place should be given to François Quesnay and Anne Robert Turgot, to the former as innovator (the startling *Tableau economique*, c. 1758), to the latter as systematic thinker (the profound *Reflexions*, 1766). The social program of physiocracy was easy to understand, for it simply advocated rapid investment in large-scale agriculture, a capitalistic agriculture freed of restrictions and controls. The science that was intended to rationalize this *laissez-faire* was not as obvious.

Surplus for the physiocrats had virtually the same boundaries as it would later have for Adam Smith and Statistics Canada. Their *produit net* is indeed the archetype of surplus. They added to this unifying concept however, two ideas, that would not be much used by Smith. The first was the excellent conception that in order to explain the origins and the use of surplus it was necessary to deal with the economy as a whole, as a system in which all the parts were interdependent. The second was the appealing mirage that surplus originated in a specific portion of the economy, and (unsurprisingly, in view of physiocratic policies) in agriculture itself. There were productive activities which contributed to surplus and unproductive or sterile activities which did not. The second idea is plainly inconsistent with the first, for if the economy is a single structure, surplus must arise from its entirety and not from a separated part. Physiocracy nonetheless had sponsored irreparable confusion, for few commentators on economic affairs thereafter have been able to resist naming favoured activities as productive and less favoured activities as unproductive. Bureaucracies are endlessly assigned to one category or the other in the Canada of the 1980s.

CLASSICAL ECONOMICS AFTER SMITH

We can now turn to those successors who for nearly a century responded to the *classical* pattern Smith had imposed. David Ricardo (perhaps the best scientist economics has produced), in his *Principles of Political Economy and Taxation* (1817), transfers attention from the *growth* of surplus to its *distribution* among labourers, capitalists and landlords. The harmony of interest emphasised in Smith's capitalism is subordinated to a competition by which one social class loses when another gains. Ricardo thus substituted *statical* theory for the *dynamics* of the *Wealth of Nations*. As a result he greatly improved on Smith in analysing *international* trade (in domestic trade, labour and capital move easily, in international trade they do not) and in explaining rents (surplus distributed to the landowning class because land has been *appropriated*). He also came upon the fact that surplus measured by costs ("value") will be different from surplus measured by commodities ("riches").

His deferential rival was Thomas Robert Malthus, famed for his work on population, but whose reputation within economics owes more to the later *Principles of Political Economy* (c. 1820). Malthus accepted the classical framework but apologetically asked for at least two important modifications. Productive occupations might still be given a nominally superior status with respect to surplus, but Malthus insisted that unproductive occupations were essential if products were to find markets. He caught the significance of economic interdependence even more strikingly in his pessimistic denial of capitalism's automatic ability to create surplus. Goods are *supplied* under one set of rules by one group of persons, but are *purchased* under different rules by different persons. Nature cannot be counted upon to match supplies with purchases and thus constitutes a most unreliable base for the orderly production of surplus. Malthus was able to predict both limited crises in prosperous countries and chronic economic failure in much of the rest of the world. For backward countries, the gap between technical limits to surplus and corresponding institutional limits might prove both large and unchangeable, a remarkably prescient opinion.

There is not enough space here to develop the subtle arguments put forward by that "one-book" economist, John Rae (1834), who was almost a Canadian. But it would be irresponsible not to mention that Rae closely anticipates German attacks on Smith for having ignored the role of the state, and Austrian attacks on Smith for having ignored time and capital!

As economic science progressed, problems with the first formulations multiplied more rapidly than did solutions. John Stuart Mill, in preparing the first edition of his *Principles of Political Economy* (1848), had expected that he would modernize a basically sound structure and then embed a polished, finished science of economics in an ambitious but barely begun science of society as a whole. But as his project evolved from edition to edition of the *Principles*, he found that clarification usually revealed questions of fact or theory with which the classical system did not, and perhaps could not cope. His studies became a call for major new ideas rather than a planned consolidation of old ideas.

Mill clarified such basic ideas as "demand" and "supply," but could then not ignore that the classical system said very little about "demand" and even less about how "demand" interacted with "supply." He described with considerable precision the conventional connection between "natural liberty" and surplus: but he was then struck by the overwhelming weight custom and culture would always have in determining surplus within real societies. Mill observed that there was not much evidence that the classical system achieved its stated goal of improving living standards, and concluded that an alternative to sponsoring economic growth would be to restrain population and improve education. Reflecting on the dubious ethics of "natural liberty," he pondered whether in time cooperative forces might be at least as efficient as self-interest in producing surplus, and much more equitable in its distribution. In brief, Mill speculated on alternatives and modifications that are still the stuff of political economy, and did so in Hamlet-like style that pleased friends and infuriated enemies.

Karl Marx rarely brought Hamlet to mind and had no doubts about the destiny of classical capitalism. Like Mill he offered a sweeping critique on which the evidence is still being gathered. (Marx's influence on affairs has of course been without even distant comparison.) He becomes easier to understand when it is noticed that on technical matters he is often an especially conservative classicist.

In *Capital* (Volume 1, 1867; Volumes 2 and 3 brought out by Engels, 1885 and 1894), Marx made the term "surplus value" one of the hallmarks of his political doctrines, yet this evocative surplus is neither notably wider nor narrower than the surpluses used by his classical forerunners. Marx reported on the machinery of "natural liberty" with even less attention to breakdowns of competition than Smith's work or Mill's had shown, and he used a labour theory of value only a trifle more elaborate than Ricardo's on some points, a trifle less elaborate on others. Marx followed the physiocrats in attributing surplus in an interdependent system to particular actors, differing from them only in naming labourers and labour rather than landlords and land.

From such conventional axioms, Marx deduced neither the beneficent future expected by Smith nor the doubtful future described by Ricardo and Mill; rather he deduced the certainty of crisis in which capitalism would be destroyed, a far bleaker prognosis for "natural liberty" than anything Malthus had observed. This would be total collapse rather than chronic malaise. Capitalism was a set of social and productive relationships like others (e.g., feudalism) and contained as they had sources of *contradiction*, for capitalism the violent contradiction between inevitable expansion and the smothering forces expansion must set free.

His arguments merely *applied* these axioms. Capitalism is indeed greatly productive of surplus, but is so by means of a technology that displaces workers and creates a "reserve army" which competes intensely for jobs. In labour markets workers can win little but subsistence. Competition directs almost all surplus to the control of industrial capitalists, and then distributes it among the whole set of capitalists (entrepreneurs, monied capitalists, landlords, and so on). Out of surplus, however, capitalists must save and accumulate to offset the competition from other capitalists that would destroy their status as capitalists. Admitting Smith's claims of a mightily productive system, Marx produces the paradox of welfare being reduced for the "exploited" but possibly even for the "exploiters"! What is more, as accumulation proceeds the giant investments that must be made are less and less likely to be calculated correctly (an extension of Malthus's idea), and imbalances will lead to crises: the dangers grow as capitalism grows. Finally, Marx decisively concluded that such remedies and preventatives as Mill has considered are outside the reach of a system that is inherently competitive and so cannot organize collective, cooperative cures. "Natural liberty" has the Midas touch.

POST-CLASSICAL ECONOMICS: THE 1870S

For those studying economics, the decade of the 1870s is likely to be the watershed in their research. They find a burst of creativity with respect to technique that has defined the general style of textbooks to the present day, for there is little in the ingenious constructions of recent years that is not the elaboration of those early ideas. They will also find, however, that pure technique has made slow progress with the larger questions that troubled the classical critics.

Carl Menger's *Foundations of Political Economy* (1870), William Stanley Jevon's *Theory of Political Economy*, (1871), and Leon Walras's seminal *Elements of Pure Political Economy* (1874), are sometimes represented as independent co-discoveries of new techniques. There is some truth in this, but scattered anticipations were already in existence and the three innovators assembled their constructions according to very different patterns.

Menger can be credited with integrating "demand" into economics on a *quantitative* basis, using a measurable utility that increased (but less and less rapidly) with successive units of a good. Where costs had been dominant with Ricardo, marginal utilities (as they came to be called) governed events for Menger, so much so that goods however remote from consumption gained their significance *only* from consumption. New measures of surplus would soon be proposed.

Menger rooted his analysis in social history, an approach that only recently has regained attention. Jevons quite deliberately chose to borrow from mechanics, and argued (with success that may have been unfortunate for economics) that to recast the framework of the classical writers as near as might be to the physicist's "statics" would take the subject as far as could then be scientifically justified. He applied the calculus to maximization of utilities (as less noted mathematical economists had already done to other problems) and to a derivation of most of the rules of efficient markets; he invented "trading bodies" as a dubious device to homogenize behaviour; and he speculated that to explain *exchange* between trading bodies would prove the key finding for all economic theory. He also attempted the empirical work required in genuine science, becoming an innovative leader of the legion of econometricians who adorn the profession today.

In his *Elements* Walras showed hypothetical markets for a whole economy, a numerical exercise in reporting surplus that would still have been as understandable to a physiocrat as it would be to a national accountant in Ottawa. His results contained what was undoubtedly the first essentially complete analysis of economic interdependence, the nature of "general equilibrium," and of the forces within a connected system that might allow economic events to be predicted. After the *Elements* had appeared, a serious economist would always have to consider an economy as a whole, either explicitly or by calculated abstraction from effects hoped to be small enough to be ignored.

POST-CLASSICAL ECONOMICS: ITS EVOLUTION AS A FIELD OF STUDY

Not much more should be added to the *taxonomy* of economics as a field of study, for by the turn of the century categories of research and debate had become very durable. The development is well illustrated by the economics of greatest fame written in this century. Knut Wicksell published brilliantly on money and interest and on public finance, and was father-figure to a distinguished, still influential Swedish school. He worked, how-ever, on creating specialized knowledge where general boundaries had al-ready been drawn. Vilfredo Pareto and Alfred Marshall were of greatest influence in the specialized choices they made of methodology. Pareto in-verted the use Walras had made of "general equilibrium", for he *decided to assume* the existence of this impossible state and deduce the circumstances the postulated existence would entail. A certain sterility in economics, now widely complained of in economic journals, owes much to Pareto's inver-sion. As to Marshall, his methodological choice was to search for economic laws by *severe* abstraction from general equilibrium but then to invoke the customary scientific test of whether good prediction would or would not ensue. His pragmatic approach has seemed inescapable to those who believe that the Paretian method nullifies interventionist economic policy.

When the legendary John Maynard Keynes supplied his famous *General Theory of Employment, Interest, and Money* (1936), he argued that an economy might be in equilibrium with vast unemployment and much reduced surplus, with unemployment immune to classical tendencies to general equi-librium. He therefore called for such modest interventionist measures as a "somewhat comprehensive socialization of investment." Everyone has read some of the outpouring of opinion on his great polemic. It is still true, however, that Ricardo and Malthus would have seen in Keynes a close reflection of their own debate, and that Mill and Marx would have had no trouble in reviewing Keynesian reforms that they themselves had long ago assessed. It is plain, too, that Keynes's choice of methodology is precisely that of Marshall, as is much of his apparatus.

More or less the same tone can fairly be taken about the reaction to Keynesian theorizing expressed in the 1960s and 1970s by Milton Friedman (the chief sponsor of "monetarism") or the still later reaction to interven-tionist policies promulgated under the name of "rational expectations." Wicksell would have been sympathetic to Keynes in the domain of policy, but his treatment of money and interest is the foundation for Friedman's treatment. Walras's epistemology is unambitious compared to that of the rational expectationists, but it is a simple version of similar ideas. Today political economy may invoke Smith but its methodology more often derives from Pareto.

CANADIAN ECONOMICS

Canadian history has been too short to have given birth to a distinctive Canadian economics or a special Canadian field of study. Canadian expe-rience comprises the raw materials of much Canadian research, but the style of investigation is part of a more general economics that borrows much of its political economy from the United States. There are many excellent technicians in Canadian universities, and the level of technical training available in our largest schools is not much inferior to that of the better schools in the United States. Advanced work in both English-speaking and French-speaking schools often reflects American training, attitudes, and thinking, and work at all levels is now increasingly that of a branch-plant industry. True, Harold Innis of Toronto was an exception to this pattern; his "staple theory" reflected a genuinely original view of Canadian economic development (the successive dominance of exported staples) that perhaps created a small Canadian school. The exception unfortunately testifies to the rule.

CHAPTER SEVEN

The Attack Upon the Democratic Left

The most important fact about the Canadian economy is the attack upon the democratic left that has gathered strength throughout the seventies. I intend to deal with the strength and weaknesses of the economy in terms of that threat. What is the "democratic left" supposed to define? The obvious people and institutions the various organizations of the labour union movement, the ordinary working men and women whether organized or not and in whatever occupations, their families, the unemployed as well as the employed, and the political bodies that are the democratic allies of labour. This does not imply that industrial organization and political organization are one and the same thing. It does propose a shorthand to define those who are under attack.

UNEMPLOYMENT AND MORE UNEMPLOYMENT

Four years ago it was possible for any independent observer of the North American economy to predict the highest rates of unemployment since the great depression. A classic cause of depressions had shown itself in the unexpected shock from the energy crisis. What would have been unthinkable a few years earlier became probable, unemployment rates to remind us of the nightmare of the thirties. The worst that has happened, of course, has still been far from matching the events of those pre-war years – we live in a wealthier society – but it has also been quite unlike anything experienced since in 1945 the Canadian government committed itself to full employment.

The predictions of four years back can be repeated today. There is nothing in sight to turn the situation around. The waste and hardship will continue.

Reprinted with permission from the Douglas Caldwell Foundation. First published 1978. This text is Weldon's adaptation of a presentation he made to the 1978 Ontario Federation of Labour Education conference on "The Canadian Economy: Strength and Weakness."

Ottawa and the provincial governments could intervene effectively but they will not. Though the commitment to full employment of 1945 was not technically unrealistic, there is neither the *intention* nor the *apparatus* for intervention on the necessary scale. Rhetoric may be lavishly provided by the authorities, but the machinery of a full employment programme they cannot provide. Why not? It has never been built. Unemployment at *eight per cent or more* is therefore a responsible estimate of how the Canadian economy will perform, for a year ahead and probably for much longer, and with the 'or more' being an essential part of the estimate. The horizon, in brief, is as far away as it was four years ago, receding as we try to reach it. When some degree of cure comes it will have waited for natural forces or for favourable accidents that will have done the work of calculated policy.

INFLATION

The usual exercise in economic prophecy has come to mean giving a pair of figures, one for unemployment and the other for inflation. This is harmless, I suppose, except as it has allowed the myth to spread that we are reporting upon equal evils or even that inflation is more damaging than unemployment. It is a myth that in this country has been specially nurtured by the Trudeau regime. From the late sixties to the present day a battle against inflation has been waged that has had the political virtues of being endless, popular, and a splendid excuse for inaction on social programmes. It is no matter that the generals in this war have had no victories. They are engaged in holy war; and when we say they have had no victories we have to be careful about language. The nominal enemy of the Anti-Inflation Board has been inflation – hence the inspired and witty choice of its name. The existence of the Board, though, has undermined the basic purpose of the labour movement, to improve wages, and has demoralized and confused the democratic left. If inflation is more or less where it would have been without the Board who will say that unions have been equally unaffected by this political instrument? If the Board controls wages, why pay union dues?

The fact is that while unemployment *must* leave resources unused and reduce the goods Canadians consume and invest, inflation has such effects only at second hand, in comparatively small amount at levels such as we have experienced in Canada, and is – with reasonable measures to counteract its impact on fixed incomes and on low incomes – an inconvenience rather than the source of deadweight loss unemployment is. Inflation is unpopular with Ottawa because it affects most people a little but enough to cost votes. That unpopularity easily overcomes Ottawa's concern for the more localized groups who carry the great burdens of unemployment. It would certainly be better to have less inflation than we do have or are going to have, other things being equal. There are, however, no *remedies* that would leave other things *equal*, and such remedies as we have tried have had small benefits and enormous costs, and especially for the democratic left.

In this roundabout way one comes to prediction. I do not think that anything has happened to change the tendencies of the past several years. The amount of inflation that the statistics will report depends on the statisticians one listens to, but only within limits. A hundred thousand price changes can be summarized in a great many different single numbers, but almost always in numbers that show some sort of overall behaviour. I say this to support two points, first, that for most of us inflation will continue to be the same feature of life it has been for the last few years, neither much worse nor much better, and second, that in terms of the most commonly reported numbers inflation may be a little lower than it has been recently BUT will be (and not to waffle, WILL BE, not may be) much higher than the average of the post-war figures. The first year of the Anti-Inflation Board showed numbers accidentally low, the second year of the Board showed numbers correspondingly a little high, so the third year should therefore show something like inflation at seven and a half per cent.

The reason for concern is not that inflation at seven and a half per cent can do us much harm of itself – if our governments would show any capacity to govern. There is not going to be some large and destabilizing gap between our inflation and inflation in the rest of the world. The things that are frightening are the effects at second hand. Our governments have shown little capacity for offsetting the harm from inflation they cannot control. They then hide behind the harm that inflation undoubtedly can do when compensation is not provided. Certainly many pensioners are going to be hurt if inflation they did not foresee is not offset. Instead of providing compensation, though, governments have found it easier to attack the democratic left. Unions are too strong, they say. The welfare state has been developed beyond our capacity to pay for its safeguards. The public sector is too large. We are living beyond our means, and so on and so on. All of this is delivered in the name of Warriors Against Inflation. The imbecility of saying we are living beyond our means when each month we are told how many of our resources are not being used, presents no problem to the propagandists of the right. Contradictions have never bothered them. They point to the seven and a half per cent, and expect (not without justification) that to weep about it will excuse contradictions and make inaction look like policy. The physicians of the Middle Ages had the same formula for the plague: weep, blame, bleed the victims but do nothing else.

AND THE CONSTITUTIONAL CRISIS?

Before going on from prophecy about the economy to attempted explanation, one can hardly duck the economics of the so-called constitutional crisis. It is *the* news of the day. There is the theology of sovereignty association to report, and if not that, then the dreary analysis of how the Royal Canadian Mounted should best burn barns.

As an anglophone from Quebec I naturally and inevitably hope the Confederation will be preserved. But it is just as natural, and just as inevitable, that many francophones have hopes of a contrary kind. Hopes of either kind are not likely to count for much. The election of the Parti Québecois on 15 November 1976 did not mark some drastic change in our affairs. On the one hand Quebec has never been a province like the others nor will be in the future. The trends by which the francophones of Quebec are claiming and seizing equal citizenship were underway long before November 15th. They are trends that should not be resisted and in any case cannot be prevented. On the other hand the Confederation will continue much as it would have continued without November 15th. There is nowhere the will nor the apparatus to produce separation or divorce. We shall spend the months ahead in debating whether one collection of meaningless language pleases us more than another.

In brief there is the long-continued evolution of French-Canada to observe, with great sympathy I hope, but that is all. There *is* a diversion, though, of attention from real events to ghosts. The dismal state of the economy has fostered tensions amongst cultural groups, as economic depression has so often done. Rather than dealing with the realities of the economy Ottawa has chosen to make the sham battle over the constitution the outlet for such energy as it has. Indeed the contest may allow Mr. Trudeau to run successfully against the unspeakable M. Levesque and M. Levesque to run successfully against the ineffable Mr. Trudeau. How helpful to all mystics if the nuances of sovereignty association take our minds from the economy! Federal and provincial governments alike have found it very difficult to organize serious economic policy, but not because they have ever approached closely their constitutional boundaries. To claim that constitutional constraints prevent action, though, is a NATURAL defense, and especially if it shifts debate to how to rewrite the constitution. The Great Trek of the Sun Life is a good example: how should it be that the governments of Canada must beg a mere corporation not to subvert the country itself, begging because they have no economic apparatus that would allow direct control and refusal. There is nothing constitutional that would have prevented such an apparatus being built: *somewhere* in this society there is sovereignty.

AN ATTEMPT AT EXPLANATION

So there are the predictions, a not very cheerful collection: it is time to offer some sort of explanation of their pattern. I have not seen anything in the post-war years to suggest that for basics we need go further than Keynes.

Great effects have great causes – that is the central idea. For several years past we have had a stagnant and ill-functioning economy, and for the years ahead can hardly hope for anything better. This is surely a great effect. Where do we look for the great cause? I think the search is as easy as it would have been in the thirties. Then we found the system shaken for a decade by the collapse of its financial markets. Now we find it shaken by the abrupt change in energy markets, a shock of the first magnitude to the whole of the industrialized world. There are always causes of causes, but I shall treat the "abrupt change" as a first cause. It is not surprising that many years pass while the system adapts to so drastic a change, and that there will be protracted depression while the system adapts to so drastic a change, and that there will be protracted depression while adaptation is underway. One might have looked at some other pages in Keynes to discover that governments are supposed to offset the effects of such great shocks, but governments in general have done very little. Canadian events are not unique.

There is the marvel of the current depression being accompanied by inflation, something said to be out of phase with the usual cycle connecting falling prices and recession. I do not see anything particularly puzzling in the facts. The shock was linked from the beginning to an all important price increase, the remarkable rise in the price of oil. It was inevitable that the balancing out of prices in general would take place by increases of various amounts rather than by a mixture of increases and decreases, and certainly not by a mixture of decreases of various amounts. Far too many markets are biased towards rising prices for other outcomes to be possible. The monetary authorities have had no option but to supply the funds to support the inflation.

Another aspect of the connection between energy and inflation has been the fact that much of the payment for the oil imports has not come from current production of goods but from paper transactions. The importers simply have not had the resources for immediate settlement and have had to use IOUs. The creation of so much monetary paper has been a source of inflation not only for oil but for commodities of all kinds and throughout the trading world. So the inflation for two rather different reasons has been accompanied by a great deal of monetary expansion, but it is the realities of oil that have created *both* the monetary expansion and the inflation. We have not been the victims of some spontaneous madness by the central bankers. They, poor souls, have lost their security blankets of fixed exchange rates and gold or U.S. dollar standards.

This may sound theoretical. Perhaps, but it points to a *critical* issue of policy. One of the more sensational conversions since Saul went to Damascus has been the acceptance by the Bank of Canada of the new Monetarism – a creed that has been spreading amongst the government bureaucracies here and in other countries. As Monetarism comes in, Keynesian economics leave. We are dealing with code words. The world is unjust: the cure is to let it cure itself (Monetarism) or to attempt change (Keynesian economics). The theoretical theme of Monetarism is that money counts so much that we should do nothing with it, and of course should do nothing with any other instrument of economic policy. Let the system look after itself! But here is the significance of deciding whether the energy crisis had generated the inflation or whether the cause has been irresponsible policy, monetary policy or any other policy. In the given situation, with the success of the OPEC cartel a fact, I do not see how substantial inflation could have been avoided or can be brought to an end now. To accept the monetarist arguments would be to leave the real world for a phantasy, and would endorse the most reactionary of economic policies, *namely to abandon policy*.

The basic explanation of our economic situation is a classical Keynesian explanation, a great shock to the system which much produced disturbances that must last over a good many years. This time round the shock had a special form that not only produced recession and direct waste as most of these shocks do (the exceptions, unfortunately seem to be chiefly the shocks that come with wars), but was a guarantee of inflation. There is no startling paradox to explain: *this* amount of unemployment and *this* amount of inflation have been a predictable result of *this* particular shock. "Stagflation" is a surprise only to those journalists for whom the sun rising is a surprise. Where there is a surprise is the discovery that the classical Keynesian remedy *has* been discarded, that government today is little better prepared to prescribe and cure than was government of the Great Depression.

WHY HAS THE ECONOMY BEEN LEFT TO CURE ITSELF?

This indeed is something to frighten the democratic left. We have been taken back forty years and more not only in policy of a real kind but in the philosophy of economic policy. Perhaps there never was much policy of a real kind – I want to develop that idea a little later on. The retreat to primitive *laissez-faire*, though, to the comforts of benign neglect, thus an explicit policy has not been invoked till now by any government since the war. Even the most foolish editorialist can pose as a hard-headed realist by reciting the ancient formulae, that the best government is the least government, that at the most public policy can only mitigate calamities a little, that there is no policy like endless patience, and that nothing is the realistic route to something.

Let me refresh memories, if I may. At the end of the second world war the Minister of Reconstruction published (in April 1945) the famous assurance that the "central task of reconstruction" was "to maintain a high and stable level of employment and income," a task the "Government (adopted) as a primary object of policy." Government, the assurance said, was not thereby selecting a "lower target than full employment." Would that if we are in the constitution-writing game that that assurance had been made a constitutional guarantee: what an assurance that might have been!

You ask about this full employment that government had promised and how it was to be implemented? For answers we can still do worse than look again at Keynes (which of course is what the Minister of Reconstruction and his advisors had done in 1945). We have full employment when people can readily find jobs in occupations appropriate to their skills and in places within a reasonable distance from their home. This does not mean (as the bright young reactionaries would suggest) that the unemployed cease to be jobless if they are women or less than twenty or belong to a household where someone else has a job. The central idea in Keynes is that when the system is subjected to certain large shocks unemployment develops which (unknown to *laissez-faire*) has no self-curing properties, or none that would operate within socially acceptable intervals of time. *Correction must come from government.*

This is where confusion appears. Many were ready to accept the Keynesian diagnosis and the prescription, *supposing only* that the prescription could be reduced to token intervention, the use of some budgetary totals, say, and perhaps a small dose of monetary policy. The fact is that Keynes saw intervention on a large and detailed scale as being necessary. The system could not be repaired on the cheap. On page 380 of the principal edition of the "General Theory" he writes to those who would like to have it both ways:

Whilst, therefore, the enlargements of the functions of government ... would seem to a nineteenth century publicist or to a contemporary American financier to be a terrific encroachment on individualism, I defend it, on the contrary, both as the only practicable means of avoiding the destruction of existing economic forms in their entirety and as the condition of the successful functioning of individual initiative.

And how extensive are the enlargements of the functions of government? Since Keynes had little faith in either rhetoric or cure-alls like monetary policy it should not be astonishing to find him saying (p. 378):

I conceive, therefore, that a somewhat comprehensive socialization of investment will prove the only means of securing an approximation to full employment; though this need not exclude all manners of compromises and of devices by which public authority will co-operate with private initiative. But beyond this [!!!] no obvious case is made out for a system of State Socialism which would embrace most of the economic life of the community.

The whole of the final chapter of the "General Theory" is worth reading by anyone who wonders why madness can displace commonsense, for nothing in the Keynesian analysis is less attended to than the scope and detail of the public policy the thought necessary to correct situations like the one we are now enduring. Keynes is perhaps guilty of writing softly about hard facts, writing to widen support for his views but at the expense of these views being misunderstood and diluted. To deal with unemployment requires activist government, activist in a degree we have never experienced in peacetime. There is no aspirin cure, *there is no aspirin cure*.

This is the reason why the economy has been left to "cure" itself. It has become clear to our governments that to intervene substantially in the economy means being activist far outside the range of their view of political realities. In the years just after the war, when memories of the Great Depression were fresh, any such abdication would have been impossible. But governments were lucky. Then there was no recession to fight. By now, though, governments have found the political dangers have faded, partly because memories have dimmed but chiefly because unemployment has discriminated between those who have little political power and those who count politically with our governments, at least as our governments perceive power.

There is a critical implication that should be made explicit. If there is no apparatus now in place for managing the economy, it is also true that there can have been *no* apparatus in place since the war. There have, however, been extended periods in which the economy has functioned well, so that observers have been tempted to speak of a Keynesian revolution checked only briefly in the early sixties until the counter-revolution of this decade. I think the inconsistency is resolved when we remember that accidental pressures can assist as well as damage the system. The Canadian version of the welfare state had its beginnings at the end of the war, and was still being extended during the sixties. We came out of the war with an enormous backlog of unsatisfied demand for goods. We lived in a world where our neighbour has engaged in two substantial "second-order" wars. There has been an expansionist economic policy during many of the years before the seventies, but it has been accidental rather than Keynesian. We note the same bitter ironies that Keynes pointed to so frequently, that Keynesian policies appear not from deliberate intention but as side effects of such lunacies as second-order wars or the building of pyramids. One wonders if any monetarist would dispute that Canada would return to full employment within months if only we could find a safe little war to wage.

AND SO THE ATTACK ON THE DEMOCRATIC LEFT

The attack on the democratic left has many exemplifications and each has its own rather different causes, though I think there are causes of a general kind of primary importance. At the end of the war we had learnt two things.

The first was that in the right circumstances the democratic state was an enormously effective instrument of a democratic people. We had seen the magnificant things this democratic, collective instrument could perform. The second was that the horrors of the pre-war years were something a democratic society need not endure nor could not endure. Out of these lessons we created the Canadian version of the welfare state. The government of the day was not innovative, but copied others. It acted to forestall still greater advances on the left. Still, a revolution of sorts was begun.

But these great improvements in time produced certain reactions. Many of the *have-not* families became *have* families, or at least comfortable families whose members began to forget the conditions from which all families were to escape. The welfare state, as it turned out, reduced poverty but by no means eliminated it, just as the welfare state reduced and delayed unemployment without preventing the revival of the disease. Moreover, neither its virtues nor its defects were evenly spread, so that the new *have* families could settle down without much worry about the unsolved problems touching those not so lucky. Unemployment statistics that would have brought down any government in weeks in 1950 are often not even headline news today. Some who have forgotten their past, one fears, do not want to see the boat rocked by further social rescues.

There was then the reaction against the bureaucratic follies that the welfare state had brought in company with its reforms. The revolution of the welfare state, like many another revolution, had been only half-finished. It has become easy to look at public medical care or unemployment insurance and to deplore, with justification, waste and nonsense and abuse. That we are vastly better for these programmes is true and should never be forgotten; but the reactionaries cannot simply be ignored when they claim the programmes have great defects. Great social changes were constructed in the rough for their main purposes, but then were left to meander on without further reorganization or improvement. To take on the medical profession, for example, would have required a most vigorous, long-continued, and politically costly use of the state. It has been far easier to let matters slide, allowing this splendid achievement in medical care to be diminished in the public mind by the vision of an entrenched profession operating as inefficiently as it ever did.

In much the same way it seems to me that the transformation of the true and radical cure for unemployment, the provision of jobs, into the analgesic of unemployment insurance, that this transformation has brought the commitment of 1945 into disrepute. Of course there should be generous insurance where some truly uncontrollable event makes the provision of work impossible, but the substitution of insurance for jobs as a general rule has made a mockery of the promise. And so on, and so on: one could say more or less the same thing about our educational programmes and other social ventures, with an ever repeated theme. To have completed the reforms would have required an apparatus to manage the economy, but there is no apparatus nor is any planned. And so the value of the reforms fade, and the reactionaries look hopefully again for the brave world of privilege.

The attack upon the democratic left can be observed in most of our institutions. Since I see few editorials except the sanctimonious columns from the Montreal *Star*, I can only guess whether editorials across Canada have equally recaptured the moralizing detestation of the left the press of pre-war days everywhere showed. For the *Star* there has never been such a thing as a good strike. The people of Canada, so the *Star* echoes our fool of a Minister of Employment, have become soft and must learn not to be greedy. Government can do little. Suffering (especially suffering accepted by others than the patrons of the *Star*) is the tested panacea for economic distress. For some years, remember, it would have been out of fashion for even such a newspaper as the *Star* openly to declare such rubbish.

Times have become difficult for the political allies of the labour movement. I suppose in some degree the governments of British Columbia and Manitoba contributed to their own downfall. The gap between convention rhetoric and legislative performance was often too wide to prevent even the faithful from gasping. Perhaps if one had one free wish about the style of political events in Canada it would not be that the Ottawa Cabinet would be caught snuffing cocaine – Francis Fox would explain it as a cold cure anyway – but that our social democrats would be less like tigers out of office and less like lambs in office: if they want to please everybody they might as well do it in opposition, and not waste their occasional years in government waiting for a time to govern. But that is ungrateful. The governments of the left have done a far better job than the rest, and have been in as difficult a position as anyone else from the left while doing that job. The labour movement has had its troubles too. And silence may be kind comment on academics!

A notable event in the attack on the democratic left, of course, was the already mentioned institution of the Anti-Inflation Board and its associated rules. It was notable in several ways. In the first place the great majority of professional economists not in government service, regardless of political affiliation, damned the programme from its birth. It has been a kind of "redneck," anti-scientific exercise in which even its sponsors probably have had little belief. They have had little belief in it, that is to suggest, in relation to its ostensible purposes. As is worth repetition the programme could be used to subvert the labour movement by making the movement purposeless – a goal that reactionary government would always be happy to pursue.

In the second place the event has been notable for its value in causing confusion within the democratic left. Provincial governments that should have known better joined the Children's Crusade. The labour movement has no doubt found that many within its own membership have accepted the notion that something named an Anti-Inflation Board must actually reduce inflation. The success with words may by now be troublesome to the sponsors themselves, who found they could not get rid of their creation when inflation was artificially low and now are faced with the need to tell the world that nine and a half per cent inflation is a triumph.

A third element of being "notable" is the freedom given government propagandists to spread the word that all social progress should be halted till the anti-inflation programme has done its work – which at the moment looks like forever – and to attack government itself, not of course as embodied in the present regime but as an agency that is supposed to act and to intervene and to do things. The Anti-Inflation Board has nurtured short-sighted selfishness amongst some of the new "have families," who have been taught that the minor inconvenience of the inflation to the many who are prosperous is good reason for leaving the rest to bear all serious burdens. It is short-sighted indeed, for the newly prosperous are not going to be saved from the minor inconveniences, but are endangering their own recent gains by supporting the crusade.

More important than anything else, though, in this attack upon the democratic left is the attack upon government itself, upon the activist state, upon social and economic policy. It is an attack upon *the* instrument of all progress for the democratic left, for without that instrument attempts at political and social progress consist of words and posturing. Even within industry attempted progress lacks the needed institutional base when government support is absent. Everywhere one turns, to the press, to radio and television, to the political parties and even in some measure to the political parties within the left, everywhere it has become routine to denounce some enemy of all right-thinking people called "Big Government."

But *this is madness* for a civilized society in the twentieth century! A tremendous proportion of the things that allow the society to be civilized for its members as a whole can exist only because of the growth of the public sector. Government in a democratic society is not our enemy, but our indispensable servant. For the ordinary person it is the only agent he or she can look to as a means to save the society from being the private club of the rich and the powerful.

Given this view of government, the democratic left would make a major mistake to appear to want bureaucracy for the sake of bureaucracy, or to appear reluctant to erase waste in government and in government programmes with the same zeal it would erase waste in the private sector. The democratic left should make clear that it is well aware of waste in the public sector and of the half-finished nature of many public programmes. In not joining the hysterical chorus denouncing "Big Government" it is looking for *strong government*, government probably much stronger than any peacetime government we have ever had – in the basic sense of government actually able to govern. Equally, it has no interest in large government *per se*, and is as opposed as anyone to the building of offices without function or the hiring of staff to increase private armies within the bureaucracies. Size of government is never the object. Capacity to govern always is.

TWO ILLUSTRATIONS

This account of attacks upon the democratic left is far from complete. Let me close it for now, though, by remarking on two less generalized illustrations. One comes from considering the affairs of the railway unions. A few years ago, the railway unions of Canada went through the most complex set of negotiations, conciliations, work stoppages and arbitrations for twenty years in order to extract from government a formula by which a reasonable basis for industrial peace on the railways could be obtained.

The outcome was the Hall report and the Hall settlement, an outcome as remarkable for the process it instituted as for the numbers it produced. The process supported collective bargaining on the one hand, and indicated agreed bounds in terms of which new agreements could be worked out as the years passed. The unions thought it a victory for themselves and for the ordinary citizens of this country. Much might have been modelled upon the result. In the cynical and destructive action by which the Anti-Inflation Board displaced the Hall report the work of years was demolished. What the politicians gained in the short run they squandered in the long: a great advance in labour relations was nullified. Just how much will be left of the Hall report when the new railway contract comes into force one can only guess; but if it is degutted, the lesson is not likely to be forgotten in organized labour nor forgiven by the railway workers themselves.

The other closing illustration of the attack on the left comes from the flurry of activity across the country about pensions. In an earlier day, when the welfare state was being built, such activity could have signified only one thing. The community would have perceived that there is still only the beginnings of a logic and of a programme to make the years of retirement as comfortable and exciting as nature will allow. Pensions from the private sector were and are in considerable degree a swindle. Law nominally made on behalf of the pensioner in fact expropriates for the business sector a good fraction of what the pensioner has saved. Pensions in the public sector have changed the *gross* poverty of retirement into *mere* poverty, not an achievement to be sneered at but not something that has permitted the typical older Canadian to remain an equal member of the Canadian family. To equate public pensions with savings guarantees a ghetto.

Today, however, the political attack is not upon those who are obstructing further reform. It is an attack upon the democratic left for the partial reforms already in place. The agents of the insurance companies are everywhere preaching about the impossible burden that decent pensions place upon the Canadian economy. Further advances in the public sector produce warnings that would be extravagant if the Great Lakes dried up, and advice is freely given to return to the warm bosom of the fully funded private plan administered by these warm mothers called insurance companies. We are not able, these companies say, assisted by silly little men who provide purchased research on their behalf, to provide the protection for the retired that primitive societies, with a fraction of our resources, provide as a matter of course. To treat the retired (that is, all of us who live out our years when the years have passed) as belonging to the family still? Impossible: it would decrease savings. One wonders what these people think the purpose of society is, more or less as one stands in awe of those corporate lawyers in our governments who plead for shared restraint with people making a few thousand a year.

THE RESPONSE OF THE DEMOCRATIC LEFT

Some victories are being turned into defeats, so it is no time for those of the democratic left to wring hands and moan about wickedness. It is a time, rather, to plan, to examine mistakes, to develop positions for the long run without being diverted by every chance of five minutes of popularity or each opportunity for clever political accomodation. You might want to read (or read again) three papers from the democratic left that seem to me to have diagnosed things correctly, and to have stressed the need for a strategy set out for years and not months. The left will not defeat the attacks upon it tomorrow or the next day, nor will it defeat those attacks until it has examined in some depth what its own objectives now are.

You might want to read, then, the submission to government by the Canadian Railway Labour Association. The Association cuts through the net of irrelevancies used to hide responsibility for unemployment and declares without any "ifs" and "buts" that without full employment all other goals of a sane policy are unattainable, that the failure to pursue and attain full employment is the fault of no one but the Ottawa government, and that the route to full employment requires the Ottawa government to act on many fronts with a vigour and on a scale not known to peace time policy. The submission is tough and single-minded, a good sign that the democratic left has not lost its will to fight.

The second document is the famous "Labour's Manifesto for Canada," the work of the Canadian Labour Congress. As one who was not very happy about the (small) proportion of the "Manifesto" given to "tri-partism," I should stress, now that tri-partism seems to have left centre stage, how sophisticated and valuable the bulk of the "Manifesto" is. Its diagnosis of what is wrong with the system today is accurate and detailed. It then goes beyond diagnosis to the issues of prescription and remedy and develops two theses, first, that labour itself must improve its own technical apparatus for organizing economic and social policy, and second, that government similarly must create a machinery for the planning of an effective public sector. This is a powerful and correct view, I believe, and remains so even if one stops short of imagining that labour should submerge its work in these reforms within tri-partism. As someone who rejoiced to see labour get out of the Economic Council, and hopes it stays out, I have no wish to see labour surrender its identity to bastardized versions of the Council. Labour has plenty to do within its traditional organizational forms: to plan, to organize, to bargain, to vote, this can still occupy the full energies of the movement.

A third document that shows the democratic left is alive and still capable of creative thought is the "National Priorities" handbook the New Democrats were able to put together at their last convention. The style of these documents is always a bit on the heavy side, but if the reader will be patient with "National Priorities" he will find about as specific and practical a guide to how government should be organized and what it should do as exists in this country. There is here a perfectly good answer – not the only version that could be imagined, but one the left can offer with pride – to the perennial questions from the right: "Just what would you do that is different? and that is possible?"

Lest someone charge that this comment is merely propaganda from the left, let me observe I am far from assured that *any* of our politicians once in office would touch something like "National Priorities" with that invaluable ten-foot pole. Too often New Democrats have been heard who make Conservatives sound good: if we are to do without policy we might as well have those in charge who dislike policy. Too often New Democrats seem to leave serious issues to documents, unassisted by the spoken word: investment in fundamentals is too time consuming. The object of the democratic left, though surely regards the election of New Democrats merely as a means, with the policies of the New Democrats being the end. Without consistent, long-run investment in fundamentals of policy, the politicians themselves are unconvincing, one being much like another whether New Democrat, Liberal or Social Crediter.

In this assessment of the strengths and weaknesses of the Canadian economy I have made no effort to do much of a statistical kind, to review industries, to estimate export prospects, and the like, to write one of those annual reviews that the governmental agencies grind out for us in marvellously forgettable prose. This is partly laziness. To do the job properly would take a tremendous amount of time. The determining reasons, though, for the approach these notes has taken is of a quite different kind. I believe that there is a focus to the issues that have been discussed, and that in studying this focus we are studying most of what really matters about the strengths and weaknesses of the Canadian economy.

The focus is this: our governments are not technically equipped to govern, to intervene to correct things that go wrong in the economy. The most important problem for the democratic left is to work out just how interventionist policy would be designed and implemented. It is much the same business as has been summed up in phrases like "democratic planning" or the "planned economy." Our ideas in these areas have been terribly naive. We have correctly seen that without planning there cannot be policy, and that without policy economies necessarily are left to cure themselves and economic justice cannot be more than a sentimental slogan. We have not seen, however, that the apparatus and methods of planning simply are not part of our system, already in place for the democratic left to use. We have not bothered to investigate the logic of interventionist government, the logic of the state. States are sovereign, so the mythology goes, and because they are sovereign they can do anything that knowledge would say is technically possible. But the Canadian state, whether in its federal or provincial components, is capable of only a minor fraction of what present knowledge pretends to allow. Much of our discussion of policy, I think, ignores this vitally important limitation.

THE NEED TO KNOW

Accordingly if the democratic left is to defend itself, it must work hard to correct this sin of omission. It is of course necessary to defend the classical elements in its programme. The democratic left must resist attacks on the value of the state and upon strong democratic government. It must demand full employment. It must reject the apologists of the new *laissez-faire*, however much time they have spent at U.S. graduate schools absorbing the notion that their professions are without function or point. It must insist on reclaiming the fourteen or fifteen years of retirement as part of the normal life to which we are all entitled. It must not back off from or be apologetic about any of these necessities of civilized society. Yet it must recognize that it has not thought through the mechanics of government, nor worked out how even sympathetic governments can carry out its programmes. How much fails if the *apparatus* of the democratic state is weak!

The sin of omission is understandable. We have seen a public sector that occupied only a few percentage points of the economy change into one occupying nearly half of the economy, but the change has been *gradual*. We have seen a geographically scattered society concentrate itself more and more in urban conglomerates, but the change has been *gradual*. We have seen business take on forms that are linked across products, industries and even countries, but the change has been *gradual*. So it is not that astonishing that we have left ourselves with the administrative, managerial governments appropriate to societies in which governments had little to do; we have entered a world where a pre-condition of effective government, democratic and civilized, is the creation of a strong policy making and policy implementing apparatus. If you wonder, by the way, at the use and re-use of the adjective "democratic," it reflects the conviction that if strong and civilized government are to be created I cannot imagine them – in advanced societies – as being anything *but* democratic. In societies emerging from tyranny, totalitarian regimes may for a time be the best that is possible, but without the usual democratic liberties what can government serve but those who govern? and what could be a weaker instrument of the civilized society than dictatorship however described?

To create the machinery of effective government is naturally in part a political problem, but in its technical aspects a task to be approached as a piece of social engineering. Under our parliamentary forms Cabinets organize policy, if in theory only. They must in these years of large public sectors organize policy in fact, becoming for most of their working life policy cabinets. But if they are policy cabinets they must have supporting policy bureaucracies. Policy cabinets and their supporting policy bureaucracies must then have the assistance of legislation about procedures to make their goals attainable. And with all of this the most difficult part of the social engineering remains, for policy cabinet and policy bureaucracy must have as motive a desire to govern in the interests of a civilized community. Because this is already a long paper, I shall leave this theme, observing only that the temptation is great for the best of politicians to wish to be activist never now but after the next election.

In Canada we encounter a further great hindrance to effective government, and in an extreme form. The issue of centralization versus decentralization is everywhere debated, sometimes related to a contest between Ottawa and the provinces, sometimes to paternalism as against self-reliance and sometimes to public as against private choice. I think there are traps for the democratic left in allowing these many ideas to be compressed into a single choice. We need stronger governments than we have at *all levels*. We have no interest in the distribution of duties amongst governments except as it assists the overall outcome of policy. To go to the barricades for federal or provincial rights would be about as sensible as crying "the Winnipeg Blue Bombers or death!" Surely the democratic left is *centralist* in wanting Ottawa to have ample authority to control the economy in the large, both as to output and regional equality in the distribution of output. And just as surely, I think, it is decentralist in wishing to see choices within the totals made at provincial, regional and municipal levels. This is the old and valuable theme of participatory democracy. Efficiency and equity both gain from having choices made by those whom the choices affect. There is in any case more than enough for governments to do at every level: so we are centralist and decentralist both, according to the tasks considered.

For the democratic left to defend itself, in brief, it must be realistic and pragmatic, not Utopian and sentimental. But the democratic left should notice that much presented as realistic is in fact Utopian. To deal in the politics of the short run, as though that could change events, instead of investing in basic ideas for the long run, *that* is not pragmatic but Utopian. To expect the democratic state to govern simply because it has been given a government, *that* too is Utopian. To build an extra 50,000 or even 100,000 units of public housing a year in this country would be no great technical challenge. Sensibly located and supplied with complementary facilities their being built would benefit the overwhelming proportion of our population. The building would be no financial challenge and might not be even much of a political challenge. It certainly would be no challenge to the needs and wishes of the democratic left. Yet I suggest it would be a greater challenge to our apparatus of government than to replace the monstrosity called the Bank of Canada Edifice with the Great Pyramid of Cheops.

By all means let us vote as many of the rascals out as we can. Let the labour movement make no peace with anti-inflation boards or their successors. Let the democratic left continue loyal to its goals. But let us nonetheless ask ourselves the urgent question: *how then do we enable our state to govern*?

CHAPTER EIGHT

On Social Policies in the Canadian Economy, 1986[1]

PRELIMINARIES

So that the message is not altogether hidden by the narrative, let me point to three ideas that the message will contain. First, in social policies our relative situations certainly do have, and probably should have, much more weight than our absolute situations. Second, the rationale of social policies is how best to respond to inescapable uncertainty. Third, social well being – the wealth of nations, the wealth of Canada – must be defined by moralists for the economist, not by economists for the moralist.

With a topic like "social policies, 1986," I think the argument has to be *self-contained* to be testable, and has to be *testable* to be worth a reader's attention. The discussion of "surplus" that immediately follows is directed to the *units* in which economic policy has been described for three hundred years. "Surplus" is then related to the kind of policy that has been central to Canadian debates in 1986 and for a long interval before, the policy that would manipulate "surplus" by subjecting it only to private property and private markets. All of this amounts to stage-setting, how the results of policy are described, what the focus has been of policy as such.

From this formal beginning I have gone on to actual events, and have chosen themes by no subtler rule than what seemed to me important. This has produced mixtures of description and (intended) explanation, of policies committed *and* omitted, of economics normative as well as positive.

There is a long account of "full employment," a goal that has always been feasible but that has been abandoned politically. With full employment, so the argument runs, interventionist *political economy* is possible; without

An edited version of this paper appears as: Jack Weldon, "Public Policy and Full Employment in Canada since 1945," in Crawford Pratt and Roger Hutchinson, eds., *Christian Faith and Economic Justice: Toward a Canadian Perspective* (Burlington, Ont.: Trinity Press, 1988), 55–75.

full employment it is not. In economic affairs this Canadian democracy has lost confidence in its authority, in its capabilities. There is then a great deal of discussion about *process*. What I have in mind is the way in which governments (and certainly democratic governments) seek to influence the future. Everyone knows that the governments of 1986 cannot commit the governments of 1996. There is neither the needed prevision nor the needed power. Governments instead legislate about *how* things are now calculated, in the hope of instituting rules that their successors will replicate. Here has been the core of interventionist policy in the Canadian system, and here is the domain in which moralists and the population at large instruct economists about the future.

One omission is deliberate. In this essay the outside world is a given. Issues in relation to the great powers, issues in relation to the Third World, these are so vast that one leaves them entirely to other studies and better informed writers. I think that reflection on *domestic* policy (facts and logic both) is a precondition for serious work about the outside world. Such "serious work," though, would need its own framework.

ON SURPLUS: AMOUNT, RATE OF GROWTH, DISTRIBUTION

For the few hundred years in which political economy has had the form (if not the achievement) of other branches of science, its focus has been upon *economic surplus*. A community organizes its affairs so that after a year, say, it has managed by production and exchange to make good all depreciation of the goods with which it began the year, but then has also managed to make available for accumulation or immediate use a *surplus* additional to its original holdings. The notion appears in many variations, in such familiar conceptions, for example, as net national product, national income, Marx's surplus value, Marshall's consumers' surplus, and the net revenues of Ricardo and Smith. I add a caution about measurement. Surplus is always measured completely and finally at a point of time, usually the here-and-now. Since it is fed by future prospects as well as "present" events its magnitude will be greatly affected by how uncertain the future appears.

I have no intention here of taking up other conceptual points or of reviewing particular forms of the idea (although a vast amount of debate has turned upon nuances of considerable importance). What is sufficient and prudent here is to assert that social policy is almost always related to the *amount* of surplus this or some other defined community produces, to the *rate of growth* of surplus, and to the *distribution* of surplus amongst the members of the community. Judgement about the worth of social policy then turns first upon how policy affects "amount," "rate of growth," and "distribution" quantitatively, and next upon whether the quantitative results are desirable. Take for example the lively debate about free trade with the

United States. Advocates of the policy claim a treaty would somewhat increase surplus, would notably increase the rate of growth of surplus, and would supply larger amounts of surplus to many persons and subtract surplus from only a few; and they then go on from these "quantities" to the assertion that the threefold effect is desirable. I believe their "facts" are as mistaken as their judgement is naive, but agree that *their* "facts" and judgement is where debate is properly joined.[2]

ON THE RELATION BETWEEN SURPLUS AND "NATURAL LIBERTY"

Within the western group of industrialized nations there is, of course, *one* instrument of social policy against which the merits of all other instruments are regularly measured, specifically, the *authority* given to private enterprise and the marketplaces of private enterprise for determining "amount," "rate of growth," and "distribution". From the *laissez-faire* of the Physiocrats and the *regime of natural liberty* of Adam Smith to the confessions of faith by academic and political leaders in 1986, a doctrine has been proclaimed that proposes to let social policy be the outcome of the decisions businessmen will take in a world of free markets. "Every man, so long as he does not violate the laws of justice, is left perfectly free to pursue his own interest in his own way, and to bring both his industry and his capital into competition with those of any other man, or order of men." So spoke Smith about a complex philosophical position[3] and so speak those to-day whose simple slogan is "free enterprise". If the doctrine has never been practiced as vigorously as it has been preached, and if it has at times fallen into disrepute, it all the same has been a doctrine *much* practiced, and a doctrine most resilient as to reputation.

Adult discussion of social policy would be impossible were so pervasive a doctrine about property and markets to be treated as something more than an instrument, as an end in itself or as a moral (or immoral) imperative. It is perfectly true that propagandists for "free enterprise" manage to add it to freedom of speech and freedom of religion in their own charters of rights, and it is also true that those appalled by the translation of selfishness into social virtue plead and demand that selfishness be renounced. No doubt the first attitude is ridiculous while the other is sublime, but in relation to a mere instrument of policy neither attitude seems relevant.[4] I shall be arguing that in Canada the democratic State has been correctly chosen as the only instrument of policy that is both means and end. Its authority in economic affairs has often been challenged and so has its competence, especially so in the past decade; but in assessing the challenge I have no intention of treating "free enterprise" either as an alternative government or a system of morals.

An agreed point of departure perhaps would be to notice the virtues that serious people have attributed to Smith's "natural liberty." Three claims come particularly to mind. That program to support the "Wealth of Nations" might in the first place achieve an efficient allocation of resources, and so assist a large surplus. In the marketplace agents of production will be moved from where they produce little to where they produce much. Next, the program might provide an outlet for entrepreneurial skill, an outlet for imagination and invention, and so again assist a large surplus. Creativity is rewarded, old methods are replaced by new. Thirdly, the program might allocate the making of economic decisions to units small enough to make decisions well, and by this decentralization also assist a large surplus.

All of this deals directly *only* with the amount of surplus. What would the program have to do with rate of growth and with distribution? Advocates sometimes engage in double counting, arguing that if there is a large surplus there will be a large amount of saving and a large amount of investment. Growth itself might then be large and, as the free gift of "natural liberty," would surely be welcomed. As to distribution, however, even double counting would lead nowhere. "Natural liberty" must be assisted by property rights, by notions of ownership that have the same beginning as history. In businesses and markets original endowments will strongly mark the sharing of surplus; the talented will do well and the rich will do still better. Advocates in this instance need to argue that only property rights that endure can support "natural liberty," and that only "natural liberty" supplies surplus in amounts worth having; and to escape a little from "distribution" that would then at best be accidental rather than just, its advocates can argue that by the time surplus has become large most wealth must have been newly created, so that surplus can be said to arise not from ancient inheritance but from recent earnings and recent endeavour.

While in principle one could discuss Canadian social policy without this background, that might suggest all questions are open and all answers have new beginnings. My preference, however, is to look at social policy at the margin of what now exists. In relation to that resilient doctrine of natural liberty just described, it is common knowledge that for more than a decade there has been a considerable ideological shift in Canada and the United States that would *actually* subordinate all social policy to the marketplace; and while that shift in ideology has been very much larger than its realized effects upon social policy have been, the change of climate has already significantly affected real events and could greatly affect them should that climate persist two or three years longer. I shall discuss social policy, then, at "the margin of what now exists" not to escape serious issues but in the belief that today especially it is at "the margin" that those serious issues are to be found.

There is one more preliminary. I shall say little more in this exercise about the "virtues" attributable to the marketplace. This is not intended to imply by silence that those "virtues" have little substance. Classical writings from Adam Smith to Karl Marx, from Joseph Schumpeter to Milton Friedman, give testimony about vigour, efficiency, decentralization that no student of social policy could reasonably ignore. Here I stipulate (but do not review) the importance of that literature, just as I stipulate (but do not review) the worth of the critical literature on social policies which emerge directly from the democratic state.

What I do not merely stipulate is my concern with the new, vulgar, uninformed orthodoxy that has been shaping ideology at the "margin," and that is as intolerant and subversive of reasoned argument as any of the parent orthodoxies that have plagued the economist's profession. In departments of economics within Canada and the United States the dogmas of "free enterprise" have in general become as binding on the upwardly mobile as cult economics in the Eastern bloc. Political fashion has been the *cause*, the scope of economics and the way economic problems are formulated, these have been the *effects*. For the time being the mainstream of economics has been displaced by a kind of dead sea.[5]

Whether to begin with general principles and then go on to illustrations or to use illustrations to develop principles is, I suppose, a matter of taste. With *social* policy the argument perhaps goes better by leaving abstraction to the end.

FULL EMPLOYMENT OF LABOUR

For classical economists full employment had very little to do with labour but was associated instead with the utilization of fixed capital. Even at that, full employment was not measured against *all* fixed capital but only fixed capital in the market sector of economies where markets were not exclusive and might not even be dominant. Since the Great Depression, however, full employment in Canada and in other "western"[6] industrialized states has been a bench-mark based on statistics about *paid workers* and those seeking paid work, about the employed who wish paid work and have it and the unemployed who do not.[7] Towards the end of World War II, policies of full employment of labour were firmly declared both here and abroad, partly because of recollection of the 1930s, partly because the war had created strong, interventionist governments, and partly because "Keynesian" ideas had been coupled to political programs.

It seemed enough in the next decade to let "full employment" be a shorthand for all cures to which the Depression had pointed, to define the remedy by its disease. So casual a definition may have been appropriate to

1945, but it later was to leave policies of "full employment" without a reference by which to gauge success or failure. A political economist in 1986 does much better to begin with the "involuntary unemployment" of [Keynes's] *General Theory* and with that concept well established, should go on to argue that a commitment to full employment must mean that Canadians should be able to find jobs reasonably suited to their skills, jobs at going wage rates, somewhere near their homes, available without extended delays. The commitment would be so near absolute that occasions when it could not be respected would be extremely rare and would require compensation; and the commitment would accordingly be supported by extended, local, "microeconomic" intervention. Such a commitment was to go (and would still go!) far beyond anything to be hoped from the marketplace, and, of course, far, far beyond the dismal record of recent experience. Still, while policy in relation to full employment was given much of this flavour when it was first promised, it was policy emerging from a catastrophe that at any cost was not to be repeated and policy then presented for a future vaguely described, an autonomous future.

Inevitably there were afterthoughts. What precisely *were* those burdens and injustices that unemployment had placed upon Canadian society? There *was* waste, persons unemployed, machines unemployed, surplus much reduced from what it might have been. There *was* injustice, for unemployment had not been a shared feature of everyone's life, but afflicted persons, families, and regions in patterns that were both dispersed and cruel. There was a weakening of social bonds: part of the community had seen itself as giving charity and part, as receiving charity; progress in women's rights had been brought to a halt; youth had been rescued by war from a dependent existence with dismal prospects. Perhaps all of this was given weight. Was it necessary nonetheless to place the marketplace in trusteeship, to demand unqualified "full employment" as an imperative for policy *and* reform? And though the answer was at first emphatically "yes," as the years passed there was a murmured "no" here and there, and by now the unabashed "no" that is said to come automatically from any realist. No matter that intervention had been successful. By the new axioms it was Utopian.

Any interventionist commitment from Ottawa made at the end of the war became politically more demanding as authority to govern drained from the public sector. Few economists noticed at the time how unusual the state of things was in the first postwar decade. A great war following upon a great depression had given Ottawa authority, purpose, and competence, gifts that would persist for a time but not gifts that were natural features of this federal society. Planning at a microeconomic level gave way to crude manipulation of fiscal and monetary aggregates, so causing Canadian policy to mimic the only Keynesian model that could be accommodated in the United States. By the end of the 1950s, a crucial divide had been passed. Policy with respect to full employment had promised jobs. There was now substituted nothing stronger than the hope that the unemployed would be compensated for their jobless state rather than blamed: jobless they would remain. The commitment to erase unemployment in the large was explicitly abandoned and so was the even more ambitious commitment to erase unemployment arising from drastic industrial changes or from uneven regional prosperity.

In the years of achievement strong government had proved necessary for full employment and full employment had proved necessary for strong government. Later, failure to satisfy these reciprocal requirements was the first cause of retreat. The rationalization of retreat could hardly be expressed in such a confession of weakness and so paradoxes were invented about behaviour: commonsense was claimed to be in error, for the pursuit of full employment would against all expectation diminish rather than augment surplus. Direct public intervention would lead to inflation, would reduce exports, would encourage flights of monetary capital, would make markets inefficient, would crowd out private borrowers and entrust economic decisions to bureaucracy; and so direct intervention would put marginal resources to work at the cost of making *all* resources less productive.

It was in some such manner that governments politically incapable of intervention excused their change of front. The rationalization may be understandable but all the same has to be disputed: whatever its origin the weakness it hides has had calamitous effects. Unnatural unemployment has been tolerated as natural. Costs of the failure have been defined out of existence. Probably the greatest damage has resulted from gross miscalculation of how that wasted surplus should be measured which unemployment puts at risk. The effort to rationalize failure has altered the way the Canadian public counts the costs of unemployment, or more precisely, has half persuaded the Canadian public to deceive itself as to what the costs are.

One classical authority after another had long ago pointed out that economic welfare for a society was *not* the summation of welfare for its members, considered person by person as though in isolation. It was not the summation of absolute and independent totals of well-being, but was a total greatly affected by relativities amongst persons, by the pattern of distribution throughout the society. On the whole the significance of whatever riches constituted *surplus* turned at least as much upon how the riches were *shared* as upon the *total* of riches that might be shared. Now it is evident in everyday usage that social welfare is likely to be measured in this way whenever the calculation is reflexively made, whenever it immediately reflects commonsense. Editorialists have no difficulty at all, for example, in praising the prosperity of the 1950s and contrasting that prosperity with the unhappy record of the past ten years, and doing this against a statistical record that shows the conventional measures of surplus per head (real net national product per head, say) are far higher *now* than *then*, perhaps twice as high!

Our editorialists have judged the matter implicitly as William Petty did in 1662 (*Taxes and Contributions*) judged them explicitly. "Let the Tax be never so great, if it be proportionate unto all, then no man suffers the loss of any riches by it. For ... if the Estates of them all were either halved or doubled, would in both cases remain equally rich". John Rae in 1834 (his *New Principles*, perhaps written in Canada!) develops the theme that so much of surplus has little use except to confirm social status that one absolute level will serve "vanity" quite as well as another. J.M. Keynes in 1936 (*General Theory*) contends that the movement of wage rates up and down depends far more on relative than on absolute levels. Veblen, Galbraith, any number of others from within the profession have given similar testimony. Here is ample authority and authority, as far as I know, that may be ignored but is not disputed.

There is no need to concede that surplus from the crude measures of the marketplace has to be sacrificed if full employment is vigorously pursued. On the whole the evidence points strongly in the other direction, with rules of thumb often reported that would give an extra surplus of one to two percentage points for a one percentage point reduction in reported unemployment. Comforting as that evidence may seem it is a perilous support for interventionist policy. Its use accepts that should the computation be overturned the policy has lost its rationale.

Not so: probably intervention *would* reclaim the wasted "billions" so often reported as lost to unemployment, but even if it left crude surplus untouched, even if it cost something in crude surplus, it would add enormously to the well-being of Canadian society. Who can possibly much care whether the absolute surplus per head in 1986 is where it was in 1982 or where it may be in 1990? Who indeed but the professional statistician knows or will know?[8] But who of those employed in 1986 would regard unemployment with anything but fear? and who of those unemployed would see themselves as equal members of the community? Dependency and equal membership cannot live together.[9]

There are at least three further consequences. First, a commitment to full employment is a public decision to intervene strongly and systematically in the economy. Here is a political requirement that political economists cannot leave unreported. Second, such a commitment points to other gains and losses that are tied to the availability of jobs. There are any number of technical and industrial changes that threaten one group or another in a system that tolerates unemployment, but that if implemented would be very likely to increase conventional surplus. With the assurance of full employment, however, and supposing that the assurance is believed, the threats to particular groups are much diminished or disappear entirely. Full employment allows the community to make free use of invention and to prosper from new methods. Third, a commitment of this kind gets rid of the ghettoes that are created when unemployment is assuaged rather than erased. As D. Bellemare and L. Poulin-Simon have often emphasised,[10] from a technical point of view full employment is very much a public rather than a private good. By diminishing those who do not have jobs, unemployment diminishes those who do.

From all of this it follows, I think, that social policy of any vigour must be tied to an unqualified promise of full employment. Where the ghettoes of unemployment are tolerated, not only is welfare dissipated but extended ghettoes are created by almost any use of government one might name. Economic policy is deprived of a rational base, of a moral base. Whether a policy of full employment of itself is more important than other policies is semantical. It is a *prior* policy, it describes preconditions. Here to my mind is the first axiom for political economy in the Canadian federation.[11]

THE SOCIAL WAGE

A small Canadian family happens to earn from the marketplace, say, $20,000 a year, largely in wages but perhaps with some rents and some payments for "capital." Given the predominance of wages one might speak briefly of its private wage. But this will not be the share of surplus that this family receives, for there will be a great range of additions and subtractions to the $20,000 arising directly and indirectly from social programs (from taxation and its incidence, from family allowances, from provisions for pensions, for medical care, for education – the list is very long). One might speak of this socially modified total as the family's social wage.

Notice (it is often not noticed) that in the immensely complicated apparatus for producing surplus that surrounds us in the Canadian economy, we can be certain that the surplus *only* exists because of our collective activity that puts the apparatus to work. When the theorist is tempted to ask precisely what part of surplus the Prime Minister created or a shop steward at General Motors or a surgeon at the Montreal General, the *prudent* theorist soon puts the temptation aside. A question that might have had a clear answer on the island of Robinson Crusoe either has no answer at all within the society of which we are actually members, or a pseudo-answer that repeats the "Crusoe" answer in an extended form. The total of surplus is attributable to the total of persons, and cannot in any general way be further assigned.

If these assertions seem to challenge the *logic* of the elementary textbooks[12] they are assertions badly expressed. In the markets of an industrialized economy, shares of surplus will be distributed to persons and "classes" in some rough relationship to a theory based upon original endowments, upon competition, and upon a specific technology; and they will still be distributed so that this "textbook" theory is recognizable in the facts even as departures from "textbook" markets take analysis closer to reality.

It will be possible for an economist to declare from time to time that such and such a "share" might have been predicted by computing a marginal product for some *extra* person or thing added to everything else employed. Jones indeed may have a higher marginal product than Smith and perhaps will be paid proportionately more. Where *non sequiturs* appear, however, is in the notion that these pieces of arithmetic connect distribution to Crusoe-like contribution to surplus, and in the still more bizarre idea that the pieces of arithmetic show what has been earned, what people have done with their *own*, what distribution need be or should be. In no other context that I can think of has elementary arithmetic been invested with such social virtue.

Out of the marketplace come private wage rates (part of a pattern of privately determined distribution of surplus). Societies such as our own undoubtedly make great use of such rates as an initial reference for computing acceptable shares, and do so with widespread agreement that the reference is efficient, fair, and natural, not only for those who receive wages but for that considerable *majority* who do not. It is well understood, however, that the level of private wage rates greatly depends on the prior distribution of property, that wages earned on private account are further distributed by custom (outside the marketplace) to family members and others, and that an "initial reference" for shares in surplus has to be ratified by how successfully it is adapted to social needs. Within Canadian public policy, the centrepiece has for decades been how to transmute *private wage rates* into *social wage rates*.

Only in textbook models, of course, have there ever been societies presented in which private rates are *not* transmuted. As John Stuart Mill pointed out over a century ago, custom and convention, the existence of secondary economies, public transfers by state and church, these things together were always more influential on social rates than were all the direct effects of market wages. Would this have left much room for a further separation of private and social wage rates? In fact, since the end of World War II, we have experienced in many parts of the world the creation of the *welfare state*, a revolution perhaps uniquely successful, far-reaching, pacific, and durable.

As against the *unrealized* hope for *full employment*, here was the *realized* hope for *social wage rates* of which private rates would be no more than a component. In describing the scale of change as "a revolution" I have no worry about a charge of hyperbole. For those members of Canadian society (the vast majority) who periodically or continuously are separated from markets as their immediate source of income, the economy of 1936 can hardly be recognized in the economy of 1986; and for all members of the society the facts of the *social wage* have drastically altered perceptions of what is normal and just.

In principle the young without exception are provided with schools and education. In principle the elderly without exception are provided with public pensions. In principle the sick without exception are provided with hospital and medical care. In principle women without exception share equally with men in both private and social wages. In principle workers *almost* without exception are provided with laws that assure rights to organize and to bargain collectively. Here are particularly clear examples of both the dominance and novelty of social wage rates in 1986.

The theme can be taken a little further. Taxation has always been seen to create after-tax wages that are social rather than private, and so to require guidelines as to equal effects or fair effects. Nowadays deliberate redistribution, supposedly progressive, is an announced goal of almost every budget. One should emphasise, though, for the point is often confused, that while redistribution is *part* of the social wage, it is only part, and is *independent* in its qualities of other parts. And as to conditions in the working place, where the social wage was assisted in the first part of the century by limiting *abusive* exploitation (length of the working day, safety and health in the workplace, compensation for industrial accidents), more recently it has been assisted by superimposing benefits the market must supply (minimum wage rates, statutory holidays, vacations, all of which are in effect taxes to be paid in money or subsidized leisure).

In the repetitions above of the cautious "in principle" I intend to draw attention to two rather different things. There is the difference that can always be expected between programs as they are wished for and programs as they are executed. A good deal that has been promised has not been delivered. When compared to its "in-principle" form the social wage is incomplete (retirement income, say); is badly administered (education, say); has only partly been given a logic and definition (health care, say); and in some aspects is a more or less deliberate fake (women's rights, unionization, progressive taxation, say). There are on the other hand the *actual* principles that must underlie the social wage when one speaks of it "in principle." One such principle, of course, is the primacy of the social wage (an end in itself) as against the private wage. A second is the principle of *universality*.

Usage varies, as recent debates testify, but always points to universality describing benefits available by right, without any sort of means test or "users' fees."[13] The attack upon the welfare state confesses respect for the social wage but proposes that its purposes are better served if it is applied *selectively*. More could be done for the truly needy by exempting the better off from, say, family allowances or universal pensions. A year or so ago the parable of the good bankers entered Canadian folklore. Why, a spokesman asked, must we who earn $500,000 a year share in these social grants so important to the poor? The attack was given an extra thrust by invocation of the moral obligation of the advantaged *vis à vis* the disadvantaged.

Defenders of the social wage have naturally been careful *not* to appear as antagonists of St. Paul, but have been well aware that selectivity and false prophets would be fatal to the welfare state. Selectivity has been the principle underpinning the current reactionary social experiments in the United States, epitomized in the conception of the safety net that saves even the unworthy from falling below subsistence. Substituted within the programs of the welfare state it creates two classes, those for whom society becomes a giant, impersonal charity (the workhouse and poor laws reborn) and those who administer and finance this charity, public trustees who tax themselves as lightly as the self-image of benefactor will allow. Benefits by right are to vanish. Only the means test is to be universal.

In pre-industrial Canada the family had carried out many of the functions of the welfare state (and along with religious organizations *was* the welfare state of that simpler society). With industrialization and altered family structures (reduced authority but larger tasks) new institutions were needed and were slowly, painfully developed item by item over all the years since World War I. Selectivity would return us to that long and bleak period when those new institutions were only partly in place. We would again have two-tier medicine, education that would create as well as confirm class antagonisms, and ruthless disregard of the vulnerable (those widows on pittances that every census reveals). Surely, though, an unsentimental critic would object, there is something paradoxical in complaining about inequalities in general while insisting that equal benefits be piled upon those inequalities. Not at all: for egalitarianism in that direction, for the immediate redistribution of surplus, income taxes and other packages of taxes are the established instruments. Selectivity so directed would not only ruin the composition of the social wage but would do very badly what taxes can do well.[14] The class of the disadvantaged is fragmented into ghettos.

ON FORMULATING PUBLIC CHOICE

The contest about universality in Michael Wilson's first budget is well remembered. So spectacular a failure as Mr. Wilson superintended undoubtedly had lessons to impart, lessons for friend and foe alike since neither anticipated the outcry that forced retreat. What had not been understood, I believe, is the immense function the social wage fulfills in dealing with economic *uncertainties* that are part of everyone's life, the uncertainties that count so heavily in the measurement and perception of surplus. Consequently the extent of political resistance was badly underestimated, resistance that would follow upon even modest initiatives to revive uncertainties now overcome. I should elaborate, for it is easy to confuse support for the social wage with a simple-minded egalitarianism, and to overlook its complementary basis in unexciting but classical self-interest.

Economists of 1986 perhaps differ more on how to deal with uncertainties than on any other matter. Let me assert, as the foundation of my own position, that it is quite impossible to see more than a short interval into the economic future, quite impossible to have foreknowledge of the great economic causes of events. Who can look back to the 1970s and pretend that the horizon for solid prediction was ever more than two or three years distant? Oil, inflation, recession, oil again, monetarism – these identify some of the *facts* about uncertainties to which an analyst should point in a debate that can only be about facts. If I am correct about this experience with facts, then economic models which abstract from uncertainties belong to fantasy, and so do models which attempt to transform uncertainties into risks and models which attempt to list all possible states of an unknown future.

A rationale for the social wage that is quite separate from redistributive policy lies in the attempt every community makes to control its uncertain future, to plan now for *process* appropriate to unpredictable events.[15] Here in the determination of *process* is all that can possibly be achieved, here is a large fraction of what has been attempted, here is the more or less "conscious" and deliberate basis of most of the social programs we have.

By itself this assertion is abstract, unhelpful, even dogmatic. I must illustrate! Income in retirement provides a familiar example, a representative example. Notice a controlling fact: such income *cannot* be absolutely determined by actions and plans established in pre-retirement decades, whether the decisions emanate from the individual or the society.[16] You and I may store up values in any form we choose but cannot determine what (for example) the most gilt-edged of bonds would signify to us a decade hence. You and I belong to one community today and are subject to a particular government; but we would certainly find a changed community in place ten years from now and a changed government. We can neither predict nor control the absolutes of those changed circumstances. Plainly, though, income in retirement is of great concern both to individuals and to the society that would plan for its members. It is of great concern to *any* society, whatever views the society may have about distribution or redistribution.

What cannot be done about income in retirement must give way to what can: those who *earn* existing surplus can be taxed and the proceeds then transferred to members of society now in retirement. Any rule that connects the pattern of "pension" taxation to the pattern of transfers is a *process* that certainly can be applied here and now, and might be imitated and repeated in the future. The government of today has at hand the chance to offer those it now taxes a *quid pro quo*, the likelihood that a suitably chosen process will commend itself to successor governments for renewed application.

Everything indeed turns upon the rule, upon the process, upon the *quid pro quo*. The government of today cannot possibly determine that income in retirement a generation later will be what it was today, or such and such a multiple of what it was today. Nonetheless it provides something very valuable to those now taxed if it can attach believability to the "pension law" under which their income in retirement will be determined. As an element of the social wage, retirement income has indeed been repeatedly attached by governments to a single theme, namely, that in retirement one should keep pace in living standards with one's younger peers who have not retired. As is well known, where such process is not in place there is generally an abrupt change in "relativities" when retirement is reached: comfort and status alike are sharply reduced. Against this threatened discontinuity *process* supplies a prospect of continuity, and in doing so relieves fears that trouble almost everyone.

Arrangements for medical care show the same principle at work. The services of hospitals and physicians can safely be promised to Canadians *now* for ten, twenty, and thirty years ahead, to be financed almost entirely, for those who will then need them, by taxes the healthy will pay. No one pretends to know today what the state of the art in medicine will be a generation from now. Individuals will rarely know more of their future medical needs than that they are uncertain, inherently so, and may be urgent. Society cannot even foretell how it will define "good health" in the years ahead and what level of good health it will decide to support. In the face of such constraints it would be absurd to imagine describing the outcome of *process*, but it would be unthinkable (as our social history shows!) not to institute process.

Much the same evidence would be found in the rest of the catalogue from the social wage, but would add little except repetition to the weight of things. Family allowances have obviously been framed in terms of process from the very beginning, although they illustrate that a program can take several different forms while debate about "best" process is still underway. One pattern of allowances would replace another without destroying the belief that family allowances were firmly in place. Unemployment insurance has been encumbered by the expedient attempt to present it as "insurance" (analogous to those pension "premiums" that are not "premiums" but part of the desire to disguise the social wage); but unemployment insurance has plainly established itself by the process it supplies rather than by worthless "guarantees" of such and such distribution of surplus. Even the sorely missed commitment to full employment would give Canadians no idea at all of the levels of surplus per head in 2000 AD – no, not even in 1990 AD! – but would assure process allowing people to count on having jobs.

So when Mr. Wilson set out to fight deficits by "de-indexing" public pensions, he could not foresee the opposition he would arouse because he did not understand (and doubtless did not intend) the damage to wealth and well-being he would have inflicted. He had after all the precedent of the "6 and 5" program as protection against critics from his Liberal opposition, and perhaps expected a lacklustre defense of the welfare state from other "official" critics.[17] Resistance all the same turned out to be massive, politically overwhelming, for it had a popular base, not merely "official" or institutional.

Mr. Wilson faced the hostility of those already in retirement, for pensioners could foresee the direct expropriation of their benefits compounded at 3% a year.[18] They would realize, too, that their plans to cope with uncertainty had been undermined, and that even the substantial immediate loss was not a ceiling to subsequent loss but a floor. Mr. Wilson also faced the hostility (far more consequential I believe, and little anticipated) of those for whom retirement would be more or less distant but who must plan for it *now*, and who would be doubly concerned about the misfortune of their elders. Their parents and grandparents would have lost immediate protection, and they themselves would have lost *now* the protection for events to come. He had not seen that pension law was part of well-being throughout the society, and that to reduce its integrity reduced wealth for almost every group in society, young people as well as old, rich as well as poor, women as well as men.

There was other instruction given by the episode. For both those sympathetic to Mr. Wilson's hopes and those unsympathetic, one lesson was that once a social wage is in place its durability has little to do with sympathy or its absence. The social wage in the main looks after itself. Most of the well-being *process* confers arises from protections provided against the future, from its believability as something that will be present in the future. Particular political figures organized the parliamentary majorities that created the various elements of the social wage. Such figures are necessary for *process* being born but they cannot be required for its life thereafter: not the least of uncertainties is the sequence of first ministers and of ideological cycles.[19]

In brief, process and the social wage have to be *perceived* as self-perpetuating if they are to have any real existence in the first place. It is because of the addition to wealth that they represent that they are automatically defended, and it is because they are automatically defended that they *are* perceived as self-perpetuating. The stakes in these contests about the social wage may be higher than the adversaries realize. They would be higher, that is, if the contests were real and the adversaries actually decided their outcome. So far, though, Canadian experience has pointed to a stability the contestants have little affected. There has been confirmation of a sort from recent experience in the United States. After all, a less friendly political environment for the welfare state can hardly be imagined. Under that aberrant regime, ideology in terms of redistribution, in terms of military spending has swept all before it. Nevertheless ideology in terms of most of the social wage has had to back away and leave *process* intact.

AND FINALLY SAVING

A visitor from distant parts might say after a week with our newscasts, that social policy in Canada seems to turn not on such issues as universality and employment but only on the terrors contained in deficits. I have no wish to follow the visitor in *that* diversion, but I would offer a suggestion instead about how the mythology of deficits is connected to real concerns. The link is based on *saving*, the part of surplus presently received which is set aside to provide claims on the future. Economic theory has no trouble with saving by the individual. It deals with such saving as it deals with the purchase of breakfast cereal. Theory has found, however, that knowing what the individual does about saving, knowing what *every* individual does, explains little about saving by society as a whole.

A large fraction of saving-as-a-whole is in fact decided upon socially (as manifested in governmental surpluses and deficits, in positive or negative balances of payment, in the choice of taxation), so much so that in relation to a predictable total of "private" saving, savings-as-a-whole becomes wholly a *public* choice. To what end is one number chosen rather than another? Governments routinely distinguish between public debt financed by foreigners and public debt domestically held, chiefly because such debt in itself is an offset to wealth that Canadians own. Governments express concern about domestic deficits with some such distinction also in mind: the accumulated total of savings is less than it seems or it might have been.[20] Governments (however mistaken they may be in their computations) see accumulated savings as being of great importance to public policy, and reralize that they will affect totals of savings by inaction as well as action.

Governments thus face the dilemma to which Malthus pointed 150 years ago. Were accumulated savings freely available to Jones or the state, more would surely be better than less. All saving, however, must reduce present enjoyments. Jones or the state can choose too much or can choose too little, and has no reference outside "Jones" or the "state" to decide on a best amount. And so we come back to *process*. Process can add, does add greatly to well-being. Process can only exist when its continued existence is believed. Process is the more believable the greater the accumulated savings of society. Whatever other motives it has for making the national total high, then, the "state" finds a powerful motive for accumulation by its need to support *process*. Obviously it is a motive constrained by immediate costs, but governments do not often dwell upon rates of substitution.[21]

NOTES AND REFERENCES

1 An earlier draft was provided with various editorial suggestions to which this draft is a response. Those with an editorial role (constructive and welcomed!) have been M. Cooke, C. Pratt, and R. Hutchinson. Colleagues at McGill have also discussed portions of the text.

2 This is not the place to attempt anything systematic about bilateral free trade.

In passing I would observe, though, that advocates seem oblivious to the costs of uncertainty, costs that seem overwhelmingly large when the economist returns to Canada from a Ricardian blackboard.

3 Adam Smith, *Wealth of Nations*, Modern Library Edition (New York: Random House, 1937), book 4, ch. 11, p. 651. For Smith and others who rejected Hobbes, out of the "nature" of things came good: a regime of "natural liberty" operated through many channels to provide, inter al, efficiency and socially valuable savings. Elaborations stretched over hundreds of pages, including two hundred and more pages on the role of the State. Vulgarization of the scheme flourished early, but perhaps never more vigorously than in the "free enterprise" and political economy of 1986.

4 My point is technical. Ultimate questions about social policy are, of course, ethical and moral. Attempted answers that would *sanctify* greed (George Gilder and the divine Marquis come quickly to mind, though they certainly have had associates more formidable than themselves!) have been given a chilly reception by religious leaders who find *tolerating* greed a sufficient strain on conscience.

5 Here again is a large topic that can only be dealt with in an aside. It seems to me that in the chain of causes the political drift to the right has been prior to the sterility that academic economics has chosen to proclaim. From this point of view such a scholastic phenomenon as the Fraser Institute, say, would not be of much interest in its own right – in contrast to the "Conference" of Roman bishops (which gives priority to the debate about values). As to *cult* economics, I do not, of course, regard either Smith's "natural liberty" or Marx's grand dynamics as part of the pseudo-science that invokes their names. It is such great writers who have defined the "mainstream".

6 Here "western" must be made flexible enough to include, for example, Australia and any other states that were technologically advanced and made substantial use of markets.

7 For details see Statistics Canada's monthly publication *The Labour Force*. Fine points aside, a person belongs to the labour force if he or she is fifteen years or older and wishes to be hired for pay. The labour force then divides into the employed and the unemployed, and reveals shortfalls from full employment according to the kinds and amounts of unemployment.

8 Imagines a history that plots surplus per head against the calendar. Whether we are a few years ahead or a few years behind some hypothetical alternative is a matter barely noticed and soon forgotten. We well remember 1848 or 1914 or 1929, but not in the least for any such triviality.

9 In speaking of dependency I have in mind unemployment "insurance" for the short term, welfare for the long, and am contrasting both with the calculated provision of jobs.

10 See particularly their forthcoming *L'option du plein emploi* (Québec: Presses université du Québec, 1986).

11 *Ibid*. As European experience testifies it is rejection of the axiom that is un-realistic, not its acceptance.

12 Tautologies can be instructive, as *professional* mathematicians most surely hope. In economics enormous use has been made of the idea that a business-man who maximizes profits must be sure that he hires anything that adds more than it costs and nothing that adds less. One should never, of course, dispute identities but need not approach them with awe. In the text above the basic idea is presented in a somewhat amplified form: it is still truistic or false.

13 I emphasize "by right" and "without any sort of means test" as the qualities that matter for the present discussion. A full taxonomy of the ideas found in this overburdened term would need another paper.

14 I should remark, no doubt, on the ingenuous inversion of this point in the astonishing catalogue from the MacDonald Commission. There the panacea is *not* selectivity but global redistribution produced solely by taxes. This is logi-cally equivalent to total faith in the market. Property rights can be modified, and then all other problems succumb to demand and supply.

15 Notice again the composite nature of the social wage. Progressive taxation is an element in creating a social wage different from the private wage. Family allowances, say, are another element. Either element is largely independent of the other.

16 There exist by way of Statistics Canada records of recently established sur-pluses. A not-too-demanding measure of absolute pensions would employ units based upon those *real* experiences. The point is that control in absolute terms is technically impossible over any significant interval of time. Reality may in this sense disappoint the academic, but seems to be little affected by its failure to please.

17 The parable of the good banker had captured minds not only amongst oppo-nents of the welfare state but amongst its creators (who seem often to have imagined the social wage as being mere redistribution).

18 Where benefits had been indexed to offset all of inflation (increased by x% when inflation was x%) they were now to be indexed to offset only inflation over 3% (increased by [x - 3]% when inflation was x%). It seems to be widely expected that inflation will be larger than 3% for many years to come. If so, benefits in terms of purchasing power would be expected to fall by 3% in a year, by 3% twice over in two years, and so on. For those aged 50, for example, there would be very little left of the real pension once they were well into retirement (3% compounded for more than 15 years). That antici-pated loss, of course, affects well-being *now*.

19 I have Canadian parliamentary democracy as institutional background, but would observe that the theory of process extends to other systems not exclud-ing authoritarian regimes. Process best flourishes, one would speculate, where strong government and democratic government are correlated.

20 One is reporting attitudes, not trying to put right the endless muddle about
   these ill-favoured terms!
21 Jargon may be better than patois ("trade-offs"). "Saving" is desirable,
   "spending" is desirable, but more of one desirable thing may require less of
   another desirable thing. Governments must choose, governments must offend.

PART TWO

Selected Topics in Economic Policy

CHAPTER NINE

Wage Controls and the
Canadian Labour Movement

Mr. Orlikow: "Seriously, Mr. Bouey, did the Bank do any studies of the effects on wages and prices and the cost of living in the three years when we had the Anti-Inflation Board in operation?"

Mr. Bouey: "Well, there are certainly studies around. I do not recall that we did any. But I think that one could look at the price indices and that sort of thing and draw some conclusions, without a great deal of study."

(Minutes, Standing Committee on Finance, Trade, and Economic Affairs, 3 June 1982, p. 97–141).

I am calling on everyone to help Canada make the difficult transition from the 12-per-cent world that has mired us in recession to the 6-per-cent world that will bring recovery .... Increases in pay of other employees in the federal sector will be constrained to no more than 6 per cent in the first year of the application of the program to them and 5 per cent in the second year ... It will cover more than 500,000 federal employees.

(A.J. MacEachen, budget, 28 June 1982, extracts from page 4).

A PREAMBLE AND A THESIS

In early June the Governor of the Bank of Canada does not recall whether his staff has prepared any studies of the effects of the Anti-inflation Board. In late June the Minister of Finance has a scheme in hand to transform inflation and prepare recovery in a "6%" year followed by a "5%" year. Whether the memory of the governor was faulty, whether the pace of research was dramatically accelerated, whether monetary policy and incomes policy

---

Jamieson Lecture, University of British Columbia, September 1982; publication no. 10, Canadian Centre for Policy Alternatives, Ottawa, 1983. This text has been edited in order to make it more accessible to persons with limited training in economics. Editors' notes have been added to supplement a number of technical discussions and to provide additional information about what may be obscure references for some readers.

Appendix A contains an evaluation of an econometric study that was in the main body of the original text. Appendix I and Appendix II of the original text have been omitted.

were totally compartmentalized as between the governor and the minister, I do not know; and whether the missing studies (newly compiled or redis-covered) would have had very little to do with policy-in-action, I can only guess. Certainly by mid-September the governor was prepared to make wage restraint the centrepiece of his public utterances. In Ontario the government had assisted restraints with a draconian bill that would, for half a million public employees, *inter alia* suspend both binding arbitration and the right to strike, giving some hope (I imagine) to those who still regret the repeal of the Combination Acts.

A SETTING FOR THE DISCUSSION

It might have been more seemly to emphasize in the title phrases like "price and wage controls in Canada" or "anti-inflation policies" or "incomes pol-icies." The alternatives appear to me misleading on social and technical grounds. It is Canadian events one chiefly wants to consider, and for the past dozen years or so. In this country and during that period, there can be no doubt that inflation has been a preoccupation of our governments, but little doubt either that so-called "price and wage controls" have been a heterogeneous collection of responses in which political theatricals have usually had a leading place. So far as the responses *have* been directed to the control of prices, they have (with minor exceptions) been directed to the control of the prices of labour in the first place, and only by derivation and at second hand to an influence on some of the prices in the "consumer price index." To speak of "price and wage controls" indicates a parallelism that does not exist. Wage controls there certainly have been, and in a bastardized form [these] have been renewed in the months since June; but price controls in the same degree have been present only in slogans.

There is the possibility of stressing "incomes policies," but just as "price and wage controls" puts two things on a parity that are very different, so "incomes policies" excludes from the centre of discussion the central fact of the fortunes of the Canadian labour movement. If there are incomes policies that are to determine how the production of the country is to be divided, it is no small matter if their shared assumption is that the labour unions of Canada shall be more or less constrained from interfering with the higher justice supposedly represented by those policies. In a memorable testament to the worth of a tax-based incomes policy, Sidney Weintraub put the thesis clearly: "This position [is not] anti-union but anti-collective bar-gaining."[1] His fellow petitioners express the same contradiction.

I do not reject for a moment that there are tangential bits of apparatus likely to be attached to wage controls in Canada, and that these tangential bits, like the wage controls themselves, will have causal effects on economic variables throughout an interconnected system. Nor do I reject that some who propose incomes policies would wish to sustain the contradictions of loving labour leaders and labour unions but destroying their purposes. With this agreed, as I hope it may be, I wish to let the title stand and to consider an actual anti-inflation board, say, or an as yet hypothetical tax-based incomes policy (*et hoc genus omne*) under the deliberately restrictive language of the title.

In providing a setting for the discussion, two facts, I think, have to be taken especially into account. There is on the one hand an immense amount of positive economics surrounding wage controls in Canada, an economics arising from the elements both of competing *justifications* of controls and of competing *condemnations* (justifications and condemnations within the narrowest bounds of economic theory, within historical narrative, based upon legal forms and announced purposes, and argued in terms of a much disputed statistical experience.) There is on the other hand the effect of wage controls (actual or hypothetical) upon social structures, upon distribution of income, upon the fortunes and nature of Canadian labour unions. I am perpetually astonished at the silence in the Canadian economic literature about the existence of these repercussions and their possible costs or benefits. That their costs may be very great indeed is surely a thesis that cannot be ignored in any responsible study purporting to advise the Canadian authorities how to approach the problem of inflation.[2]

The economist cannot plead that such institutional matters fall outside the domain of economics. At every Canadian university courses are offered, I speculate with some confidence, on labour economics and industrial relations. The economist cannot plead unawareness of how destructive the leaders of Canadian labour calculate the advent of wage controls to be. The economist, or at least the economic historian who knows even fifty years of Canadian social history, is well aware of the severe, the violent contests that gave the labour movement its present marginal footing in Canadian society. The quashing of the movement might be attempted directly, but it would be more effectively attempted by letting the movement live in suspended animation by cutting it off from its objects and functions.

In his important and influential address to the Canadian Economics Association in May of 1981 Professor Richard Lipsey inserted a placatory paragraph.

But if present policies do not work, I would be prepared to try controls as part of a full policy package which I shall outline in a moment. There would of course be constitutional problems and labour's hostility would be understandable ... prices did not fully follow wages [under the AIB] ... It should be made clear that the controls are solely an anti-inflationary policy, and we expect to come out of controls with an unchanged distribution of national income between wages and profits."[3]

Suppose against experience that Lipsey's hope could be translated into labour's belief. With unions or without unions, the translation would be identical; and so actual unions would have been deprived of their *raison d'être*. Perhaps the silence about the effects upon labour unions – I have in mind not so much Lipsey now, as those who do not even acknowledge the collectivity implied in the term "labour's hostility" – emerges from the difficulty of bringing these effects to some sort of monetary measurement (intramarginal surpluses rather than accounting at the margins, social rather than private gains and losses, and so on). The problem is not simplified but erased. This excuse will not wash. It is *social policy* that is at issue, and it is inevitably miscalculated if great social effects are ignored.

John Stuart Mill put the matter well in Book 5 of his *Principles of Political Economy*:

The ends of government are as comprehensive as those of social union. They consist of all the good and all the immunity from evil, which the existence of government can be made directly or indirectly to bestow ... [But] the practice of setting definite values on things essentially indefinite, and making them a ground of practical conclusions, is particularly fertile in false views of social questions.[4]

If wage controls are to be praised or condemned in relation to practical conclusions, then major elements in their practical effects cannot be suppressed from consideration; and if so central an element as the effect upon the labour movement is difficult to measure, the difficulty is not overcome by quietly treating it as commensurable *and* zero. I wish to return to this business of the labour movement repeatedly, but stress at once that whatever wage controls may do to inflation they do it with accompanying effects – to my mind, appallingly destructive effects – upon the labour movement.

On the other side of the discussion, it is just as necessary, of course, to be careful in reviewing the relationship of wage controls to inflation as such: evidence that wage controls could cure something as unpopular as inflation should no more be ignored than the effects of controls upon the labour movement. Parenthetically, one would observe the social harm appears quite as difficult to quantify in the one case as the other; the once popular (if always absurd) measure of the burden of anticipated inflation (lost consumers' surplus *à la* Cagan) seems to have vanished, and the now popular measure of the disease of inflation by the production given up to its "cure" has the qualities of circularity and question-begging.

The point can fairly be put even more strongly. Not only are the two kinds of effect similarly difficult to quantify, but they are assessed in practical affairs almost exclusively according to their political weight, as to how social consequences are perceived individually; the head count of those who dislike inflation (in any degree) is set against the (net!) count of those who fear the weakening of the labour movement (and again in any degree). The Governor of the Bank of Canada, I surmise, does not recall studies in those areas either, although in this area the absence of studies and recollections would be understandable enough. In a sense the contrast becomes an election between a private good and a public good, and as an election it is one in which the outcome has complex and unsymmetrical sources.

Any review of wage controls in Canada gains many more dimensions as these two large themes are divided. The variants are many in principle and – in their hypothetical as well as actual applications – considerably different in their possible effects. Wage controls may be employed *coercively*, they may be self-imposed under guidelines, they may be hybrids of these purer forms, and they may contain an admixture of extralegal persuasion. Wage controls may be for a short term, a long term, an indefinite term, an infinite term. Wage controls may be universal, they may be selective as to occupation, they may be selective as to the levels of wages, and they may be selective as to employer or constitutional jurisdiction. In their ancillary features the variety of forms becomes countless; and in those ancillary features that are framed in terms of commodity prices, in terms of profits, in terms of still other sources of income, in terms of 'mark-ups', the *principal* types are not simply variations on a theme. There are questions of the availability of theory with a microeconomic base, of theory with a macroeconomic base; there are questions of administrative feasibility and of political feasibility, and there are certainly the crucial questions – to which the questions of theory and expected feasibility can only defer – of the effects actually observed of wage controls upon wages, upon distribution, upon social power, upon inflationary expectations, upon inflation. With so many issues open selection is necessary, but one can attempt to speak directly to large or representative issues and say something at least by implication on some of the remaining matters.

ADMINISTRATIVE FEASIBILITY:
BREVITY VERSUS CUMULATION

I shall begin with administrative adjuncts of wage controls, and shall for a number of reasons use so-called tax-based incomes policies as the illustration in chief (and within the group, the elaborate scheme of Sidney Weintraub).[5] The reasons are: first, that I have paid much more attention to the minutiae of this scheme than to those of any other; second, that it is certainly a scheme of *wage* controls in the strict sense; third, that it lives (at least in the acronym TIP) in virtually any discussion one encounters of the next Canadian venture in wage controls[6] – a new anti-inflation board is its only superior in that respect, and even then, has become a board supplemented and extended by a TIP; and fourth, that the *dilemmas* within the programs of wage controls, which seem to me inherent to them in any form, are explicit and confessed in the scheme. I might add for completeness that the Prices and Incomes

Commission instituted in 1969 consisted wholly of guidelines; that the Centre for the Studies of Inflation and Productivity born in 1978 seemed to be a makework program for economists more than anything else; and that the Anti-inflation Board and the program of the budget of 28 June [1982] are the only *realities* that on the administrative side clearly require further comment in their own right.

Administrative feasibility is pretty clearly connected with the lifespan of wage controls, or to be exact, with the lifespans of experiences with wage controls. Controls suddenly introduced for, say a week, would presumably require no administration except that they be published (although against a history of such interventions, odd effects outside the boundaries of the week might well be encountered); but their administrative simplicity would leave Canadian statistics sadly unaffected by policy. Controls less frivolously brief would probably also be undemanding of administration, not so much because of good behaviour (as the controllers would see such things) but because, for the actors, to avoid their boundaries would be simple; and now there *would* probably be effects on the statistics but of a speculative, wasteful kind. As far as I can see the cases of interest are *exclusively* those in which *ex ante* the wage controls are long lived either because they are instituted for a lengthy fixed term; because they are a repetition of earlier controls or are linked to conditional repetition in the future; or because they are of unspecified or contingent term.†

Weintraub's scheme for wage controls (let me call it simply the plan in the paragraphs that continue from this) unambiguously fits the formula. First, he identifies the instrument of policy as the average wage rate of those employed.[7] †† Second, he is firm about the role of unions. "It is with the unhampered power of unions to eke out excessive wage settlements that we must deal."[8] Third, he is specific that the plan has no predetermined termination and must be conceived of by the public as extending for many

---

† For example, the controls could remain in force until the rate of inflation fell below some specified level.

†† "A proper gearing of average wages to average labour productivity can establish price stability in Canada. Sometimes the rise in average wages would have to be subdued somewhat below the average productivity gain; for example in circumstances of pronounced inflation abroad. When other countries were containing their price level, a more relaxed relationship between average wage gains and average productivity gains could prevail in Canada. ... TIP contemplates an extra corporate income tax of 5 per cent on firms whose average pay hike ... exceeds a guidepost of perhaps 5 per cent a year. The surtax could be designed along progressive lines, with the first staged levy on firms whose pay advance topped 5 percent but was less than 6 per cent, then an extra impost on hikes above 7 per cent but under 10 per cent, and so forth. Also, to ensure that corporate income tax revenues were not raised in the aggregate and total investment capital from retained earnings eroded, the ordinary corporate tax bite could be cut. Hence the total corporate income tax intake would not be increased." Sidney Weintraub, "A Prices and Incomes Policy," in David Crane, ed., *Beyond the Monetarists: Post-Keynesian Alternatives to Rampant Inflation, Low Growth and High Unemployment* (Ottawa: Canadian Institute for Economic Policy, 1981), 70, 73.

years. "Perhaps after an experimental year or two of restricting TIP to the largest firms, the plan could cover most firms, or firms with over 50, 100, 200 ... employees, as judgement dictates."[9] Lipsey, it is worth noting, suggests that the "wage-price controls [of immediate application] can then be used in an attempt to cut through the inflationary inertias [in a] package [that] should include some post-controls policy ... A temporary TIP might even follow the removal of controls, to be used for two or three years."[10] Professors Clarence Barber and John McCallum, it is worth noting, advise a similarly sequential program:

For a program that is intended to last for only two or three years, this greater effectiveness of outright controls leads us to favour them over a form of tax-based incomes policy. On the other hand, the prevention of a re-emergence of inflation is likely to be a problem for years to come ... . Accordingly, our policy recommendations include the use of some form of TIPs.[11]

So the plan is high on the list of economic advocacy and would belong to *enduring* policy. It would not only belong to enduring policy in its own right but would have descended after a short interval from that other "plan," the anti-inflation board, and in a latent sense would become permanent.

A long-lived plan, however, cannot escape the charge that administrative complications are always substantial nor the much graver charge that complications are *cumulative*, so that hardly any early difficulty is erased by time. Instead, complications build on complications and, in the eyes of the sponsor of the plan, appear to do so speedily and at an accelerating rate. One of the often-expressed fears that the anti-inflation board inspired was that its life would ensure that new boards would be procreated, and this same fear must be reinforced by current events and discussions. Success or failure would mean no more than the success or failure of generals in the middle of World War I. Indeed, disastrous failure might be the better guarantee of repetition. Without the Somme, said the General Staff of 1916, imagine how much worse the military position on the Western Front might have been! Professor John Kenneth Galbraith has some authority on these questions and has not misled us about the time scale of schemes like the plan: it is permanence or nothing. (If I heard him correctly on the Canadian Broadcasting Corporation during his last visit, it was also "Canada-after-the-United States *or* nothing," if inflation was to be contained here. That these amplifications wholly contradict most of the programs of the disciples does not prevent Galbraith being reverently invoked.)

My count of major elaborations of the plan runs at least to more than a dozen, most of them obviously required elaborations, elaborations required within quite brief periods; and that as each "cure" corrects an anomaly, it thereby creates induced anomaly and the need for further elaborations. There is no such thing as *the* plan in final form or even *the* plan in predictable form. In the beginning only a couple of hundred of the largest employers – it is said – would have to be included, no more than seven lines on an income-tax form would have to be added, and a "control force" of as little as two [*sic!*] persons would be able to process and enforce the content and implications of the 1400 lines by which wages would be controlled (and derivatively, inflation of consumer prices restrained).[12] "If TIP succeeded, for literally pennies a real GNP prize of $5 to $10 billions could be captured",[13] a benefit-to-cost ratio beyond compare even in the rich domain of economic panaceas.

The *beginning*, however, cannot sustain the plan except momentarily. Government is "to contain increases in money wages, on the average, to the gains in average labour productivity,"[14] although a pragmatic government might allow itself the use of a slacker rein.[†] The increases in money wages, however, are required to have the same economic significance from one year to the next, and so are the increases (or decreases) in average labour productivity. Since these are composites of the most intricate kind,[††] even in the absence of the plan, both numerators *and* both denominators would only by chance have the desired continuity of meaning, and (along with the plan itself) would be affected by the new incentives. Almost everyone affected by the plan would have to learn how to contrive new ratios (a skill that would entail learning by doing). Still, for its author the plan is to be protected against the vagaries of the statistical base and the forces of false incentives. The average wage in any one of the 200 enterprises loses economic continuity in its denominator if the pattern of occupations and status is altered, or at least, if standardization via a fictional denominator is not successfully applied.[†††] In the plan whenever the "net value added per full-time equivalent employee" is reported – extra lines on the form, extra inspectors of the forms – as having fallen, the denominator of workers should be reduced proportionately. The enterprise that might wish to bid away talent by some padding of its rolls with the unskilled is thwarted, albeit by the supervision of so amorphous a magnitude as "net value

---

[†]   A "slacker rein" might add, for example, some part of the ongoing inflation rate to the trend rate of increase in average labour productivity in forming the guidepost for allowable wage increases.

[††]   The money wage would be represented by the total wage bill divided by a measure of employment. Productivity would be indicated by a measure of output (for example, net value added), divided by labour input (for example, full-time equivalent employees). This productivity measure is expressed as net value added per full-time equivalent employee.

[†††] A fictional denominator in calculations of the average wage rate could, for example, modify the measurement of total employment by making adjustments for workers' skill levels. The contribution of more skilled groups of workers (that is, higher paid workers) to the overall employment index would be increased by a factor that depended on the size of their wage relative to the wage of the least skilled group of workers.

added,"[15][†] a particularly vague magnitude in the multi-plant, multi-product enterprises sizeable enough to be included in the 200.

Yet the plan has its *raison d'être* in an inflationary environment, so the conversion of the labour forces into wage units is unlikely to be convincing in nominal dollars. "Corrected average productivity is needed, i.e., net value per employee, in *constant* dollars,"[16] an amendment that may add little to complexity but adds something to the risks that an unfavourable rather than a favourable price deflator will be used. Perhaps more troubling to anyone who would implement the plan is the possibility that particular gains in productivity would be blocked. An enterprise might genuinely seek to improve its techniques by changing the structure of its work force, and find the change witlessly prohibited by the plan. Still another elaboration offers a form of remedy: the "corrected average productivity" for the enterprise is compared with the "corrected average productivity" for all 200 enterprises (or perhaps for the grand total of enterprises for which statistics are available), and in the event that there is an advance, "one third the gain [say, may be] added on to the permissible pay hike."[17] Another arbitrary element is added, another administrative complexity is accepted, and another false incentive is incorporated in the system. Both the constraint and the exemption have the quality that they indistinguishably improve profits, whether by escaping the first or exploiting the second.[††] Further, by now the plan has to be seen in long-run terms, and will have succeeded in trisecting the once unified family of firms; thus, the 200 enterprises we have been considering, the innumerable little firms, but also the "more firms, small as well as large" who would not be left to their own devices (with the minnows) but might "at least for several years" be governed by the barebones rules only.[18] Again there must be margins; crossing the margins is inevitably profitable, and profits will be the more attractive as the plan is extended.

I shall deal summarily with other aspects of the evolution. The plan might seem to be biased in favour of profits unless the original tax rate were changed: a "neutral" calculation of a higher rate can be devised (of little effect unless one can foretell the future, and perhaps making the uncertainties facing businessmen still less certain). Failure to adhere to the plan might

---

[†] A firm could increase the proportion of low-paid employees, which would tend to decrease its average wage rate. This would allow for increases in compensation to higher-paid employees that would have not been possible without incurring TIP penalties. However, this manoeuvre is likely to cause a fall in the labour productivity index because of the increased proportion of low-paid, less skilled workers employed on plant and equipment with a given technology. Administrators of TIP would then decrease the fictional employment denominator (see note above) in calculating the average wage, thereby raising the calculated average wage increase.

[††] If pay hikes are prohibited when productivity increases, other things remaining the same, then profits will increase. If only one third of productivity gains are passed on in increased wages, other things being equal, profits will increase.

carry varying instead of fixed penalties (although elsewhere the penalties are spoken of as though they should be unbearably severe).[19]

Elaborations on a more monumental scale are still to come. "Some firms with low current year profits, but with large past and prospective profits, might be ripe candidates to be victimized [*sic*!] by wage and salary raids"; and so to forestall the raiders, the plan conceives that the "surcharge might be levied on the *highest* pre-tax profit of the last three (or five) years."[20] Two thoughts present themselves, the one being that the ratio of profits to wages is after all not a very basic distributive measure (*pace* Barber and McCallum), and second that the link between present behaviour and its historical causes must be allowed to lengthen till nothing simple and direct about the Plan is left. "If the TIP features are directed to apply only to the largest, ... smaller firms might conceivably become union targets ... repercussions would flow to larger firms whose pay practices would be condemned as unrealistic, even exploitative." On this basis the dramatic extension above noted arises: "Perhaps after an experimental year or two ... the plan could cover *most* firms."[21] (Emphasis added.)

Elaboration on a grand scale appears to repair misallocation from small beginnings. In a twist that has its ironies, the plan will control wages in the private sector, and allow wages in the public and extra-market sectors to be modelled upon those private controls (the inverse of 28 June which went first to the public sector and looked to "moral" suasion for transmission of its control *there* to the private market). Imbalances as between these two giant divisions of the labour force would be inevitable "but every two or three years ... could be ... revised where appropriate".

It seems the plan is hesitant about farmers and others who are self-employed: "farmers and professional employees *could be* exempt," by "the power of substitution" it would appear. Since firms are born from time to time, the plan will provide them with a constructed history where an actual history is missing."[22] One would guess the vital statistics of firms would not be insensitive to the *ad hoc* inventions of the plan. Regrettably, the labour movement might at times be intransigent. Under the plan, labour's opponents as a penultimate resort could be assisted by public subsidies – how far do those who invoke the help of the Plan understand how firmly it will operate? – and as an ultimate resort could be assisted by, e.g., "a denial of union recognition or curtailed unemployment benefits."[23]

Some elements of this evolution might be said to be peculiarities of the plan, and to caricature alternative, much superior plans. I know competing schemes of the genre abound, of course, but I do not see that the plan ex-Weintraub has been disowned or expelled from the pantheon of such plans, or is different in fundamentals from any of the competitive versions. In the current debate no one writes that when he or she speaks of using TIP, the choice of form greatly matters. The plan as sketched at worst may appear a little worn at the edges, but in substance it is quite satisfactory. The dilemma the plan points to is intrinsic. Without cumulation the plan fails in its own terms, and with cumulation it must endlessly become cumbersome. Admittedly, if the facts in retrospect testify that the dilemma *is* resolvable, the facts override the speculation; but I have no fear that the facts will so speak.

How one thing leads to another in these schemes is shown from rather a different angle in some bleak sentences from the Barber and McCallum version of wage controls. "It is proposed that there be a three-year program of wage and price controls patterned in some measure after the Anti-Inflation Board plan."[24] Some pages later the authors note realistically that,

the government would undoubtedly face opposition in introducing wage and price controls, but if, in the course of its implementation, the program was seen to be both effective and equitable, then it is possible that the co-operation of the various interest groups could be enlisted in the design of post-controls policy ... guidelines or a tax-based incomes policy .... In the absence of improvements in this area, the results of this study raise the spectre of permanent or at least recurring wage-price controls as the only long-run remedy for this country's inflation problem.[25]

Alas, to exclude any number of non-remedies adds nothing to the prospects of some remaining candidate.

Barber and McCallum are as concerned with equity as Weintraub and are more sensitive than he to "the importance ... of a role for collective bargaining." Their well-intentioned suggestions fall foul, I think, of three actualities. Their corrective devices encumber what is already too cumbersome. A role of collective bargaining that preempts redistribution in favour of the labour movement is not a role the movement can accept – consult, say, Marx, Rawls, or McDermott.[†] A satisfactory role – Barber and McCallum search for something serious – is not available from those who would impose wage controls; redistribution is not part of their political agenda. Fairness ends at not making unfairness worse.

"Perhaps most important, the program should take account of the phase of the business cycle at the time of the introduction ... so that companies are not permitted to maintain profit margins at the peak levels that were experienced in some industries in the past one or two years."[26] After the fact, some believe they can read phases of the business cycle from the statistical entrails. As the cycle unfolds, not many (I suspect) would wish to commit themselves to the *phase* of contemporaneous events. For the

---

[†] Denis McDermott was the president of the Canadian Labour Congress when this article was written. John Rawls is an American philosopher who has written on the relationship between government, individual liberty, and income distribution.

program to operate retroactively would be a horrendous administrative challenge. Further, as the authors point out, "with a 100 per cent tax rate on excess profits under the old program, there is evidence that some companies chose to make unnecessary or wasteful expenditures rather than pay such a tax." It is doubtful whether distribution as the national accounts report wages and profits much concerns the labour movement, but if it does, *this* plan to put things right may not convince many of its practicality. Such sweeteners for labour as being "allowed to bargain for a one-time cash bonus or share of profits" or being put in expectation that in "non-unionized firms, the employer could also offer a profit-sharing arrangement or a cash bonus" – such vanities would be nonstarters in Canadian industrial relations.

Barber and McCallum foresee the "apprehension among workers and unions that this will involve a reduction in real wages" and suggest the possibility (Galbraith again, I expect) of offering "workers a real wage guarantee." But if the productivity figures are misforseen (as the authors note is a likely possibility), then a host of compensating adjustments – all applied to "averages," remember! – have to be contrived. An alternative approach would be to provide a "wage share guarantee rather than a real wage guarantee." Calculated repairs have turned into *ad hoc* improvisations.[27]

I have no quarrel with the assertion that government "could take steps to treat unions as legitimate and valued institutions in Canadian society rather than as barely tolerable entities to be ignored, contained or weakened as the opportunity arises," and am not alarmed that this civilized view is presented as a means to an end, or showing government how to act if it "wishes unions to behave in a 'socially responsible manner.'"[28] It would be ingenuous to regard the Canadian labour movement as embodying all private and public virtues, but its purposes are as plainly known as those, say, of Canadian universities. Barber and McCallum comprehend these purposes, recognize that the purposes extend to social policy in many dimensions, and see that the social contract they seek is perilously close to social tyranny if the labour movement is forced into compliance. Unfortunately, *the sequence is critical*, for the labour movement cannot be a partner to a social contract until it has gained social recognition (and can offer very little for recognition-yet-to-come); and to provide social recognition is an enormous administrative and institutional change. The wish is (in my view) admirable, but it may well be, alas, a hope for action that is at the same time essential and impossible. Much of Barber and McCallum brings to mind the old exchange. "I do not like strawberries and cream." "What? Come the revolution and you will have strawberries and cream and like them." The agencies of *social* democracy are far fewer in Canada than in the countries of *social* consensus to which Barber and McCallum longingly look. Probably those agencies are far from sovereign remedies for inflation, but they may mitigate its severity and do much about the discriminatory harm it inflicts upon the vulnerable.

The obstacle remains that those agencies which do not exist cannot be reasonably well mimicked by administrative decrees. If one wants the benefits of a strong union movement, then one will have to begin by assisting it to be built, and in a cold climate. The substitutes, I fear, are simply anti-unions, at the best delusions.

ADMINISTRATIVE ASPECTS OF
THE ANTI-INFLATION BOARD

Most of what I wish to say about the Anti-inflation Board may be put under a later heading, for only then does the inescapable question arise as to whether there is a case to meet. Let me interpolate here, all the same, two themes about administrative aspects of that program, for judgements appear to vary enormously about whether the board was (surprisingly) simple to administer (whether the cumulation factor was really not large) or whether the board was unnecessarily complex in relation to a tax-based incomes policy (whether the feared cumulation proved inherent and was part of experience). The board (and more precisely, Bill C-73, the Anti-inflation Act, and all other statutory action immediately connected with that Act) surely is not to be regarded as a single intervention born on 16 October 1975, defined at that moment as a uniform force to exist smoothly through a preordained life of three years and then to be buried whether or not its goals had been achieved. This manner of controlling wages for some three years was notably varied throughout its history – one remarks on this only to note how the phenomenon should be appraised, not as some special flaw in its orderings.

The *Financial Post* of 16 October 1976, has an excellent diary of the administration of the first year that well illustrates the point. Price guidelines were, of course, never price controls but derivative formulae everchanging. By 18 December 1975 the "product-line method [existed], with price/profit rules added to cost pass through and net-margin rules." On the same day "Ottawa [unveiled a] first attempt at spelling out the rules ... 60 pages of highly complex regulations together with explanatory booklets ... [and instituted] a special 100% levy on increased corporate profits from exports sales ... 90% of it refundable [under various terms]." By 28 January 1976, "the Board orders 6,500 companies [instead of] the original estimate of 1,500" to report by 27 February and by 14 April it was able to make a "general announcement about reporting and compliance requirements for professionals." But then in May, on the 25th, the "Federal budget ... [included] a major review of the price-profit rules" and those rules were changed again on 7 September. With one year nearly gone on 23 September 1976 "rules for banks and other financial institutions were announced" and two days later the news is available that "the profit-line test for calculating profit margins and excess revenues is to die." On 14 October the "AIB has a staff of 850 – down from the peak of more than 900 in August." So much for the helpful memories from the *Post*.[29]

As is well remembered, during that same year, in one way or another the provinces attached their public sectors to the scheme (hesitantly, at times, because adherence might have its political costs). In the case of Ontario the process was challenged in the Supreme Court, and in the case of Quebec the direct link had a short lifespan because of the famous electoral change of 15 November 1976.

There was continuous speculation about whether the three years would be aborted or extended (and some still relevant speculation about how many inflationary emergencies the Constitution will accept). In the upshot, at the end of the second year – 20 October 1977 – "the Minister of Finance announced that the AIB *would be* phased out during 1978, slightly ahead of schedule."[30]

It seems to me difficult not to regard the Anti-inflation Board as a series of quite heterogeneous happenings.[31] For some time before the board was introduced, the idea of its coming was in the air, very much so with the railway unions who feared that their investment of years in the Hall formula and controlled disputes was at risk.[†] Perhaps these speculative murmurings can best be let pass, and the intervals of the board be dated from the Act.[32] In the first year, the apparatus of wage controls was tacked together from month to month, although admittedly it was with respect to the derivative "rules" that improvisation was most marked. In the second year, there was an apparatus in being against which the forces taken note of by Weintraub began to be felt. In the third year, the apparatus was officially under notice and was wound up or allowed to disintegrate. There has been, however, a fourth interval, for if the board has a beginning not that awkward to date, its ending as an economic phenomenon would come when its structural effects had disappeared (and this date is not at all agreed).

As to the second theme about administrative aspects, I observe only that the cumulation that would undermine the plan seems to be matched virtually point for point within the cumulation of the board. The exercises in dealing with markups, product lines, and taxes on export profits may seem additional complications for the board, but their primary purpose is to exhibit "fairness" – at any cost – just as similar gadgetry is found within the plan. In the domain of wages I can see nothing in principle that separates the two schemes, for the punitive taxes of the plan are in intent prohibitive; and since wage controls are at the core of the plan and board alike, there is not much to recommend the one rather than the other or to separate the two schemes on administrative grounds.

---

† In 1974, the Hon. Emmett M. Hall, in his role as arbitrator in a national railway strike, wrote a decision that provided a framework for collective bargaining of compensation issues. The Hall formula, as it came to be known, contributed to the stability of labour relations in that industry.

POINTS OF A THEORETICAL KIND

In considering some theoretical questions I have two rather different objects in mind. There are a few elementary objections advanced *against* the plan, or the board, or anything in their image, that have been made many times over in Canadian discussions and no doubt in any similar discussions of wage controls. Their existence flows into administrative feasibility, and is indeed founded in theory of the very simplest kind; but they seem to me to have no simple responses, and so can be recited once again. The other object is to consider some of the theory advanced *on behalf* of wage controls, and particularly the ideas associated with "relative shares" and with "social consensus." As might be expected we encounter again the logic of union behaviour, what it is unions are supposed to attempt, what they are supposed in fact to do, and how economic policy is supposed to adapt to the presence of unions.

Let me begin with the "elementary" objections, and since some of them have been on stage earlier in their applied forms – the discussion of the plan – repetition can be minimized by using a summary list.

Item, in an economic system as open as the Canadian, much work done here ends up in items that are exported and much is employed on items that are imported. *Vis à vis* the rest of the world, Canadian authorities no doubt wish to sell dear and buy cheap, yet in relation to wage controls the authorities apparently desire uniformity of wages across industries and unchanged ratios of profits to wages. Appropriate taxes and subsidies exist, I suppose, but are beyond calculation. *Item*, in a scheme where workers are "controlled" in groups, the fortunes of any particular worker are arbitrarily determined (subject to custom or to putative regulation of individual fairness by the controllers). The Judas-union naturally has neither the administrative powers nor the legal authority to provide safeguards, and in the longer run, to assist efficiency. *Item* (and most important), under a scheme of wage controls the motives of the actors are altered in direction if not in form, for profits and advantage are now to be gained where before they could not. Even custom will be threatened by these motivations.

Item, wages are a part only of the labour-derived income of the Canadian worker. Within the workplace, wages are supplemented by earned benefits in many forms, from "paid" holidays to dental plans to complex pension plans (sometimes little understood by employers, let alone the pseudo-union). Outside the workplace labour-derived income is finally complemented in the social wage (as, for example, in unemployment insurance or benefits under the Canada and Quebec pension plans). Wage controls affect these elements unevenly. The narrow wage may be easily accounted for, but not the labour for which it has been compensation. Unexpected effects on productivity will surely follow. Other earned benefits will probably be included in group compensation, but they are arbitrarily valued in normal times and become more artificial under new incentives. As to the supplements found in the social wage, these seem not only computationally difficult to locate and limit but because of their collective qualities, conceptually impossible to isolate. *Item*, while it is true that in an economy growing and known to grow at a steady rate, changes in the growth of wage scales are also changes in average hourly earnings, a near corollary is that the wage scales and average earnings rarely move in step. Again, the difference that is merely accidental without wage controls becomes an object of corporate policy and profit when the plan or the board appears.

Item, in the derivative features of these schemes of wage controls, prices of commodities and services are the end result of the tracker action the governing organist uses. Variations within a single name for a commodity or service may be literally infinite. While this may be of minor significance without the schemes, it is an inevitable attraction to higher profits *as soon as "names" become endogenous. Item*, and in the same style, wherever the schemes invite all to do voluntarily what economic incentives deny they should do, then clearly the gainers are those who most quickly realize the wicked are about to inherit *that* corner of the earth. *Item*, whenever the schemes discriminate amongst groups, then economic incentives are established to change membership from one group to another (firms reorganize, promotions are accelerated, people change jobs). *Item*, and finally, wherever the schemes succeed in holding relative prices or relative wages fixed, their effects on inflation and absolute prices interfere with substitution and dictate economic status. Over very extended periods – periods the plan asks for but in the real world will naturally not attain – social hierarchies would be fixed.

These are illustrative of any number of similar objections. I might turn now to the broader question (not necessarily more important question) of "relative shares". In the Lipsey address there is a good point of departure.

Wage rates are relatively insensitive to the cyclical emergence of excess supplies of labour. Downward inflexibility of money wages seemed a mystery to most of Keynes' critics. "Money illusions", they shouted ... Keynes used the correct hypothesis that there are many, many different kinds of labour ... [and] added the hypothesis ... relative wages are an important argument in the utility functions of wage earners.[33]

There is much surrounding argument in the address, and interesting references to supporting sources. Still, I think the heart of matters is already exposed and is anticipated or made use of in earlier statements by M. Kalecki, say, or Joan Robinson.[34] It is fair enough to be concerned here with the argument, whatever its source, "rather than what Keynes himself thought," but the Keynes of the aggregate supply and demand schedules seems to me sufficient for the main ideas, along with the Keynes of the somewhat casual remarks about the behaviour of workers.[35]

In the basic functions, capacity considerations and rising marginal prime plus user costs are captured by the aggregate supply function in its "wage unit" form. If aggregate demand increases, say, in intervals where the supply schedule is significantly rising, then as A. Asimakopulos has emphasized, events are better traced with the schedules in money form.[36] Workers who seek with some success to offset the experienced increase in the prices of wage goods will name higher wage rates – and the supply schedule rises. There has so far been a *single* inflationary fact (shown in prices and wages), but the enforced increase in wage rates now causes prices to rise again and inflation in the continuous sense is underway.

It seems to me that the all-important asymmetry is whether there are or are not unions, and as a matter of degree, whether the labour movement (locally or generally) is powerful in relation to employers. In an important sense, Weintraub was quite correct in saying that, at bottom, it is with the power of unions that wage controls must deal. If workers are in full competition with each other, if there is no organization explicit or customary, then any individual who seeks to recoup higher prices in higher wages will surrender his job or his hopes. "Rigidities" of any kind will find a place either in the shape of the aggregate supply schedule, the possible instability of the schedule, or its rate of displacement. Ratios of men to machines, markup formulae, cartel arrangements, all such affect the force of unionization in this construction, but they are additions to the single essential of the construction. The theory of wage controls, when connected to relative shares, amounts to diluting union power so that the upward shifting of the aggregate supply curve is slowed or stopped or even reversed. It is correct, I think, to regard the imposition of wage controls as the creation of a union, but with the peculiarities that the new union is the creature not of labour but of the state, that it chooses to exercise zero or negative power by the yardstick of a competitive situation, and that it regards *present* relativities of wages as just – they can be fairly perpetuated by this new or pseudo-union – and even that it regards the *future* relativities of wages to commodity prices as just. When Keynes takes note of the resistance of workers to wage decreases, which are seen as particular and disturbing to relativities, and their comparative inaction in relation to price increases that are general, he is observing basics of union behaviour: outside a labour movement there is no such phenomenon because there is no power to resist either variant.

Lipsey remarks guilelessly in support of Keynes that "every economist I know who first came back from an arbitration assignment finds himself accepting with more or less surprise and reluctance [that] relative wages are an important argument in the utility functions of wage earners."[37] He fails to distinguish wage earners and the labour movement and allows a variety of motives to appear without differentiation. A wage earner no doubt might be a simple or complex Paretian, rejoicing directly at the good fortune of some other wage earner, or rejoicing at the possibility that such good fortune is a portent of an improvement in his or her own situation. I do not see that in either case the worker outside of the labour movement affects market wages at all by a regard for relativities, wherever or if they appear in utility functions. Still, in an arbitration assignment one is likely to be encountering part of the labour movement, as contrasted with "wage earners." An economist who came back from providing union evidence to the tribunal would no doubt have noticed at least two goals that unions have in mind. The first is to improve the position of those who are union members as against those who are their employers or who are non-union members; and the second is, *caeteris paribus*, to reduce income differentials. These are certainly far from a complete catalogue of motives; they are not continuously in force; in some remote period, perhaps, they cannot be wholly successful and consistent both; but nonetheless they are routine guidelines within the labour movement when wage demands are prepared and are the more considered when demands are seen as breaking new ground. The enquiring economist who attends a few meetings within the labour movement will easily discover that the relativities of today are likely to measure *only* what has so far been accomplished and what remains to be accomplished. Few would be found to testify that they represent a tolerable final pattern of distribution, something to be perpetuated.

It seems to me that the significance of the relativities lies in quite another place. Knowledge of their existence, and defence of their levels against external control, are instruments by which the labour movement is able to act in a coordinated and purposeful way. From the relativities the movement, which in Canada is decentralized, partial and fragmented, can all the same create some sort of coherence in overall policy. Indeed, it is from the relativities that the movement extends its influence in some measure over quasi-unions and the large fraction of the working force outside the movement, and it achieves this influence even as it seeks to make the advantages of membership even larger. Lipsey observes that "Keynes used the correct hypothesis that there are many, many different kinds of labour selling services in many, many imperfectly linked labour markets."[38] He goes on to asymmetries in labour behaviour as to real wages that are altered by prices in general and those altered by the relativities of a wage rate; but he might have concluded, I think, that the concern for relativities is an obvious concern by labour about the ability of the movement to function in one or the other environment. Unions make use of the principle, and so do state anti-unions. So far as the execution of the program of the budget on wage controls had any economic logic, it seems to have been precisely of this kind. From a base in the public sector, the state anti-union will make use of preexisting relativities throughout the economy. The results of such programs, of course, if they were successful, would freeze relativities in amber.

In Barber and McCallum there is a thesis about "social consensus" that seems to me to have similar roots to the ideas associated with "relative shares." "The theme of their first chapter is that the rise of inflation in the

Seventies was a 'social consensus phenomenon'"[39] and they almost immediately ask "what determines the degree of social consensus?"[40] It seems to me there is a critical hiatus even here, for an economist can hardly avoid the fascinating question as to what *social consensus* is, not something at all obvious. Suppose we are in a Marshallian world of representative firms and representative consumers. All persons are alike but all are maximizers of personal fortune; consensus on anything but the existence of the state would seem to be nil. Suppose we are in a world of devout egalitarians. Consensus may be almost as complete as it is in Albania, but it is hardly a consensus that is matched by anything else in the real world. Consensus perhaps is generally experienced happiness, but then it seems to exist regardless of human *relationships*. It appears from the text that the scenes Barber and McCallum would judge as portraying consensus are those one might notice in social democratic states, in welfare states, in fully employed states.[41] It also appears that complementary scenes are those in which there is contentment about the distribution of incomes,[42] the settings which connect "social consensus" with the texts just discussed on distributive shares. In the upshot, though, "social consensus" is taken from the domain of philosophical meditation and made specific. "Long run strike activity [is] taken to be a proxy for social consensus" and more specifically still is a proxy counted by "days lost per 1,000 employees, 1950-69."[43]

It would be disproportionate to be especially critical of *this* use of a proxy variable simply because it is a proxy. The device seems to me suspect or at least redundant in most applications. Here I am troubled not only by the displacement of a qualitative conception by a quantitative conception but by the great range of images that the qualitative images invoke. We are left in the end with a number that does not seem close either to some single image or even to a kind of representative image. "Strike days lost per 1,000 employees," for better or worse, is given no extra depth, to my mind, by being vaguely connected with the poetry of consensus. (I certainly do not object to the earlier images of the welfare state and social democracy, but I would not be comfortable in trying to convince the skeptical that they translate numerically into the strike statistics.) When Barber and McCallum come to the concrete version of social consensus, they leave me wholly unconvinced that the numbers have anything like the same meaning throughout the countries and period in their sample, that their meaning from 1950-69 can typically be extrapolated, and (of course) that this homogeneity is not lost very rapidly as one moves from those references. The composition of the Canadian labour force is very different structurally now from what it was in 1960, and so is the structure of the Canadian labour movement. Strikes are uncommon for political purposes in the United States, say, as compared to strikes in France, and do not take the form of one day mass protests. Social consensus in its proxy form – outside the sample range – may well be as high in South Africa as in Sweden or in the Canada of the 1920s as the Canada of this decade. What is the idea that matches the proxy?

The area of dicussion Barber and McCallum have widened is well worth the work that has been invested. It can be agreed that the authors have been ingenious in attempting to contain their conclusions within their data. With that much conceded, I protest about the extensions of the results to anything so drastic in Canadian affairs as the creation of an anti-union, and an anti-union that could well be permanent, latently if not overtly, and interrupted quite as much by periodic administrative collapse as by concern over distribution. Social consensus that would freeze the distribution of the national dividend (and at second hand, the distribution of status) simply does not exist in Canada. Any enquiry of the leaders of the Canadian labour movement makes that clear. If one believes a social consensus could be reached and a social contract constructed by the voluntary choice of a more or less universal labour union, then whether the belief is naive or practical, one makes the voluntary choice the precondition of the social contract. The imposed union in Canada, as in Poland, is an anti-union. On this kind of choice the labour movement has long been clear that there are no neutrals: the tune is well known.[†]

WHETHER THERE IS A CASE TO MEET:
THE ANTI-INFLATION BOARD AND INFLATION

It had seemed to me until recently that there was really no case to meet on the question of wage controls and their *publicly declared* purpose of curing, or making a substantial contribution to the cure of, a Canadian inflation that is sizeable and protracted. The experience with the Anti-inflation Board had been a test case of a reasonably representative kind and had been generally judged to have had negligible or at most exceedingly modest consequences in relation to "declared purpose." Such consequences could not begin to balance the administrative costs, social costs, and their cumulation over time. Publicly declared purpose may be the guise rather different purposes would take, such as the advance of political fortunes for one party or another, or the gift of an opiate, or the deliberate alteration of the social structure. References abound on the suspicion that such disguised purposes have in fact animated the political adventures from the Prices and Incomes Commission to the budget of June last. It is only with the publicly declared purposes, however, that the economic critic presumably should be concerned, for the hidden purposes are of interest only so long, so to speak, as they are successfully hidden. They do not stand inspection in day light.

[†] "They say in Harlan County / There are no neutrals there; / You'll either be a union man / Or a thug for J.H. Blair." From "Which Side are You On?", a song that originated during a miners' strike in Harlan County, Kentucky.

R.W. Crowley had written in the autumn of 1981[44] that "there appear to be few long-term effects [on the structure of collective bargaining] other than a dampening of wage (and perhaps price) levels. And even that may be temporary." Lipsey in the cited address remarks matter of factly that "the AIB had some modest restraining effect on wages, but that prices did not fully follow wages is a good example of Lucas' warning that the empirical relations of one policy regime cannot be expected to stand up under another policy regime."[45] Lipsey also cites his judgement of 1976 about "more evidence of some modest restraining effect on wages than on prices, and thus that incomes policies may sometimes be more effective in redistributing incomes from wages to profits than in restraining price inflation."

In their often cited study the "Guelph" group of D.A.L. Auld, L.N. Christofides, *et al.* found that "the cumulative wage effect [for its first two years] of the AIB is on the order of 3.2 per cent in the private and 4.6 per cent in the public sector" but in their "summary and conclusions" they do not venture a word about consequences for general inflation. "While the wage effects of the AIB appear fairly clear, the crucial issue is whether these restraining effects will persist or reverse themselves in the post AIB period."[46] F. Reid, similarly cited, studies the full period and finds similar effects on wages. "The reduction in wage settlements estimated in the present paper is of very substantial magnitude." He observed, on what seems to me *the* question, that it is obviously of crucial policy importance to assess also the impact of the Canadian controls program on the expectations equation and the price equation, but he remarks that unfortunately very little rigorous research on these topics has yet been done. "It is fairly clear that the substantial reduction of inflation during the first year of controls and the subsequent rise in inflation during the second and third years of controls were due primarily to this cyclical behaviour of food prices rather than the effect of controls." As recently as last summer, D. Wilton (of the Guelph group, but now at Waterloo) summarized from a very informal model that if the AIB is judged in terms of prices it was trying to control (the CPI excluding food and energy), the underlying inflation rate was significantly lowered during the life of the AIB from 10% to about 6%. Unfortunately (exogenous) food price increases and the government's phased-in energy price increases

shocked this underlying inflation rate (CPI less food and energy) by almost three additional points during the AIB period ... Since the raison d'être of the AIB was to 'reduce inflationary expectations' and lower the long run inflation rate, the AIB obviously failed to achieve its major objective. Even if the AIB may have won the battle on the wage front, it lost the war against inflation expectations.[47]

If such a summary is representative, as seemed to me plausible, the argument about *publicly declared* purpose was over. Wage controls would be part of another domain, a roundabout way of attacking public waste or public services or both, a constraint on unions as such, a beginning with supply side economics, or the creation of a scapegoat for economic distress.

Had the evidence been otherwise, one would still not, of course, have accepted wage controls as being worth their price, which is the subversion of the labour movement. The search for other remedies would have to go on, and in the meantime as much of the hardship inflicted by inflation – erratic inflation particularly – would be erased in as compensatory way as possible. Others, though, might have weighed both factors and come to a different estimate. Now Barber and McCallum claim unequivocally there is evidence of a strong effect from the controls of the Anti-inflation Board. "The difference between the actual and forecast change in inflation between 1975 and 1978 is 6.3 percentage points and this amount may be attributed to the impact of the Anti-inflation Board."[48] A little later they remark that

as was made clear above, the AIB had a substantial effect on price inflation. This result, which is new to the literature, contradicts the view that controls affected wages but not prices. Our results suggest a reduction in price inflation of about two percentage points in each year of the controls program, an amount equal to the official target reductions of two percentage points per year and quite close to the existing estimates of the effects of the AIB on wages.[49]

How one should interpret that earlier literature is perhaps not *that* clear cut, as the preceding paragraphs show. P. Fortin, for one, cites the items I have mentioned and others to the effect that "all of the studies of the effectiveness of controls have arrived at the conclusion that controls did help wind down inflation and that there has been no post-control rebound" – "controls shaved about 1–1.5 percentage pt/year off the inflation rate."[50] Still, 6 percentage points is higher than 4.5 percentage points and double 3 percentage points! If Barber and McCallum are correct, one's impression of *this* aspect of the program was mistaken, and there *is* a case to meet.

So far I have had time to consider the text only on its internal evidence. [The results of these considerations are contained in Appendix A below.]

ADJOURNMENT

A paper is composed at a certain date. After the text above was written there remained the obvious task of replicating the Barber and McCallum numbers and further testing their results. My skepticism has been increased in this first run, but there are factual questions certainly still open. They are opened still further by materials received from J. Helliwell (his own work) and from C. Archibald, but received after the event (though Helliwell's results had been available since the "annual" meetings). Helliwell in particular finds a sizeable anti-inflationary effect for the AIB from a general model, though an effect that would seem to call for repeated AIBs to be sustained. The late statistical news is therefore stronger than I expected, and will no doubt require review on all sides to see just how strong. This text is adjourned as of 30 September 1982.

APPENDIX A

The narrative relied on is abbreviated, the underlying equations are not much elaborated and are set out in language that may not have been correctly edited. Raw data are not given. Further, there are references to earlier work by the authors that would no doubt help in interpretation of this piece. I know very well it will be easy to get the "externals" from the authors, but that will have to wait. As to the internal evidence I asked for advice, especially on the econometric technique and especially from my colleagues, Robin Rowley and L. Soderstrom. Attributions follow in the usual way, and responsibility for the reading and use of the advice is naturally mine.

Let me recite the sources of the "estimated equation" using $G(X)$ to mean the annual rate of growth of X and a series of subscripts to distinguish the several indices of price that the equation contains, thus, F to identify food; $\sim$F to identify the variable for anything *but* food; E for energy; and M for imports. An asterisk shows an expectation and -1 subscripts a lagged value. $G(W)$ is wage inflation; $G(\$)$ is the rate of growth of the monetary stock; $G(Y/L)$ is the rate of growth of real productivity per person employed; and U is a kind of involuntary unemployment, thus, the excess of actual over equilibrium unemployment rates.[†] There is a price equation, a wage equation and an expectational equation.[50]

$$G(P_{\sim F}) = G(W) - G(Y/L) + \alpha_0 G(P_M/P_{\sim F}) + \alpha_1 G(P_E/P_{\sim E})$$

$$G(W) = \beta_0 + G^*(P) + \beta_1 G(Y/L) + \beta_2 U$$

$$G^*(P) = \delta_0 G(P_{-1}) + (1 - \delta_0)G(\$)$$

δ_0 is now set at unity ("confirmed by empirical tests") and the expectational equation is replaced effectively – something must be wrong in the editing! – by $G^*(P) = G(P_{-1})$.

Further, β_0 is provided with a value by supposing that in "the long run" there is a "long run productivity growth," already known, identified by, say $G^{LR}(Y/L)$, and U will be zero. Then $G(W) - G^*(P)$ will equal $G(W) - G(P)$, and $G(Y/L)$ in turn will equal $G^{LR}(Y/L)$. Thus, whatever these "long run" adjectives mean, $\beta_0 = (1 - \beta_1) G^{LR}(Y/L)$.

---

† [In Barber and McCallum this is the difference between the actual and the "natural" unemployment rates.]

Substitution from bottom to top gives

$$G(P_{\sim F}) = (1 - \beta_1)[G^{LR}(Y/L) - G(Y/L)] - G(P_{-1}) + \beta_2 U$$
$$+ \alpha_0 G(P_M/P_{\sim F}) + \alpha_1 G(P_E/P_{\sim E})$$

or in a further stage, from $G(P_{-1})$ approximated by

$$\alpha_2 G(P_{F-1}) + (1 - \alpha_2)G(P_{\sim F-1}),$$

$$G(P_{\sim F}) = G(P_{\sim F-1}) + (1 - \beta_1)[G^{LR}(Y/L) - G(Y/L)] +$$
$$\beta_2 U + \alpha_0 G(P_M/P_{\sim F}) + \alpha_1 G(P_E/P_{\sim E})$$
$$+ \alpha_2 G(P_F/P_{\sim F-1}).$$

In fitting the estimated equation to 1957–81, with the Gs in percentage points, β_1 acquires a value of 0.86; β_2 a value of –0.36, α_0 a value of 0.05, α_1 a value of 0.14, and α_2 a value of 0.12. A dummy for the control years of 1976, 1977, and 1978 acquires the critical coefficient of –1.85 and a second dummy for the "bubble" year 1979 acquires a value of –1.27. The equation as in fact fitted differs, apparently, from the equation of theory: an intercept appears with the value of 0.38.

On the methodological side, Rowley points out that (as the text stands) the dependent variable has been allowed to appear on both sides of the equation, assuring bias and affecting all coefficients and their reliability. He remarks on the unlikely method of forming expectations about a series that has risen for several years, and yet is expected to stand still (though the text and the equation seem to be saying different things where this difficulty arises).[51] α_2 can hardly be a constant over time. β_0 could have been allowed to find its own value, but is eliminated via a strange "long run productivity growth." As far as I can see, the "long run" of the model has at least four different meanings under the same frame, thus, distant in time, hypothetical equilibrium here and now, an *ex post* historical adjective, and *ex ante* logical tendencies.

Robin Rowley also emphasizes the introduction of the constant in the estimated equation: accelerated inflation is built into the prophesies. Soderstrom draws attention to the specification of the wage equation and the extraordinarily high coefficient linking $G(W)$ to productivity (the 0.86 which would transfer almost all growth in productivity at once to growth in wages). He draws my attention to (*e.g.*) work from what I called before the Guelph group who – assisted by the Anti-inflation Board – report that "in *all* cases the profit and productivity variables enter the wage equation with a *negative* but typically insignificant effect."[52] Sparks and Wilton, for another example, fail to pick up anything like the productivity effect on the wage equation implicit in Barber and McCallum.[53] S. Ingerman added the point, that comes from much of his own work, that the productivity variable

is suspect from almost every point of view (railway negotiations are illu-
minating as to how rich *that* menu of ambiguities is!). Computations based
on an interval where "real GNP per person employed" has a rapidly changing
meaning – the participation of women, of part-time workers, the growth of
service industries – are on the face of it unconvincing. It is not surprising
these difficulties appear, for the basic price equation is close to the Wein-
traubian form for Canada, that is, an equation with imports included, and
then the fact of energy inflation added. The wage and expectational equations
combine to fill the markup role. Perhaps one should then add the point that
it seems misleading to date the Anti-inflation Board as an economic force
with the exact period of its legal existence. The predictive equation had
surely begun to go wrong for many months before the AIB could have
influenced anything, and it surely should not have continued to go nearly
as wrong in the final year when its disintegration was promised.

NOTES AND REFERENCES

1 See S. Weintraub, "A Prices and Incomes Policy," in D. Crane, ed., *Beyond
the Monetarists* (Ottawa: Canadian Institute for Economic Policy, 1981), 86. I
shall cite the pagination of the paper as delivered rather than as reprinted.

2 It is, of course, legitimate to explore a part only of this or any other policy,
but then there is the problem of clarity in reporting the scope of advice and
the problem of disproportion.

3 *See* Richard Lipsey, "The Understanding and Control of Inflation," *Canadian
Journal of Economics* (November 1981), 569.

4 John Stuart Mill, *Principles of Political Economy*, 8th ed. (London: Long-
mans, 1878), Vol. 2, book 5, chapter 2, 393. Mill is cited in context: his
concerns are about spurious accuracy in weighing taxation.

5 S. Weintraub, *Capitalism's Inflation and Unemployment Crisis* (Don Mills,
Ont.: Addison Wesley, 1978). This text is connected with the U.S. economy;
from it comes the much briefer variant on the Canadian economy, cited in
note 1 above.

6 See the principal proposals discussed below; also, for example, see the entire
edition of *Canadian Taxation* (summer 1981).

7 Weintraub, "Prices and Incomes Policy," 5ff; Weintraub, *Capitalism's Inflation*, 44ff.

8 Weintraub, *Capitalism's Inflation*, 124.

9 Weintraub, "Prices and Incomes Policy," 15.

10 Lipsey, "Understanding and Control of Inflation," 570.

11 Clarence Barber and John McCallum, *Controlling Inflation: Learning from
Experience in Canada, Europe and Japan* (Ottawa: Canadian Institute for
Economic Policy, 1982), 40–1.

12 Weintraub, "Prices and Incomes Policy," 15.

13 Ibid.

14 Weintraub, *Capitalism's Inflation*, 129.

15 Ibid. For most of these points, either the Canadian version of the evolution of the plan could be cited or the parent conception from the United States. More importantly, the difficulties that Weintraub seeks to overcome might be approached from other directions than he suggests. But, as he correctly sees, they must be approached from *some* direction. "Cure" and problem, once in place, continue to coexist for the life of the project.

16 Weintraub, *Capitalism's Inflation*, 130.

17 Ibid., 131.

18 Ibid., 133.

19 Weintraub, "Prices and Incomes Policy," 14–15.

20 Weintraub, *Capitalism's Inflation*, 135–6.

21 Ibid., 140. This is in the text for the U.S. version. Where the boundary might be reached in Canada would be presumably at still smaller enterprises.

22 Ibid., 141.

23 Ibid., 142.

24 Barber and McCallum, *Controlling Inflation*, 100.

25 Ibid., 109. Reflect on the significance of these admissions!

26 Ibid., 101.

27 Ibid., 101*ff*. Within Keynes, the guarantee would be a contradiction.

28 The problem is that Barber and McCallum point to two opposed programs as though one did not have to choose between them. The anti-union of an anti-inflation board and the federal budget of 28 June are contradictory of free, widely based trade unions of the kind that might be able to enter into a social contract. I am uncertain still of the practicalities of social contracts, but I would find the thrust of the book much different if the asides on social contracts were required preconditions for the rest of the argument. Still, Barber and McCallum at least *speak* to the issue, albeit briefly.

29 All quotations in this paragraph come from the *Financial Post*. The somewhat cryptic quality comes from the tabular method that the *Post* reasonably decided to use.

30 Borrowed from D.A. Wilton, "The Case for Controls," *Canadian Taxation* (summer 1981), 62.

31 There are more elaborate and more complete histories, of course, although in all cases I have seen, they are of a narrative or episodic kind. My own reaction to the record of improvisation is that Weintraub, if anything, understated the problem of cumulation, except in the sense that *rational* response to difficulties in practice has a lower weight than he demands.

32 Or perhaps not: the improvisations of the Anti-inflation Act casually set aside a long and intricate evolution by which labour relations in the railways had at last been given a coherent form. On the one hand, the range over which collective bargaining in this pace-setting industry had been constrained from both

sides promised coherence for the future. On the other hand, developments *via* the imaginative Hall formula might well have been a pattern for many other industries. All of this was wasted overnight.

33 Lipsey, "Understanding and Control of Inflation," 522.

34 I was a little surprised to find neither referred to on issues that they seem to have written about with some authority and in close harmony with some of Lipsey's themes.

35 The key passages seem to be those of chapter 2, section 3, of Keynes's *General Theory*. Keynes has a more or less competitive labour market as particular arguments need more or less competition. The labour movement is fragmented, or else it would bargain in real terms (which, fragmented or not, it often seems to do). It is far from wholly competitive or there would be no groups whose concern about relative wages has any practical consequences. Certainly, *this* asymmetry is required: that substantial union power exists.

36 Aggregate supply (chapter 3) can be read as connecting employment to either "aggregate supply price" in money or to money divided by the wage unit. In meditating on inflation, the first is clearly better. For further ideas on the aggregate supply schedule of Keynes, see A. Asimakopulos, "Keynes' Theory of Effective Demand Revisited," *Australian Economic Papers* (June 1982).

37 Lipsey, "Understanding and Control of Inflation," 552–3.

38 Ibid., 552.

39 Barber and McCallum, *Controlling Inflation*, 1.

40 Ibid.

41 Ibid., ca. p. 11.

42 Ibid., 11*ff.*

43 Ibid., 8.

44 R.W. Crowley, "Income Control Policies," *Canadian Public Policy* (autumn 1981), 546.

45 Lipsey, "Understanding and Control of Inflation," 569.

46 L.M. Christofides *et al.*, "The Impact of the Anti-inflation Board on Negotiated Wage Settlements," *Canadian Journal of Economics* (May 1979).

47 D.A. Wilton, "The Case for Wage-price Controls," *Canadian Taxation* (summer 1981), 66.

48 Barber and McCallum, *Controlling Inflation*, 21.

49 Ibid., 25.

50 Ibid., 117.

51 Ibid. Compare the successive definitional statements.

52 L.M. Christofides *et al.*, "A Microeconomic Analysis of Spillovers within the Canadian Wage Determination Process," *Review of Economics and Statistics* (May 1980), 213*ff.*

53 G.R. Sparks and D.A. Wilton, "Determinants of Negotiated Wage Increases: An Empirical Analysis," *Econometrics* 39(5): 739–50.

CHAPTER TEN

On Private Plans in
the Theory of Pensions*

INTRODUCTION

In an earlier paper we set out a simple theory of government pensions, illustrated by an account of some of the features of the Canadian pension system.[1] Here we would like to extend that conceptual framework, adding private pensions to the theoretical structure and connecting both government and private pensions to savings. The models used are highly stylized, and are not intended *to describe* pension arrangements either as they are or as they should be. Our purpose is rather to identify what seem to us the essential abstractions in an economic system where the generations are linked, where the future can only be dealt with conditionally, and where savings have a collective as well as an individual basis.

The sequence of the argument is as follows. We begin with definitions and vocabulary, sketching the conception we have of the problem, descriptively and in an institutional setting. To formalize this outline, we set up various simple models, and in particular, basic "pure private" and "pure government" pension systems and a combined superimposing government on private plans, though only for a population of the self-employed. We then go on to a world where there are employers, and where firms, governments and other organizations have their own pension plans. The theme that emerges is that the employer-employee relationship can introduce substantial government-like elements into private plans. We conclude by relating the theoretical material to a few issues of a practical kind, and in particular to the ambiguous role of public policy in relation to these employer transfers.

* We would like to acknowledge a grant from the Canada Council which has helped us prepare this paper. This is a revised version of a paper read at the annual meetings of the Canadian Economics Association at York University in June 1969.

With A. Asimakopulos. Reprinted with permission from the *Canadian Journal of Economics* 3(2): 223–37.

PENSIONS: DEFINITIONS AND SETTING

Pensions are payments made to individuals either because they have reached a certain age and have retired from the labour force or from a particular job, or simply because they have reached a certain age. These payments may be the result of governmental action (e.g., the Old Age Security Act, the Canada and Quebec Pension Plans), or of a pension plan at the individual's place of work (e.g., the General Motors Company), or of the individual's own action (e.g., the purchase of annuities through a life insurance policy, or through contributions to a Registered Retirement Savings Plan). Any given individual might receive payments from plans which fall under each of these categories.

Pension payments must be based either on the prior accumulation of savings or on the transfer of the command over resources between generations, or on some combination of these elements. It is useful in examining actual pension plans and in considering the theory of pensions to define two "pure" types of plan which, we argue, alone or in combination contain the essential features of all plans. By a "pure government" pension plan we mean a scheme whereby government exercises its command over goods to provide income for pensioners and instructs successor governments on the rules to be used in determining future pensions. By a "pure private" pension plan we mean a scheme in which payments come only from capital that has bee specifically accumulated, in one form or another, by or on behalf of an individual. The definitions are based on the differences between social and individual methods of providing pensions. Government has the power to tax and use the revenue for pensions, while an individual can, on his own, provide for his retirement only through savings built up during his working life.[2]

A pure government pension arises from the application (perhaps implicit) of a social welfare function to the consumption possibilities open to the workers and the retired. The distribution of the command over goods of individuals in these two groups, in the absence of government pensions, has been judged by the community to be inappropriate, and transfers are used to produce a more equitable distribution. The social welfare function may have various forms, e.g., its only concern with the consumption of the aged might be that they have at least some minimum "subsistence" level of command over goods, or it might, say, provide additional payments to the retired related to the earnings of similar types of workers presently active. No matter how complex the social welfare function employed by government in determining pensions, the basic principle of the pure plan is that the payments are tranfers.

Actual government pension plans, which we construe to include *all* the legislation associated with the introduction of government pensions, may also be designed to produce savings, at least for some considerable period of time. Planned savings might be forthcoming from a government pension plan because of government's direct concern with the level of total or public saving, but also because of its concern to increase the likelihood of projected pension benefits being paid by future governments. The two motives are not incompatible, but can usefully be considered separately.

Private savings might be either raised or lowered by the introduction of a government pension plan. Theoretical arguments can be marshalled in both directions. If an individual were assured of a government pension he would only save for his retirement enough to make up for the difference between his desired pension level and the benefits from the government plan and his saving would be correspondingly less. Where, however, individual foresight is limited and the desired level of pension is a vague and remote concept to the individual making his consumption decisions, the effect of a government plan on saving might be much less than complete information would determine. Indeed, a negligible effect on saving could be expected if the pension provided was of the minimum subsistence variety and the scope for individual discretionary saving on the part of a large proportion of workers was small. Further, the implementation of a government pension scheme might bring a reasonable degree of financial independence during retirement within reach of individuals and act as a stimulus to increase personal saving to make this possibility a reality.[3] But even if personal saving is increased, private saving as a whole may be reduced if the government pension plan replaces employer pension plans. As a group, employer plans are important contributors to private saving. The larger the government pensions, the greater the probability that they decrease private plans and thus private saving. If an unchanged level of total saving is a matter of public policy the government pension plan must then itself produce savings.

Savings to help cover the cost of pension promises increase the likelihood of the promises being met. If the savings are used productively, then the proportion of income needed for a give level of support of the retired will be correspondingly less. Government, looking to the interests of its workers, will thus have a concern for the restraint under which its successor governments must operate. It will be remembered how much attention was given to the impact of the Canada Pension Plan upon total saving in the economic analysis that came from the Department of Finance.[4]

It is to be emphasized, though, that the savings produced by such government pension plans as that of the U.S. Social Security system and the Canada and Quebec Pension Plans are much less than those required to cover the full cost of the promised pensions. Not only does the accumulation of pension funds cease in the not too remote future, but in the years thereafter, the funds will be exhausted by the promised pension payments unless the premium rates are increased. For example, the maximum accumulation of funds under the Canada and Quebec Pension Plans is expected to occur sometime in the mid-1980s, and then, with the present rate of premiums and the stipulated payment schedule, the funds will be exhausted sometime in the late 1990s, i.e., twenty to twenty-five years after the plans reach maturity. [5] The continuation of these programmes is thus dependent on future governments levying a higher rate of tax on their workers' real incomes than today's workers pay, in order to honour the commitment made by today's government. Actuarial studies of government pension plans are often no more than estimates of the contribution rates required to fulfill the provisions of the plans under hypothetical changes in earnings and population. Whether future governments will accept the contribution rates required to pay the promised pensions in the light of actual events is another matter. Government has many resources – the inflation it allows, for example – to change the significance of past promises without repudiating their form.

PRIVATE AND GOVERNMENT PENSIONS IN BASIC FORM

For all the formal constructions in this paper a very simple setting is assumed. People work for half their lives, as employers or employees or as self-employed persons, and then retire, and subject to this life cycle are identical in tastes and abilities. Their tastes relate to a single consumption good, and (for workers) show their pattern of time preference between present and future consumption. There are no bequests or other familial ties: whatever is available in retirement is consumed. People know the parameters of the economy as it now is, and in particular know population structure and technology, but while they may estimate what these parameters will be in future, do not judge that for generation intervals they can be estimated at all closely. Part of this setting is essential to our conception of the pension problem, but for the rest, as we attempted to show in the earlier paper, is straightforward. There is no special difficulty, for example, in dealing with a varied population and with more detailed life cycles.

In this context the polar case for private pensions is to be found in the community of one person. Robinson Crusoe must be allowed a storable consumption good if he is to eat in retirement, and if it is storable and nothing more, his pension calculation consists simply of saving during his working years whatever capital for retirement his time-preference dictates. A real rate of return, plus or minus, complicates his arithmetic, but, subject to any uncertainty he may have about the rate, leaves its essentials unchanged. [6] Deliberate saving for retirement by the individual, invested according to the known technology of the period, and leading to a pension wholly determined by what the savings produce, these are the basic features of the "pure private" pension plan.

A community of persons, some belonging to the one generation, some to the other, but all relying on private arrangements and all, in their working lives, being self-employed, would merely multiply the result for the individual. With a real rate of return there might be borrowing and lending and a market for savings, but the result would still be within the domain of the pure, private plan. Everyone is self-employed, and must rely in retirement entirely on what his own savings provide, regardless of the standard of living of workers or of other pensioners.

Given this setting for the pure private plan, the convenient source for a pure government plan is the world of non-storable goods, for there Robinson Crusoe could do nothing for his retirement, and even a community of the self-employed could not as individuals provide themselves pensions in a two-generation model. Whatever the distribution of present and future goods workers might want, the goods they produce do not keep, and there is no one to whom they can supply present goods in exchange for the realizable promise of future goods. The point of this as a polar case is that pensions can only come from government (and could not come very easily from other sources even if the self-employment and two-generation[7] assumptions were dropped).

Collectively, though, the community can tax its workers to provide pensions for those who are retired. Given equal treatment of equal persons, the possibilities are contained in the relation

$$(1) \qquad c^R = (a - c^L) \, L \, / \, R,$$

where c^R and c^L are the per capita consumption of the R pensioners and L workers, and where the transfer c^R to the pensioner is the counterpart of the tax $(a - c^L)$ on the average product a of the workers. A public pension plan, in pure form, here consists of the rules or conventions – the pension "law" – by which the community chooses one of the possibilities in equation 1.

The rationale of the collective choice is, of course, quite different in kind from the simple maximization of the private plan. The view we take of government is that it is the present population acting only in its own collective interests, giving place period by period to the successor governments of the changing population. All that government can do with certainty of the outcome is to tax its workers for the direct benefit of its own pensioners, but it of course wishes a *quid pro quo* for its workers so that they too will have pensions. Pension law thus has this further quality, that it attempts to influence and give instructions to the successor government on behalf of today's workers in their retirement. The overlapping membership of successive governments, and the interest each government has in the actions of its successor, links pension policy from generation to generation.

For government to issue real bonds[8] to its workers, or to propose future pensions in some equivalently fixed real form, would in general prove either miserly in relation to the living standards of the next generation, or notably burdensome to that generation's workers. Prediction attempted over the period relevant to pensions would often lead to real promises that were wildly inappropriate. The nature of the pension law proper, as we see it, is a set of instructions expressed in conditional terms. A basic form for the present system is

(2) $U^S = U^S(c^L, c^R, L/R)$,

where U^S expresses the preferences this government has, and wishes its successor to follow, for the various combinations of workers' and pensioners' living standards, all as a function of the basic pension parameter, L/R, the population structure. The social welfare function of equation 2 set against the range of possibilities of equation 1 determines what government does about its own taxes and transfers, and contains the advice it passes to its successor about the pensions that should be paid in the circumstances that obtain a generation later. Government has no determining power in the future, but it proposes that its successor apply the same conditional function to the facts that eventually appear. Governments, therefore, are identified by a sequence of overlapping social welfare functions based on, and only on, the consumption of the individual workers and pensioners.[9]

Here as anywhere else the choice of a social welfare function is finally normative rather than positive in kind. Nonetheless there is some point to assessing alternatives, for we are judging what to postulate behaviourally in a model that links generations together; the problem seems fundamental in any system where the existence of generations is recognized.[10] In our earlier article we thought a formula of Lerner's was worth special attention. Government, in effect, looks to the workers' preference function, and then imposes the level of taxes the workers themselves would choose if they were exactly assured of the pensions their taxes now provide. Put more formally, when L/R is unity, the function 2 is identified with the workers' preference function $U^L = U^L(c^L, c^R + 1)$ – where $c^R + 1$ is a worker's consumption one period hence in retirement – so that the social marginal rate of substitution between a pensioner's income and a worker's income equals the private rate of substitution the worker has between future and present goods. For other values of the parameter L/R the social rate is changed in proportion to the parameter, the point being to reflect the numbers enjoying the two levels of consumption.[11]

As with all possibilities for function 2, this formula makes only a conditional prediction of the future. It is neutral as between equals, and uses such information as there is about inter-temporal tastes. Seen as a basis for a continuity of policy that links the generations it has a kind of familial quality. Changes in population structure and technology affect what can be paid to the retired, and can only be roughly foreseen, but the pensioner has his standard of living adapted to community standards as they now are, and

adapted also to time-preference and retirement needs as the community
assesses these things. The public authority can be seen as basing its policy
on the continuity the family provided in simpler societies.

THE PURE CASES COMBINED

In combining pure cases, but still holding to the assumption that everyone
is self-employed, we must accept as essential one feature of the private plan,
that is, the existence of capital even if it is in only so simple a form as
storable consumption goods. If we look at an economy after a certain capital
has been accumulated under private arrangements, and imagine government
now super-imposing a public plan on the system, then its choice must be
made from an extended version of equation 1 thus,

$$(3) \qquad c^R = (a - c^L)(L/R) - S/R,$$

where S is aggregate saving measured in the single good the economy
possesses, and where there is no imputed distribution made between factors.
a will have been determined by the history of the system, but neither the
distribution nor the amount of S will have been similarly pre-determined.
If we suppose that S is determinable by government, at whatever of its
technically possible values government chooses, then pension law in the
combined system can be given the same form as in the basic public system.
Government determines S and then applies the social welfare function (2)
that it has named or inherited to the extended possibilities of equation 3,
and proposes to its successor that today's workers get their pensions on the
same basis.

It is clear, though, that rather more has to be said about the determination
of S, both as to government's power to ensure its total and as to the effect
a given choice will have on the linking of policy between generations. Within
the present framework there is no difficulty on the first point. To those in
the private sector the environment is taken as given, and they respond in
their saving decisions to a government plan that as individuals they cannot
affect. Since the taxes imposed are lump-sum – imposed at such and such
a level on everyone in a given generation[12] – government could predict with
certainty the effect of its decisions on savings provided that people knew
the real rate of return on their savings and that government's pension promises had the form of real bonds. The promises instead have the conditional
form of equation 2 above, and there is some uncertainty about the real rate
of return, so government is not able to make a precise forecast of the
repercussions from its plan on private saving. Still, having made its initial
estimate, it is able to adjust from year to year to whatever experience shows
real repercussions to be. Government, then, can reasonably be assumed to
make the total of saving, after its plan has been introduced, whatever it

wants it to be (within the range of the possibilities that are technically open to it).

Once again the question arises as to what rationale there can be to the choice of total saving in the government pension plan. Those constituting today's government would in principle have no objection to saving being low today and low again tomorrow, except for the consequences they might fear from today's low saving on tomorrow's productivity. They could not be confident of persuading successor governments to continue the pension law if the law embodied deliberately low saving and even if the law were continued their workers' pensions would be reduced by the low productivity associated with the low saving. Saving at high levels would certainly displease today's pensioners no matter how agreeable their effects would be to the successor government, and so again would not be a likely basis for policy. In the pure consumption good model only the distribution and not the amount of output is affected by the government pension plan. A saving rule that would lead to the same result would require government to act to produce aggregate saving equal to whatever would have been saved without the public plan, in this sense committing itself to neutrality in relation to the capital the next generation has to work with: each generation passes on the stocks and productive possibilities that would have existed without the pension transfers.

The saving decisions of government need not have the special form just discussed. They may, for example, be partly based on a desire to increase the rate of economic growth, but to be a consistent part of public pension policy must have the same conditional quality as the social welfare function 2.[13] Government causes aggregate saving to be what it is because of present circumstances, and would have made it something else in a known way in other circumstances. The saving rule may be very simple, as the neutrality rule is, or as it would be if government chose some named fraction of national income or some pattern of growth derived from a given ratio of saving to the market value of capital, but it is clear from the fact that saving appears in schedule 3 that the conditions on which it is based are an essential part of a complete pension system. To say, though that aggregate saving at any time is included in the logic of the government pension plan does not suggest any special distribution of total saving between private and public uses. There are all sorts of reasons that lie outside the discussion of pensions why government might want to change the proportion between public and private saving, for example, government's view of its entrepreneurial function and the changing weight it may give to public goods.

EMPLOYER PENSION PLANS

The systems we have been considering here have combined government and private pension arrangements, but still have relied on the convenient assumption that all workers are self-employed. The existence of employer pension plans should now be taken into account. An employer may be an individual, a partnership, an unincorporated or incorporated firm, an institution, or government itself or its agencies. This employing entity may have a formal or informal arrangement to provide pensions for its employees, and since it derives revenues from its economic activities or its institutional position, which may continue even when a given employee has retired, it will often be able to pay pensions irrespective of whether savings have been put specifically aside for this purpose. The question that naturally arises is whether anything fundamentally new is added, or whether the complicated arrangements of employer plans can be resolved into the same components defined by the pure government and pure private plans. We conclude that the resolution into the simpler forms is always possible and that the earlier analysis covers the essentials of the multitude of employer-employee arrangements. The point is not to show that the categories of savings based pensions and transfer based pensions are indeed exhaustive, as by definition they of course must be, but to show that the pure plans are the appropriate units for the discussion of all plans.

There is a matter of vocabulary. If we identify the employer-employee relationship with purely economic motivations, then the pensions paid as a result of employer plans must be reckoned as deferred dollar payments and must be related to specific services performed at some time in the past. An employer may pay for services performed today wholly in today's dollars. He may also pay in part by pension promises, the source of the eventual deferred dollar payments. Notice, though, that pension promises may be made *at any time in the interval* between the performance of the services to which they are related and the deferred payments in dollars. Compensation paid currently for services may in the event prove incomplete, as it does for example, when an employer pension plan picks up back service or improves benefits retroactively.

The pension promises, whenever they are made and whatever their form, may be fully funded or may be funded only in part or not at all. The conception of funding is based upon the present value of pension promises, as near as the value can be estimated, and the proportion of that value placed in the control of some third party to redeem the promises. It may be that pension promises simply assure whatever a certain sum today will eventually buy, or it may be that they are specified by various conditions the eventual deferred payments will satisfy, for example, that pensions will be related to salary at retirement. We can thus speak of formula and non-formula plans, noting that the problem of estimating present values (often for possibilities inherently difficult to estimate) distinguishes the formula plans, but noting also that with non-formula plans the forecasting problem is transferred to the pensioner-to-be, at least insofar as he sees his pension needs in formula terms.[14] Formula plans are often funded, but are also often unfunded or only partly funded. Where there is commitment to full or partial funding, the difficulty of estimation is likely to be recognized, and provision made to fund in relation both to obligations as they occur and to adjustments (plus or minus) for earlier forecasts that are now seen to need change.

With this usage in mind we can take up the main theme, the relation of employer plans to the elementary systems. An employer pension plan provides a worker covered by the plan with a "claim" to a pension. This is a personal, non-transferable claim[15] which can only be exercised following provisions contained in the plan. There are often legal restraints on the operations of employer pension plans, and government legislation[16] has tended to limit the extent to which these plans (in the private sector at least) can issue pension claims without at the same time setting aside funds to cover their expected cost. In what follows, though, we abstract from such restraints.

A fully funded employer pension plan is one in which sufficient assets have been accumulated in a fund, which can only be tapped by pension claims, to enable all estimated benefits for service up to the present to be exactly met as they become due. A *money purchase plan*, where a worker's pension claims are simply the accumulated amount built up by the contributions made on his behalf, is by definition a fully funded plan. Since the benefits provided by fully funded plans are paid for by the savings set aside for this purpose they are similar to a pure private plan except insofar as they produce transfers when pension promises are made for services from some earlier period, so-called back-service. In formula pension plans, where the pension claims are normally based on some combination of years of service and average earnings over a specified period of years, an absence of complete funding is possible. In the first place the estimates of the cost of the pensions earned in any period, which are dependent on the earnings profile of the individual during his working life with the organization and on the rates of return obtained by the pension fund's assets, are subject to error. Lack of full funding may therefore be simply the result of miscalculation. A more important possibility, though, is where the lack of funding goes beyond the results of miscalculation, and is based upon the special economic circumstances that allow certain categories of employer not to fund as a matter of policy.

A completely unfunded plan, a "pay-as-you-go" scheme, where pensions for past services are paid for out of current revenues of the employer, may easily lead to transfers between generations similar to those produced by pure government plans. The correspondence between the two types of plan, however, does not always hold. In calculating the net worth of a competitive firm with a completely unfunded pension plan, an informed market would make allowance for this obligation. When the cost of the pension claims earned in any year are much greater than the pensions paid in that year the "pay-as-you-go" nature of the plan allows the firm to exercise its discretion over the disposal of more revenues than funding would permit. If this leads to higher dividends, it does not mean that the owners have succeeded in shifting the cost of the promised pensions to others, since the net worth of the firm and the value of their shares are diminished by the cost of the new pension claims. The pensions must be paid out of past savings made by or on behalf of the firm's owners. If, instead, investment in the firm were higher as a result of the non-funding of pensions, the net worth of the firm might also be higher, even after allowance is made for the pension claims, if the invested assets accumulated at their expected rate of return in the firm more than cover the cost of the pension claims. Here, too, the pensions are eventually paid out of the savings of the present owners. Thus unfunded employer plans in competitive firms, with no default on pension payments and in an informed market, are based on savings and are similar to the pure private plans.

It is where firms are sheltered from competition that unfunded plans can result in intergeneration transfers. If a firm does not maximize profits in each period because, for example, of government regulation or fear of such regulation, it may have scope to increase revenues in a later period to cover part of the cost of pension obligations incurred in an earlier period. Some of the pension costs for past services would thus be shifted forward without decreasing profits or the net worth of the firm. Intergeneration transfers would also arise as a result of union negotiations where part of the bargained increase in labour payments is used to increase pension payments for past services.

Unfunded employer pension plans in the public sector are especially likely to give rise to intergeneration transfers because government's power to tax is used to obtain the resources needed to complete the payment for past labour services from a group that will in general be different from and belong to a later generation than the one which consumed the labour services in question. In certain jurisdictions, where most taxes are levied on property or other capital assets, the expectation that taxes will be higher in the future because of the uncovered pension liabilities will lower the values of these assets. The generation that promised the pensions then cannot as easily shift their cost to others, and there is some parallel with the situation in the competitive firm. In most cases, however, the use of general tax sources and the basic uncertainty of how costs will be financed leads to shifting, and the public employer plans approach the pure government pattern, though with transfers to a subset of the retired, those who have been public employees.

At the competitive end of the spectrum of employers, then, pension plans reduce in essentials to the private pension plans of the self-employed. It might even be argued that in a regime of perfect markets the phenomenon of deferred compensation would not appear, and that employees would be left to make their own arrangements for retirement. This ignore the institutional economies that pension plans based on place of employment can provide. There are advantages for firms and workers alike from the actuarial side and in relation to the investment of savings in dealing with groups of people. It is still true, though, that for employer pension plans significantly different from those of the self-employed we must look to imperfect markets, whether the imperfection arises from, say, union activity, or oligopolistic power, or quasi-public function. At this other end of the spectrum, we find the pension plans of government, federal, provincial, and municipal, of government institutions, hospitals, school boards, universities, and government business enterprises: as we go through this sequence the likelihood of specific pension funds being kept increases, but pension funds are in fact not needed to assure that promised payments are made. The power of taxation, exercised directly or indirectly, is sufficient support for the plans, just as it was the support of pure government pensions. With employers having this power, therefore, plans will be a mixture of the pure forms. To the extent that pensions payments come from savings, we have again an equivalent of the private plans of the self-employed, and to the extent that they do not, but are based on current taxation, they are the counterpart of the pure government plan. The result, in whatever mixture, does not go beyond the combined system we discussed in the system of self-employed persons.

The intermediate range of employers consists of firms with some substantial degree of monopoly power, the large oligopolists like General Motors and the regulated utilities like the Bell Telephone Company, and of firms dealing with union organizations that are themselves possessed of substantial market power. If these entities choose to, or are required to by the unions with whom they deal, they can proceed in a partly funded or even unfunded way, for their relationship to their shareholders and to the public is such that the pension promises they issue need not result in assets being even indirectly assigned to the support of pensions. The oligopoly has a certain range of discretion about its market situation, and the public utility can pass on through its regulated rates some part of unfunded pension costs to the general public. Large unions may institute pension plans that even call for payments to those already retired and will often ask for arrangements that contain visible and substantial intergeneration transfers.[17] Their younger members who are, so to speak, taxed to pay these transfers, may well see a *quid pro quo* in the promise of union protection when their own retirement comes and they find the funded programme inadequate. As to the employers' motives in instituting non-funded pensions, and picking up back-service, it may well be that they also share another quality of government, namely, in some limited degree a measure of familial relationship to their employees.

The familial quality would in any case seem to be a major factor in the union attitude to employer pensions.

With the system as a whole, therefore, with its mixture of competitive firms, unions, monopolies, and government employers, the payment of employer pensions is only in part dependent on the existence of assets set aside for the purpose. Employer plans are not the simple counterpart of the pension arrangements of the self-employed, but do contain, considered *en bloc*, transfer elements. Part of the cost of current labour services is transferred to subsequent generations. Whether such transfers are good or bad, of course, is not at issue here. Those who like the result might argue that later generations will be so much better off they should pay part of the pension costs of the earlier and poorer generation. But it should be noted that transfers brought about by employer plans are not universal, since they are only possible for employers in non-competitive situations. The result, from a social point of view, may be an incomplete and somewhat capricious pattern of intergeneration transfers, possibly very different from the pattern public opinion would accept in a pure government plan.

We set out to show that employer plans can be conceived of as combinations of the pure government and pure private plans. What we have seen in the discussion is that employer plans contain transfer elements of three kinds, and for the rest are, of course, savings plans and the direct counterpart of the pure private plans. The transfers occur in the first instance when employers make pension promises (or even pension payments) for services performed in the past but performed without the promise of payment having been then required. The arrangement is *ex gratia* in relation to the particular employee, but has still an economic basis, emerging as it does from collective bargaining or the market structure surrounding particular employers. Transfers occur in the second instance when formula plans, as they often must, inaccurately forecast the future, and here may easily be negative. Transfers, finally, can occur where there is no funding or only partial funding, and with this, a market situation where pension promises are not reflected in a correspondingly reduced net worth of the employer. Here the relationship with government plans is institutionally as well as theoretically close, for public and quasi-public employers (government departments, universities, churches) are particularly likely to have unfunded plans with this quality. These three transfers considered, what else there is, is savings.

CONCLUDING OBSERVATIONS

A word should be said about inflation. Pension plans are instituted to help provide command over goods to individuals during retirement but are normally expressed in money terms. The real value of most pensions will be diminished when prices rise. Unless the values of other assets owned by the retired are increased sufficiently by the rise to more than compensate for the fall in the real value of pensions, an inflation which is not fully anticipated brings about an intergeneration transfer which favours younger generations. Some employers, governments and oligopolists might, if they choose, increase the money value of pensions to restore in some degree their real value. This might well be the result of collective bargaining when workers recognize an affinity with workers now retired. Such attempts can only improve the economic position of a portion of the retired, some fraction of those insulated from competitive forces, and must be discriminatory.[18] If the reduction of the real value of pensions is considered socially undesirable, then social action to deal with *all* pensions appears appropriate.

This is not to deny that if intergeneration tranfers are socially desirable, as many might judge to be the case when they are intended to offset things as unpredictable as the accepted rate of inflation a generation from now, that private adjustments and local remedies are better than no adjustments. The point is that once the case has been made for transfers it is a case that applies to the community as a whole. There is something to be said for looking after the retirement needs of academics whose depression based savings now leave them in relative poverty, but transfers to the universities that allow these subsidies come from the community as a whole and *vis a vis* the correction of what is seen as a major inequity introduce what must then be judged minor inequities.

Perhaps there is emerging in this area of public policy something like the sequence in another area of public policy, the evolution of central banking. If government policy in relation to the funding of pensions in the private sector has had its origin in considerations of safety, nonetheless present developments may be pointed more towards considerations of economic policy and social equity. Transfers via the private plans fulfilled a social need that now government has begun to satisfy. For the government, though, the continued existence of the private transfers may make a general policy that much more difficult to pursue. A test case, perhaps, is whether funding legislation will become more and more severe, and whether government will extend its effect to its own subsidiaries in their operations as employer.

The transfers that can emerge from non-funding may thus already be an understood concern of public policy. There are also, though, the transfers in the less competitive sectors that can appear even with funding when back service is picked up or pension improvements are extended retroactively. Once again those in some degree isolated from the market may lead public policy by providing transfers that offset unanticipated inflation, as we have just noted, or any other unexpected change in economic circumstance. Once again, though, the private remedy is of necessity discriminatory, and may point to the need for action in the public sector.

We might observe as lay sociologists, or at least on the basis of everyday information, that in the North American economy not only is the period to be spent in more or less comfortable retirement considerably lengthened, but so is the period which is typically spent in the high schools and universities before the worker-to-be enters the labour force. There are three generations rather than two. With this, and with a changing family structure in which the generations are less interdependent than they were, the need for analysis directed to intergenerational arrangements, and particularly of the role of government in these arrangements, becomes ever more urgent. The worker nowadays has indeed a very complicated relationship to those whose production will support him in retirement, but whom he must now nonetheless himself support, and with those who are retired and must also expect assistance and support to the extent that their private saving has been small, whether as a result of lack of foresight or simply because of the secular trend in living standards.

NOTES AND REFERENCES

1 A. Asimakopulos and J.C. Weldon, "On The Theory of Government Pension Plans," *Canadian Journal of Economics* 1(4) (Nov. 1968), 699–717. Some of the preliminaries to the argument of the earlier paper are repeated here so that this paper can be read independently. In these introductory sections where pension concepts in general are discussed, the reader should notice that definitions have at some points been modified. The changes do not affect the treatment of government plans in the earlier paper.

2 In addition to the command over goods he receives from his pension payments strictly considered, a retired person will also be able to obtain goods if he owns assets that are the results of inheritance or of saving in non-pension forms, or if he receives private transfer payment from, say, family or friends. Any discussion of the adequacy of pension arrangements must make some assumption about the size of these supplementary resources. The extensive development of government and employer pension plans in Canada in recent years seems to have been the result of the belief, justified or not, that the private means available to a large proportion of the retired population are low in relation to the country's per capita income.

3 Empirical work has tended to conclude that individuals covered by pension plans do not save less than similar individuals without such coverage, and there is, in fact, some indication that they save more. See Phillip Cagan, *The Effect of Pension Plans on Aggregate Saving* (New York: National Bureau of Economic Research, 1965); George Katona, *Private Pensions and Individual Saving* (Ann Arbor: Survey Research Center, Univ. of Michigan, 1965). The findings of these studies are summarized in Roger F. Murray, *Economic Aspects of Pensions: A Summary Report* (New York: National Bureau of Economic Research, 1968). Similar results with Canadian data are reported in P.R. Andersen, "Discretionary and Contractual Saving in Canada, A Cross-

sectional Study," (PHD diss., Harvard University, 1967). This section has benefitted from the comments made by Dr. Andersen on an earlier version.

4 See Canada. Department of Finance, *Economic Implications of the Canada Pension Plan* (Ottawa: Queen's Printer, 1964), and especially the summary observation at the end of the section on "National Saving and Investment" that "the ratio of savings to income has tended to be relatively stable over long periods of time notwithstanding social welfare measures. It would seem reasonable to suppose that this tendency will continue to operate in the future." It will be remembered that the eventual plan represented a compromise between Ottawa and Quebec. Quebec had wanted larger savings from the public plan.

5 For more information on the facts of savings in the Canada and Quebec pension plans, see Beverley Watson, "Government Pensions: An Analysis of the Benefit Structure in the Canadian System," (MA thesis, McGill University, 1968).

6 There is a choice in the formalization here as to whether to postulate that the real rate of return on an investment made now is known, or is subject to uncertainty. In either case technology is not to be supposed fixed, but to change in a realistically unpredictable way. We have decided to assume that even with the storable consumption good Robinson Crusoe is not altogether sure what the effect of time will be, so that throughout the discussion real rates are estimated but not exactly foreseen. This suggests a world in which there is some precautionary bias towards oversaving.

7 With three or more generations, intricate transactions are conceivable that would allow, for example, second-generation workers to lend to first-generation workers so that one generation later they could retire on their maturing loans, realizable at negative rates of interest. On pure consumption loans, see Paul A. Samuelson, "An Exact Consumption Loan Model of Interest with or without the Social Contrivance of Money," *Journal of Political Economy* (Dec. 1958), 467–82.

8 By a real bond we mean a promise to pay exactly some specified amount in commodity units at some specified time.

9 See James M. Buchanan, "Social Insurance in a Growing Economy: A Proposal for Radical Reform," *National Tax Journal* (Dec. 1968), 386–95, for a proposal in which a pattern of conditional payments would be explicit, Buchanan's "Social Insurance Bonds" would carry no predetermined rate of yield, but would mature in terms of the realized course of the GNP or the rate on Treasury bonds. Our view of the Canadian system has been that conditional rules of a sort already exist, although rough and largely implicit.

10 If there is to be a logic of transfers, interpersonal comparisons are at the centre of things; the issue is whether we try to do something with such increasingly important areas as government pensions.

11 We are by now paraphrasing a paraphrase. For the source conception, even

though of different form, see Abba P. Lerner, "Consumption Loan Interest and Money," *Journal of Political Economy* (Oct. 1959), 512–7. Although in our earlier article we reviewed the Lerner-Samuelson debate on consumption loans, it may avoid misunderstanding to emphasize that the issues here have nothing much to do with the merits of the debate.

12 Leisure as a good does not appear in the preference functions used in these models.

13 Indeed, the saving rule can be incorporated in an extended version of function 2 if government considers only the variable of 2 in deciding what average saving should be.

14 In our earlier paper on government plans, (Asimakopulos and Weldon, "Theory of Government Pension Plans," 699), we distinguished between savings and formula plans. The usage above uses formula in a different and, as we now see it, more useful sense. Formula and non-formula plans are distinguished by the nature of the promises made, and are cross-classified by the degree of funding. Both formula and non-formula plans may involve savings.

15 In case of death before retirement some payment may be made to an individual's estate and for death after retirement there may be payment of survivors' benefits.

16 The laws regarding employer pensions in Quebec and Ontario require that the pension plans be fully funded. This requirement provides that (i) the employee's pension rights are protected in the event the firm ceases to exist; (ii) pension rights can be portable; (iii) both current and deferred compensation for labour services performed in a particular period must be paid for in that period (except, of course, for accidental transfers arising from the impossibility of accurately forecasting the future). This latter implication of the Pension Laws in these provinces perhaps cannot be taken to imply that a value judgment has been made that employer pension plans should not give rise to intergeneration transfers, because the governments, as employers, do not fund their own plans.

17 See, for example, the Fact Book of the International Brotherhood of Pulp, Sulphite and Paper Mill Workers, where many illustrations appear. In an instruction to its officials the Union points out that if a new plan is introduced "the arithmetic must be done separately for a man's service before July 1956 and after that date." The reason lies in Internal Revenue Service regulations. Pension plans must be approved by the Revenue Service before a company can treat its contributions as expenses of doing business. The Revenue Service permits annual contributions for "future" service. But "past" service is handled differently. The Government sets a limit on what can be paid in any one year.

18 An example is the Federal Government's recent announcement of an increase in the pensions of retired public service employees by the application of percentages ranging from 2 per cent for those who retired in 1969 to 42 per cent

for those who retired in 1952 and earlier. Pensions are to be subsequently increased each January 1 in accordance with the percentage change in the Canada Pension Plan pension index, which has a maximum possible increase of 2 per cent a year. (*House of Commons Debates*, Volume 114, no. 41, 2nd Session, 28th Parliament [Ottawa, December 19, 1969], 2203–5.) The point is not that it is better to do nothing than to discriminate, but to observe that the result is indeed partial and therefore discriminatory. Many who were employed in the private sector have been equally hurt by inflation.

CHAPTER ELEVEN

Pension Policy: Practice
and Positive Theory

Politics is the daughter of culture and if culture moves towards integration, why not politics?

Robert Garaudy[1]

PREAMBLE

This will be too long a paper, even though I shall make no attempt to comment on the mass of statistics others have gathered about the living conditions of those in retirement.[2] The elderly, it appears, too often enter a ghetto upon retirement that in its economic aspects is cruel, discriminatory, and permitted only by failures of policy. Women are victims in greater degree than men: life expectancy and work histories are well-known factors in explaining that difference. Like most other papers on pension policy, this paper had its origin in such disquieting facts. The facts themselves, though, I shall take as available in other sources (for example, in the writings of Louis Ascah and valuable work by government researchers).[3] Here the intention is only to discuss pension policy, to analyze whether there is a logic and theory to public pensions, [and to determine] what the possibility is of there being at least one great problem our governments will solve.

VOCABULARY

It will be easiest, I think, to define concepts in a reasonably strict way, but then to discuss policy in everyday terms. Customary usage is neither clear nor consistent in the abstract, but it points to familiar arrangements in a

Jamieson Lecture, University of British Columbia, September 1982; publication no. 12, Canadian Centre for Policy Alternatives, 1983. The description and discussion of a proposal by Martin Feldstein to reform the United States public pension system, formerly in the main body of the original text, has been placed in Appendix A. Appropriate changes in the text have been made to accommodate this editorial change.

familiar way. Where this double standard might invite confusion the argument can be interrupted.

Pensions, in the first place, are payments made to people after they have left the work force because of age. By extension, they are also payments made to people for closely associated reasons, chiefly because of reaching retirement age even outside the work force, because of family relationship to a pensioner or because of disability expected to be chronic. Within the scope of the idea, then, the sharpest illustration is that of the payments to the worker who has become too old to work.

There are other sources of income and of consumption, however, that those who receive pensions may also receive. Some beneficiaries of the Quebec Pension Plan, for example, will also benefit from dividends and interest on their savings; some will benefit from annuities arising from private schemes for retirement; some will benefit from the services in kind of houses and other durable goods; some will receive gifts; and so on. The question arises as to where to place the boundary between pensions and these others sources, for although any clear boundary would satisfy logic, a division is needed that would be helpful with practical matters.

It seems to me that the best choice of a boundary is to distinguish sources that arise directly from *personal* savings, and those that do not, and to reserve the word "pensions" for payments coming from the second source. Alternatively, but in intention equivalently, the choice of a boundary is to distinguish sources that arise from transfers, and those that do not, and to speak of "pensions" as payments coming from the first source. A very large proportion of the sources of income and consumption[4] that need classification fit easily into either form of the dichotomy. Everything received from Old Age Security payments and from the Canadian and Quebec Pension Plans is certainly transferred income. Everything received from private possessions, from interest payments, dividends, rents, and services of accumulated durables arises directly from personal savings.

There are admittedly many sources not so readily placed in one box or the other, but I believe that this does not point to further categories that have been missed but to arrangements of a mixed kind in which transferred income and the yield from personal savings are mingled. Registered retirement savings plans are important examples.[5] The retirement plan at McGill University is an interesting example.[6] Many plans for employees in the public sector have a base in savings but are complemented by transfers. The forms of these hybrids often compound the two sources of income in so intricate a way that to search for the components has a scholastic quality. Retirement plans in regulated industries and in the great oligopolies may at first sight seem to be merely a convenient way for individuals to make use of economies of scale in saving, but the incomes they generate can be quite different from those the same saving would produce under competitive conditions. It should be noticed though that even under competitive conditions, as they are in Canada, there is still the complication of how to assign the effects of tax abatements for retirement funds; and so the comparison is one of degree.[7]

Accordingly I shall rest the argument on the notion that the two categories are exhaustive, and that "pensions" represent transferred income while everything else that complements "pensions" originates in personal savings. The two categories are to be exhaustive and also enough. The hybrids will be divided without much worry about nuances, partly on the ground that one source or the other will usually seem to be clearly predominant in any given hybrid, and partly on the ground that in Canada the hybrids are of much less importance than the easily classified uncontaminated arrangements. In principle, transferred income may, of course, be provided just as readily from persons (within families, say) as from public or quasi-public bodies. Nonetheless I shall make no effort to deal with such transfers through private channels because of the large complications that would ensue; the limit helps keep the immediate discussion manageable. This is not to deny that privately transferred income belongs within the topic, both theoretically and practically, nor that in contemporary Canada it may be still more than a minor appendage to the better documented arrangements. In fact in the later argument the treatment of pensions from the public sector will be closely linked to familial patterns.

On the basis of the restrictive assumption, pensions (strictly considered) flow only from the policies of governments. It is a redundancy to speak of *public* pensions, and true by definition that pension policy is wholly contained within the economic policies of the state. In hybrid arrangements, that income which flows from savings is set aside, no doubt in some measure arbitrarily, and the remainder is counted entirely with (public!) pensions. Pension policy, it follows, can only have a theory insofar as there is an economic logic to at least part of public policy generally.[8]

There are a number of corollaries or near-corollaries that may fit naturally in this account of a vocabulary not that far from nature. After all, no one would say that Robinson Crusoe alone could retire on a pension, although he might live from his personal savings; and most would agree that in the community of Friday and himself he might retire on a pension even if (communal) savings were impossible.

In the first place the distinction between pensions and the complementary income from savings identifies a corresponding distinction much confused in the literature between pension policy and savings policy. Let me go further. Pension policy is one thing; policy about savings is a second thing; and policy about redistribution is a third thing. All three have the greatest importance in the programs of governments and states, but they cannot be reduced from three objectives to two objectives or even one.[9] It is true that programs of redistribution such as the progressive income tax involve transfers, but they are not transfers contingent upon age or infirmity and so are not pensions. As to the level of savings in a community, the state may wish to let it be determined by the market as near as possible or it may choose to intervene in respect of, say, bequests. But in any case it has many instruments at its disposal to affect the aggregate of the level of saving and of its allocation to investors. It seems plain that the transfers that are named "pensions" are in some sense redistributive, just as the progressive income tax is; but here there is the fundamental difference that the transfers are not from the better off to the worse off but from younger generations to older generations, in a program fundamentally connected with age. This fundamental difference may provide a theory.

In the second place, then, pension policy can be organized over a very wide range of public choice about redistribution of the ordinary kind and about the level and application of saving. Because of the ultimate interdependence of all variables in an economic system, choice in one area at length constrains what is practical in another, but since so much in the decisions is merely distributive, the constraints do not seem very near or very binding. Against the fears of those who equate pensions with savings, pension policy can possibly be varied a great deal without much affecting the level of savings and the pattern of distribution outside of pensions; and these magnitudes can in any case be adjusted to change.

In the third place, the substantial independence of pension policy does not carry with it a priority for programs in this area against policies touching the level of saving or the pattern of distribution. The independence is reciprocal from each policy to the others. People may save for retirement as for any other purpose. The existence of pension policy does not of itself deny the purpose or efficiency of such choices.

Finally, the possibility of an economic theory of pension policy requires that a system of transferred income all the same provide every participant in the programs with a *quid pro quo*. At the analytical level, the existence of an economic theory would separate still more sharply pension policy from the arbitrary (nontheoretical) choice of redistribution. Specifics will occupy much of the text that follows. In broad terms, though, the paradox of transferred income to all the retired population, accompanied by the needed *quid pro quo* everywhere, is not very mysterious. Taxes are collected from the working population. Transfers are paid to the retired. The state supports some sort of pension law which persuades the working population that in time they too will receive satisfactory pensions, if they acquiesce in the current taxes.[10] There is a set of complex transactions that people generally find profitable and that have been made possible by pension law and the calculated use of government.

This is, I hope, a sufficient outline of the formal but usually implicit vocabulary that will control the analysis that follows. To force the facts of Canadian experience into this language, though, is, as I observed before, unnecessary if the strict usages are allowed a latent authority. It is clear enough by now that, apart from the publicly subsidized exemption from taxation, the usual money purchase plan in a smallish enterprise is an exercise in group savings and is quite a different thing from guaranteed income supplements or old age security payments or benefits received from the Canada and Quebec Pension plans. There should be no harm, with that understanding in place, in comparing public pension plans with the even more heterogeneous private pension plans, and in appraising public plans and private plans one by one, without at every point observing that shared names in this field are weak evidence of shared qualities. We might move on now from terminology to phenomena.

PROJECTED SCHEMES: A BACKGROUND FOR ANALYSIS

We might begin with general, hypothetical situations. I think it will be more useful to study the particular features of, say, two schemes actually projected for Canada and the United States, proposed reforms of the public pension systems of these countries that are drastic but not simply visionary. This should give focus to the discussion. [One scheme is sketched] in the "Proposal for Pension Reform"[11] of the Canadian Labour Congress; the other [can be found in] one version[12] of Martin Feldstein's advice for altering the financial underpinnings of the social security system in the United States. There are many schemes in the style of each of these examples and many others some distance from both; but between the two illustrations a good many issues of theory and practice can be stated and analyzed.

It will no doubt be sufficient to deal in first differences and to describe the schemes only in terms of changes from the existing state of affairs (or at least, from the state of affairs that existed as the basis for the proposed reforms. The qualification seems necessary because, for example, the CLC would certainly have wanted to erase the recent budgetary changes in Old Age Security accounting.) For the Canadian scheme the essential ideas within a very long list of detailed improvements are as follows:

1 Old Age Security benefits should be raised at once by one-quarter and then be doubly indexed. In the short run, indexation should reflect inflation. Every five years, indexation should ensure that the new ratio to the average industrial wage is maintained;[13]

2 Guaranteed Income Supplements should also be raised at once, but differentially, by one-quarter for individuals but by a little less than one-
eighth for couples. In the short run, again, indexation should reflect
inflation. Every five years, a second form of indexation should ensure
that, with the supplements, the package of basic benefits will exceed the
Statistics Canada poverty line for Canada's largest cities;[14]

3 as to the payments from the Canada and Quebec Pension Plans: the
controlling 25% of preretirement earnings should be raised to 50% in
equal steps over ten years (always with immediate effect), and that although the ceiling should remain the average industrial wage,[15] it should
also have immediate effect;[16]

4 as to the weaknesses of the Canada and Quebec Pension Plans *vis à vis*
households: new arrangements should be made for calculating earnings
when children are being raised, for splitting contributions earned during
a marriage, for improving equity in survivor benefits, and so on; and

5 as to the financing of the scheme: the Canada and Quebec Plans should
require taxes roughly proportioned to covered wages and at a level to
balance current payments (subject to the accumulation of a "cushion" of
two years' expenditures); and all other elements of the program should
be paid from the general revenues of government.[17]

This sketch has a legalistic tone that may have left the social goals of the
policy obscure. The purposes its advocates have in mind appears to require
a little further comment.

For the Labour Congress, the statement of purposes begins piously but
then becomes explicit without further waste. "Society has a responsibility
to make sure that arrangements are in place that will allow people to have
an active and satisfying period of retirement." Except as a vote for public
pensions, this is not really informative. Precision follows a little later.[18]
The amendments must achieve standards for retirement incomes that are,
first, above poverty levels, regardless of preretirement incomes; second,
sufficient to allow the transition from work to retirement incomes without
a decline in living conditions; and third, indexed against the cost of living.
As a rule of thumb, says the text, retirement incomes (to smooth the transition) should replace three-quarters of preretirement earnings.[19] *Nota bene*!

The scheme is thus addressed, it seems to me, to problems and solutions
of three kinds. For those in the work force, there is to be continuity of living
standards insofar as these standards have been generated by a reasonably
homogeneous occupational status and are contained within certain ceilings.

For those outside of the work force, there is to be a pattern of living standards supported by the floor just mentioned, but then affected by the vagaries of experience in the work force and by experience with private pension plans and other claims upon savings. Taxation for all three "problems and solutions" raises funds as they are needed, without significant prior accumulation.

CONDITIONS FOR A THEORY OF PENSIONS TO EXIST

Here are programs for pension policy and here are purposes to animate the programs. It is reasonable to ask what theory might animate the purposes.

Public pensions require public law, and public law requires governments; and as one government first introduces pension law so do successor governments maintain and amend that law. In the real world it may be a necessary, a satisfactory abstraction, to treat the state and its constitution as durable and unchanging, but it obviously would be frivolous to ignore that *governments* – and their policies and laws – have lifespans that are mortal and often brief. It is a cautious observation to say that any given government has such and such a view of the alternative conditions of the citizenry – has a social welfare function, believes that by its policies it can choose amongst some of these alternatives, chooses its policies according to its ranking of the possibilities, and will choose in a situation different in several ways from the situations of earlier and later governments. A given government has its own political view, sometimes even being loosely correlated with its published program; it certainly has a unique citizenry to consider, as any demographer will attest; and it is constrained by the original endowments and inherited laws of its situation. There is not much but taxonomy in any of this, but it is at least taxonomy that suggests conditions a theory of pensions would have to fulfill.

When a given government deals in pension policy it does so within the limits of its *own* social welfare function and its *own* prior constraints. Since its social welfare function is whatever it may be, no doubt having explanations – which political science may cast some light on but which conventional economics has nothing to say about – then the possibility of a theory may indeed seem remote. Out of an arbitrary social welfare function comes an arbitrary distribution, in which original endowments are adapted by the market and distributive law, and out of the same sources comes an arbitrary decision about savings; and so it might well seem that pension policy, having the same origins, must also be an arbitrary thing.

In considering pension policy, however, government must concern itself with features of the data that can pass unnoticed elsewhere in its decisions. Its social welfare decisions are formed by the well-being of those who *are* the society, the well-being considered individual by individual. From the perspective of conventional economics, well-being is satisfactorily described for the individual by the stream of consumption he or she will benefit from during the rest of life. From the same perspective, redistribution is arbitrary because it affects each stream of consumption by, say, an arbitrary rearrangement of original endowments, and the effects of savings are arbitrary because the national total has been arbitrarily chosen. With pension policy, though, a government has before it variables in the social welfare function of two quite different kinds. It can decide directly upon pensions that are paid during its lifetime but it cannot decide directly upon the pensions that will be paid by successor governments. This is so because, on the one hand, it cannot determine what successor governments might wish to do – they will have their own social welfare functions – and on the other, it cannot know the circumstances in which the successor governments will operate. The present government is not the next government, and in any case has no exact information about the economic environment of the future. Still, it wishes to maximize its *own* social welfare function despite the formidable obstacles this ambition faces.

Now, if a government cannot directly control those variables that interest it, it surely will make use of any indirect control it can discover rather than abandon the variables to chance. Any government we have known has sought to influence the decisions its successors might take, and in the field of pensions, it has done this in a most deliberate and explicit way. The vehicle by which influence can be transmitted, though, must be constructed to meet the reality of an unpredictable future. It cannot promise that so many "real" dollars, for example, will be paid to the generality of pensioners. The promise might be literally impossible to fulfill; it might be absurdly ungenerous if fulfilled; and at the moment it is made has only a slight connection with the future consumption the citizenry might depend upon and which is the missing variable in the government's calculations. What a government can do, and at most does do, is to write pension *law* in the most effective form it can do, that is, as law that says contingently such and such will be done according to the circumstances of the future that becomes known. It would be pointless to write pension law that would not be respected and continued, and so the goal of government seems to be to transmit a pension law (creating it, maintaining it, amending it, but always with a view to a final form) that successor governments will respect and transmit. Maximization, of course, only requires continuity for the lifetimes of the present population, but continuity for that interval implies continuity indefinitely.

The enquiry about whether conditions for a theory exist thus boils down to an enquiry about whether a theory for the choice of pension law exists, pension law that will in principle and more or less in practice maximize social welfare as the government of the day sees social welfare. Doubtlessly any government maximizes as best it can, for that is virtually tautological;

but there is the important, real issue of whether the process is patterned or arbitrary, has a theory or does not. The question is put in a formal framework, not at all out of the usual style for economic models. The immediate arguments of the social welfare function are the utility indices of individuals. Those indices have as their arguments personal consumption and nothing else. This is the severe utilitarian setting of economic man, where there are no externalities and private bequests would be nil. These specifications are by no means innocuous but they are surely orthodox. It appears routine also to suppose that policy with respect to national savings and policy with respect to distribution and redistribution have already been decided, so that people in similar circumstances with respect to the history of their wages can be grouped, and then counted in subgroups according to age. In the society we know, this is how we are regularly distinguished by our governments. So and so has been a participant in the labour market with such and such an experience. A government in a market economy sifts us to that degree, but not more finely. In the sifting, it will certainly encounter many, even in a market economy, who are not participants or who participate rarely: these too can be grouped, but they may not fit easily into a pension policy.

If this is accepted as a reasonable account of the setting, then one further condition for the existence of a theory seems to follow at once. To execute policy, whatever the policy may be, a government must collect taxes from those working to match exactly – savings have been determined already – the net transfers for those receiving pensions. Since it does not distinguish members of a group, whatever it does for one member it must do for all, and since distribution has already been decided, the balance between taxes and transfers must hold not only overall but group by group. But the government cannot close the arithmetic of its problem without assigning numbers to the consumption in retirement of those now working. It is true that *this* government will not assign future transfers, and it is almost certain that the future transfers will be different from the numbers used in the calculation. All the same, maximization (and a theory) require that the transfers and taxes today be calculable, and calculation requires numbers to be assigned to the future. The route to a theory is further narrowed.

A HYPOTHETICAL PENSION LAW, WITH VARIATIONS

To close out the argument, its direction should probably be reversed, and some candidates for a satisfactory pension law examined.

On the arithmetic side, suppose the pension law completes the missing variables by stipulating that in *each group* the consumption actually provided to pensions will be equal to the "consumption" entered into the blanks for the future consumption of those of preretirement age. Whether this is a good or bad choice, it determines what the government does now with taxes and transfers, and if it is continued through the tenure of successor governments, it will determine the taxes and transfers of the future. Such a pension law, notice, does not lead to future consumption equal to that used in the arithmetic (except by chance). Consumption in the future will be as the circumstances of the future allow and will be subject to the now unknown alterations of social preferences and economic experience. This particular pension law declares how the computation of taxes and transfers will be made as long as the law is maintained.

It is evident that a vast family exists of pension law formally similar to this first example. Instead of using equality to fill in the blanks for future consumption, one could use overall proportionality, or even proportions that would vary from group to group. Calculation would continue to be straightforward. Very high present pensions, however, might be literally impossible to finance, and if they could be financed, they might not inspire confidence that the pension law would long survive. On the other side, very low present pensions would defeat the purpose of pension law, as it would be judged both by pensioners and pensioners-to-be.[20] There is the beginning of theory here, for at worst the range of possible law has been reduced.

Pension law in any of these forms carries with it interpersonal comparisons of utility and – in general – continuously measured utility. It is true that, as a mathematical statement, any one of the rules could be applied from the limited information in the individual utility functions. These functions, however, have already been grouped, and neither a government nor the citizenry enquire further about variations in tastes within a group. Equal treatment within the group is seen by all as sufficiently attained by regarding the members as equals. Interpersonal comparisons may be made for want of anything better, but made they are. As to the measurability of utility, in those hypothetical pension laws which specify multiples (or fractions) in filling in the "blanks," a government and the citizenry alike again seem agreed, and judge one multiple, say, not merely to be higher than another but *much* (or *not much*) higher. The comparisons that are made in these matters apply "measurable" utility as a matter of course.

The initial version of this hypothetical pension law can therefore be expressed in alternative, much less formal language. Suppose one proposed that pensions in Canada should be calculated to allow the standard of living of those in retirement to remain on the same level, as near as may be, as that of the younger members of their group who are still working. Taxes are collected within each group accordingly and are distributed in the required transfers. Those who pay the taxes see what is now taking place, are aware of the workings of the pension law, but again are ignorant of the purposes of future governments and the absolutes of the economy when they will themselves retire. What the pension law promises is that if it is maintained, then there will be continuity in living standards as those within a group enter and live through retirement, continuity in *relation* to the no doubt changing standards of preretirement life. The variants of the initial version can be similarly expressed, of course, and draw as they did before upon both interpersonal comparisons of well-being and comparisons of *changes* in well-being.[21]

WHETHER THIS HYPOTHETICAL PENSION LAW HAS A POSITIVE BASIS

One argument that is of some comfort, if one looks for a positive basis to this hypothetical pension law, is an appeal to analogy with the small society of families in simpler days and outside the market. In any given three-generational household, the customary account runs, the grandparents would be supported by their children who, as the working members of the household, would provide also for the youngsters in the family. From household to household, living standards would vary, but in each given household the standard of living would be maintained across generations. From year to year household fortunes would show change, at times drastically, but the *pattern* of transfers would be a constant, unifying force in the social fabric. As the generations succeeded each other the pattern would continue to be applied, so that those who furnished support now would expect support according to the relativities of their own retirement period. The maintenance of living standards across generations would, of course, be considered in terms of well-being rather than goods. The needs of the old may not be *as* different from those of their children as adult needs are from those of youngsters, but very different they undoubtedly are, and it is in their satisfaction that continuity of living standards persists.

All of this appears to me very close to the form of the hypothetical pension law considered for a contemporary market society as a whole. One could easily venture further, as D. Bellemare has,[22] to treat the public response to pensions (and other welfare measures) as a forced response from the state when the new economy rendered family structures inadequate. "The advent of the industrial revolution and the salaried worker modified the nature of economic problems of other people and created, for the first time, the problem of retirement as we know it today." On the purely technical question however, the limitations of analogy, and *this* analogy, should be noted. The hypothetical law has no place for family feelings, or at least does not require any motivations that are social. The happy household of three generations may have been more myth than reality. The demography of the simple society is not incorporated into its idealized form. The continuity of the standard of living in relation to needs is asserted but not tested. Yet if the analogy failed it surely would have counted *against* the theory, so its success is reasonably counted *for* the theory.

If the hypothetical law is to hold, its underpinning must include a general belief by those being taxed that its processes will control pensions in the future. They must believe that those processes will be seen as well chosen so that they can accept them as well chosen now. The law certainly has some virtues that would commend it in this way: first, it excludes alternatives that are *prima facie* not sustainable; second, it chooses amongst possible alternatives that *single* rule which respects individual judgement about the worth of pre- and postretirement income; third, it deals with the unknowns of the future *contingently*, and not by forcing an inappropriate certainty within those unknowns; and fourth, it defends *relative* incomes against the abruptness of retirement and the special vulnerability of the retired to those economic unknowns. It achieves results not possible to any scheme of private savings, on the one hand because such schemes cannot deal contingently except by ceasing to be private, and on the other hand, because in a progressive economy such schemes guarantee a *deterioration* in relative living standards.

The upshot is, I believe, that the law *does* have a positive basis. For almost everyone in the society the law would be advantageous compared to a *laissez-faire* solution. It is not faced with competition from alternative laws, or at least from alternatives free from obvious failures. Consequently it is politically possible, or even politically inevitable, and is economically plausible. The significance of unanimity, or near-unanimity as a connection between individual preferences and social choice has had a long history in economic thought. For example, Wicksell's rule for joining the political process to market forces required unanimity as a precondition for just taxation[23] and Arrow's list of "interdicted" features of tolerable social welfare functions[24] included any public choice imposed against unanimous preferences.

In Canada, then, and in similar societies, the speculation that pension law has a particular, positive form becomes a claim to be tested by experience as any other putative law is to be tested. Since the speculation comes from a simplified statement of reality, the test of experience is directed to approximations and readily visible tendencies rather than to some exact correspondence between the hypothetical law and the facts. Sociological changes, for example, have been very great in the period of Canadian industrialization, so that what governments will be compelled to do, they may, nonetheless, do hesitantly and slowly. At the conceptual level, every aspect of pension law is under debate, so that coherence is unlikely to be instant or complete. At the level of simplification used in this text, unanimity may be thought of as supporting the law, but in the world where private pension plans are produced and sold like any other service, unanimity is certainly not to be found in pure form. A government lives in the short run and may at times maximize (or defend) its own prospects regardless of its hopes for society; Wicksell and Arrow do not canvass in byelections. Such reasons as these qualify the practical force and regularity of any positive law within economics, and they certainly have that effect with pension law. One asserts, however, with all of this acknowledged, that there is a sharp distinction between the essential arbitrariness of redistribution, say, and the economic determinism that fixes pension law.

NORMATIVE AND DESCRIPTIVE APPROACHES

There is an ambiguity that can now creep into the argument. With or without a positive basis, with or without a theory, there is undoubtedly a collection of statutes and regulations that describe Canadian pension law, and that legally *are* Canadian pension law. What then appears is the use of "law" in its normative rather than its scientific sense, in which pension law must, of course, have a theory. I think context will take care of the ambiguity, but I remark on it because of the retreat that is always available *from* theory to description or normative argument. Descriptive research would no doubt be as important to prescriptions for "good" pension law as it is for prescriptions for "good" redistributive law. Outside of economics I would not dispute that "good" law in such matters can be distinguished from "bad" by judgements well worth respect; but within economics I see the retreat as founding pensions law only upon arbitrary choice. The cost is great if positive law is indeed there to be discovered. A logic for intergenerational transfers greatly changes the way pensions should be considered but also the way other aspects of state policy should be considered, all those aspects where there are inherent difficulties of meeting an uncertain future contingently and the general advantage is calculated from individualistic tastes. Such a logic perhaps extends from pensions to environmental programs and to almost any social policies (including monetary policies) that outlive governments, and age with the lifespans of the ordinary system.

It would be pedantic, however, to regard the debate about pensions with the serene detachment of an astronomer. The hypothetical pension law has severely excluded altruism, family feeling, and all such sentimental embellishments (except as economic man may enjoy goods because he gives them away!). As the law of the land, however, the hypothetical policy must surely be strengthened by these excluded motives of ordinary people, and must be strengthened also by overlapping of the generations into a continuum that gives the force of custom to abstract law. Similarly, although one should keep positive and normative analyses separate, there is no reason to shun normative lines of thought. The positive law is, at best, far from exact and immutable, partly because what is correct about it may not be understood. Economists have never been humble about assisting history: think only of Friedman, Pareto, and the greatest midwife of them all.

COMMENTARIES: FIRST, THE "PROPOSAL" OF THE
CANADIAN LABOUR CONGRESS

The discussion might now be returned from theory to practice, and consider the Canadian scheme *ex* the Labour Congress, and then (as facts too well known to need an earlier sketch) the new form given Canadian pension law *ex* the budget of 28 June 1982.

To begin, then, with the proposals of the congress: I think it is striking how far the reforms accept the *kind* of structure that already exists, and are directed mainly to altering the dimensions of the structure. Only in the areas where great social changes have been experienced are the building blocks of the scheme really new, required to deal with changed family relationships, with more frequent divorce, with a new view of balanced rights in marriage, with changes in family size, with the spectacular increase of the participation rate of women in the work force, and in brief with a more complex connection between society as a whole and the elementary societies of which it is composed. The new social structures must present a problem, for an evolutionary conception of pension policy could not be realized, if reform had a random direction; and it would be quite as embarrassing if those new structures did not produce novelties in the law.

The proposal by the Congress that "a person can move from work to retirement without suffering a decline in their standard of living" is on the face of it very close to the positive rule. So is the "rule of thumb" in the proposal that would meet the requirement of continuity: "retirement earnings must replace 75% of pre-retirement incomes."[25] The proposal *is* close to the positive rule for the transfers but is not exactly equivalent as to scope, and the transfers are not that easy to compare with those of the positive rule. Continuity of living standards at retirement, but unindexed thereafter, is one thing; indexed to the cost of living thereafter, is another; and indexed by wage rates, is still another. The congress elects the second reading and so protects pensioners against inflation; but that reading provides an absolute standard rather than the relative standard of the third reading. In the last few years pensioners admittedly have temporarily gained by a cost of living as compared to a wage rate adjustment, but they almost certainly would fall behind in periods where productivity and wages advance; and, *critically*, they do not maintain the pattern of relative incomes on which the logic and acceptability of the law depends.

So far, though, the issues are minor. Even 75% of pre-retirement incomes seems a perfectly good attempt to capture pragmatically the business of changed needs during retirement, and takes into account, too, the finer points of distinguishing gross from net incomes. Much more consequential are the problems concerning those outside the conventional work force of the marketplace, and much more varied as well as consequential. The scheme the congress offers fits most comfortably into a world of factories and classical households. Even in that setting, though, the Congress is not altogether consistent. It would raise the one-quarter parameter of the Canadian and Quebec Pension plans to one-half, and it would raise the yearly maximum pensionable earning at once to the average industrial wage – it still lags, by at least 15%. These extensions of what exists combine with other expected benefits, especially the Old Age Security payments, to underwrite the 75% promised for continuity. Gradual phasing in of the switch from 25% to 50% and half-heartedness and retroactivity are signs that in the political world even a known goal is approached gradually; but of course such gradualism contravenes the logic of the reforms and is harmful to *living* persons however helpful to pragmatism on behalf of the future.

There are a number of places in the resumé by the congress where some such questions appear as "are Canadians going to guarantee adequate retirement incomes to middle and low income earners?" The congress continues the limit of the *average* industrial wage, and so has excluded a substantial proportion of the pension problem even within the labour force. It might, for example, have followed the program of the Fédération des travailleurs du Québec and raised the limit to 150% of the average industrial wage, keeping *a* limit for administrative practicality but avoiding the qualification of logic that contains full public pensions within the middle and lower income groups. In a sense, as earlier remarked, the caution preserves a ghetto that pension law tends to break down, undermines the *general* support pension law would command, feeds the prejudice that public pensions are a modern form of charity, and leaves a large area for private pensions to occupy inefficiently that public pensions would occupy efficiently. To reduce the scope of pension policy in this way may be explained by some fear that pension benefits won at great cost in collective bargaining might be endangered by too sweeping a public scheme, but if so, it is a fear that mistakes the nature of private pensions as well as of public pensions.

In its thematic statements about public pensions the congress naturally refers (in this market economy) to earnings, retirement earnings, and so on: as we have just seen, the major issue is linked to middle and low income earners. A still deeper question of scope is raised, though, by the retirement needs of those multitudes in our society whose earnings from the marketplace have been minimal. There are those whose work is entirely in the home, characteristically but not only housewives, those who are self-employed from time to time, those whose involvement in the marketplace is intermittent, those whose record of earnings comes from badly paid jobs, and in general those for whom the continuity of *earnings* is anything but a close substitute for continuity in their relative standard of living. For many, public pensions generated from an earnings record (the ceiling questions aside) are well adapted to the logic of pension law. For many others, an earnings record is a poor proxy or even irrelevant. In very broad terms I think those many others may be symbolized by the housewife on the one hand, and the marginally employed on the other.

As the complement to its desired expansion of the Canada and Quebec Pension Plans the congress looks to expansion of the universal, flat rate payments under Old Age Security and of the means tested payments under the Guaranteed Income Supplement. There are various philosophic bases on which this second type of expansion might be built, though they have the common property of relating to the housewife and the marginally employed. If the housewife has not entered the general labour market, then perhaps some formula for imputing income to her can be found. It seems, though, that the would-be imputer has a colossal task. One might itemize services, and so invite confusion as well as derision. One might decide that a single imputed wage rate should serve for all housewives, or with an equal sweep, decide that the imputed rate should be proportioned to the income earned by the rest of the household. An observer will be certain that any such rule will assure discontinuity of living standards where continuity is sought. The egalitarian formula would be either ineffective or would make equality a quality specially favoured by old age: and the aristocratic formula would in a parallel way be either ineffective or augment *inequality* in old age. The proposals by the congress quite rightly, to my mind, eschew such appealing inconsistencies and do what they can to treat the household of partners as a partnership, in which the continuity that is sought concerns the standard of living of the partners jointly, and not only jointly but equally – hence the suggestions about splitting pension credits, about full equality in survivors benefits, about assignments in divorce, and so on.

Admittedly there are well-known objections, but I think they are mistaken in logic as well as intention. If pension law is wholly governed by continuity in the relative standard of living, then it cannot be governed simultaneously by something else. Some who have deplored the economic status of housewives will look to remedies of form rather than of substance, and they may imagine that imputed income according to the market will confer freedoms that might (ingenuously) be hoped for were the household decreed to have entered the market. Others will have noticed the gross inequalities in income and consumption from houseshold to household of those in retirement and perhaps will have confounded the inequalities from their earlier histories with the added inequalities that retirement has imposed. They may rebel at the notion that one group of the elderly, long out of the work force, should have incomes several times larger than the incomes of some other (not easily distinguished) group, perhaps as they quarrel with a similar phenomenon among groups of the very young. All the same, this is a belated objection to redistributive policy transferred to pension policy. It does not seem morally convincing to repair society's choice of unjust distribution by redistribution

only amongst the very old (although the arbitrary basis of economic distribution does seem easier to notice amongst the very old and the very young!).

It would be rash to expect that the congress has the numbers and details
exactly right, for if the principle behind the scheme is straightforward the
society to which it applies is intricate and volatile; but I do not see any
great tension between proposed theory and proposed practice. Incidentally,
the alterability of social and family organization is why it would be very
mistaken to elevate pension law, enduring though it is expected to be, into
some sort of constitutional clause. Freedom to adapt to sociological change
has to be retained if any given form of pension law is not to become
outmoded. It is the microeconomics that demand flexibility in the legislature!

Guaranteed Income Supplements, as Asimakopulos and Bryden remind
us,[26] were "originally intended to be a transitional measure to provide
supplementary benefits for those who, because of age, would not be eligible
for full benefits under the C/QPP" – "a transition measure which would
ultimately phase itself out." Asimakopulos observes that despite this intention "by June 1982 before the latest budget, the maximum GIS for a single
person had moved from 40 per cent of the OAS to just slightly above the
OAS" ($233.89 a month for the GIS against $232.97 a month for the OAS)
and interprets this as showing that since "the 1970 amending act replaced
the limitations on the GIS ... the Government's policy on income security
began to place more emphasis on anti-poverty measures ... "selective payments based on income rather than on universal payments such as the OAS."[27]

So the marginally employed (who may of course overlap the category of
housewives) comprise the final test of the *scope* of the congress's proposals
in relation to positive pension law. There is some hesitation in the prescriptions. If pensions must be above the poverty line and must also allow a
person to "move from work to retirement without suffering a decline in their
standard of living," then the positive pension law would represent a floor
– flawed in logic but well intentioned as anti-poverty law. Closer inspection
indicates that the first rule applies essentially to the marginally employed,
and the second (always connected explicitly with earnings) is all that represents full pension law. To "insure that OAS and GIS will guarantee a level
of income to the elderly that exceeds the Statistics Canada Poverty Line for
Canada's largest cities" is to take a half-way position. It appears deliberately
to go beyond the early notion of public pensions as charity, given by a
narrowly defined community to a separate, unhappily impoverished community with which it is federated but which it controls. Bellemare's already
cited paper shows how deeply ingrained this notion has been, to regard
public pensions as charity, required only to supplement private responsibilities improvidently discharged.[28] Asimakopulos, for that matter, suggests
that in the relative growth of Guaranteed Income Supplements the notion
has had a considerable revival. Still, the congress demands something more

than charity, and it might charitably be interpreted as using the elastic phrase "above the poverty line" as meaning *enough* above to maintain relative incomes across the generational line. The relative expansion of the supplements might then be considered a second change in their nature. They *were* to have been transitional but have become quasi-permanent. They *were* to have provided a floor of subsistence levels of income and consumption but have been adapted – or, in the view of the congress are to be adapted – so that they are awkwardly constructed extensions of Old Age Security payments, distinguishable from those payments only by name and the stage of their evolution.

Which way the integration runs is, nonetheless, vital to the hypothetical theory and to the fortunes of pensioners. From the tone of current political debates, it is plain that many imagine that the social programs should be selective rather than universal, and should be reconstructed in the image of the safety net, to save the feckless and luckless from disaster by some minimum protection. If the Old Age Security payments are merged into the forms of the Guaranteed Income Supplements, then the universality of a pension law will have been lost, or to put the matter in another way, there will be a community of the elderly poor and their younger peers, and a *separated* community of the rest of society; the pleasing correspondence between *society*, government, and social welfare function will have vanished. Pension law may be imagined for the more coherent of these communities, but that strains imagination and theory both! On the other hand, from the tone of the proposals by the congress, it seems the intention is more and more to incorporate the supplements into the governing scheme of the Old Age Security payments, so that in time the only distinction left may be one of name and later not even that. If that is so, the probable battleground will be fought over in the name of "universality" versus "selectivity," and the weapons of the congress will be still more advances in the technique of supplying continuity, even where there has been little guidance from the market place.

There are many parts of the proposals on which I shall not try to comment here. In respect of finance, the congress advocates the same sort of group-by-group tax and transfer principles the positive theory would project. In respect of private pension plans, the congress makes many recommendations that would allow collective saving to be carried out more efficiently and with greater regard for the individual interests of the savers required to participate in these enterprises. But since the congress, in watching over the plans negotiated by its national and international unions, at no time pretends to convert them into substitute public plans, it is consistent in separating policy about savings from policy about transfers. In respect of reforms connected with the changes in family and industrial life, I have noted their scale and importance for a theory, but otherwise have little to say about them. As technical matters, they would have as their counterparts, say, discoveries the scientists might manage to make about longevity or senility; but the theoretical implication is again that pension law must be adapted from time to time when the social environment is altered. If the proposals *are* in fact guidelines to where Canadian pension law is heading, then I would cautiously claim they are consistent with positive law in this area; and with that said, the second claim could be added that the years ahead will sufficiently test the first claim.

COMMENTARY: SECOND, THE PROPOSAL IN THE BUDGET OF 28 JUNE 1982

For some time payments under the Old Age Security program have been indexed quarterly, according to the consumer price index (and not according to an index of wage rates as relative continuity would have indicated – although differences lately have been of more interest theoretically than practically). The federal budget of 28 June did two things to the program. In the first place "the indexation of benefits from the Old Age Security ... will be limited to 6 per cent per annum for 1983 and 5 per cent per annum for 1984. Full indexation ... will resume on January 1, 1985".[29] In the second place, the Guaranteed Income Supplements "will be increased by the difference between the [capped] OAS level and the level that would have occurred if full indexation had been applied".[30] The text is ambiguous for it is just possible that it means that full indexation in 1985 will contain all losses from 1983 and 1984, and it is probable but not certain that any such losses will continue to be a supplement under Guaranteed Income after "capping" is over. I take the most likely reading to be a permanent reduction from 1985 on in the Old Age Security payments, representing losses from "capping" of, say, 6 or 8% (in relation to current projections of inflation) but there will be permanent compensation in the same amount for the roughly 50% of Old Age Security recipients who also receive the supplements.

As Asimakopulos points out, this is "the second time in the relatively short history of universal old age pensions in Canada that indexing provisions [have been] altered to the disadvantage of those receiving these payments".[31] (The first instance was the 1971–2 experiment in pegging payments without indexation of any degree.) Taken by itself, the evidence from these episodes is discouraging to the notion that pension policy has a positive theory or at least the positive theory I have sketched. There can be a difference in how one regards such shocks, as intrinsic to a theory or as eventually negating a theory.[32]

The grubby expropriation in the June budget was especially offensive in equity, but that of course is not the issue here. Positive theory depends upon belief in the continuity of pension law as it depends upon nothing else, and it is the less credible if *ad hoc* raids upon public pensions become an important political expedient. Earlier, too, it was argued that in Canada pension policy will require the conflation of the Old Age Security payments and the supplements according to the logic of the payments. In the June budget, the danger appears of the divided social welfare function in which the elderly poor are supported under a rule of charity by way of the supplements. I have gone over this question of universality above, and will go no further with it.

The budget constituted negative evidence, but not, I think, decisive or even very important evidence. On the other side one can point to the unexpected resistance the new right met in the United States when they confused the logic of social security with the arbitrarily distributive aspects of other welfare programs. Everywhere in Canada, it seems, schemes for pension reform are advanced from government to government and association to association. On balance, it seems to me that expansion of the existing public plans are by far the favoured recipes. I repeat the theses that something like the Canadian Labour Congress proposals will be adopted, nothing like the Feldstein proposals will be attempted, and that the proposals from the budget will prove to be trivial episodes from the politics of the day.

APPENDIX A: MARTIN FELDSTEIN'S PROPOSED
REFORM OF THE SOCIAL SECURITY SYSTEM
IN THE UNITED STATES

The datum from which Feldstein works is the present ratio of Social Security payments to the total wage bill of those who are effectively within the system, and is a ratio that – he assumes – has existed *before* reform and would continue to exist to an economist's eternity *after* the reform.[33] The assumption is justified[34] by the purpose of the investigation, which is directed to the financing of a given pattern of benefits, by the fact that indexation makes use of a wage rather than a general price index, and by the characteristic methodology Feldstein employs of predicting an unknowable future by using unchanging rates of growth.[35] In his stylized version of the system as it stands, a payroll tax is in place that precisely finances the flow of current benefits. Feldstein proposes to increase that tax rate, in order to collect a continuing surplus from the higher rate, to build a fund on which interest is earned, and to continue this process of accumulation until, at some history-making date, all benefits to eternity can and will be paid from the revenues of the fund *and* the social security tax can and will be reduced to zero. There will be those who gain from the reform, and there will be those who lose. Feldstein calculates that, for a wide range of increases in the tax rate, the sum of gains will exceed the losses, and that within the wide range there will be a well-defined optimum increase maximizing the difference between gains and losses. Rapid accumulation speeds the history-making date, but accumulation either too rapid or too slow subtracts from net gains.

The central purpose of this scheme proposed for the United States seems to be nothing more startling than to capture gains from accumulation that will outweight losses imposed by the same accumulation. There are immediate consequences that could, I suppose, be considered associated purposes since they are inextricably linked with the main purpose. Under the Feldstein rules, for example, if social security benefits were to be generally increased (or for that matter, conceived of as being introduced for the first time) then payroll taxes should in the first place be imposed to cover all current payments and then further imposed to produce the fund that erases taxes of both kinds – eventually – and still can finance benefits to eternity. Any one of the myriads who enter the system after the history-making day is, of course, the recipient of transfers without ever having been taxed. It is true that he who enters still later will receive even larger transfers, but all benefits are indexed by the growth of wage rates. Since benefits are arbitrary as to scale, there is no particular connection with continuity of living standards. All who lose from the accumulation of the fund are by definition inhabitants of the transition. They contain a finite population and have had their interests weighed – unfavourably – against the interests of the infinite succession that will follow them. Finally, in this matter of associated purposes, the extra taxes collected during the transition constitute collective savings forced from those *who appear* on payrolls and which as savings are promptly invested and reinvested until the transition is over: the revenues from the accumulation are endlessly transferred to those *who have appeared* on payrolls. What must certainly happen under Feldstein's postulates presumably is *intended* to happen if these postulates are realized.

COMMENTARY

Since Martin Feldstein has written widely on social security and private saving, I should pick a representative item. The sketch from the earlier part of this argument is, recall, related to Feldstein's "Optimum Financing of Social Security,"[36] for that account is particularly systematic and easy to relate to issues that have already emerged.

Under Feldstein's rules, the heart of the matter was to increase the payroll tax for a time and then to eliminate it altogether. Social security benefits would be maintained throughout in proportion to current payrolls. Those subject to the *increase* would lose by the reform, and those who would benefit from the fund the increase had generated would gain. The reform is justified by a computation purporting to show aggregate gains far in excess of aggregate losses. It is also justified, alternatively and inconsistently, by a one-person-one-vote referendum in which there would be a resounding "yes" vote.

Within the computation, though, a difficult, even disastrous dilemma is at once apparent. If the future is known with certainty, then the arithmetic of gains and losses can at least be attempted, for the chief conceptual problem will be the usual one of finding commensurable utilities and disutilities. In a practical sense, of course, to aggregate even a known future from now to eternity usually will be disappointingly arduous except in artificially simplified models. It is a hypothetically known future characterized by handy constants and steady growth that Feldstein in fact uses, so being able to compute and to compute easily. The problem that may be totally intractable is nevertheless never the computation *per se*, but ignorance of the future; even for a generation ahead the numbers needed for computation would be mostly fiction.

Taking the numbers from Feldstein's world, with foreknowledge, steady growth, and all, we can simplify a little more – it hardly matters – and replicate the essentials of his results.[37] Working in fractions of the wage bill (for *1974*, and apparently $621 billion) the loss would be proportioned to the *change* in the tax rate, to the appropriate number of *present* "utils" (utility units) into which a dollar of the loss should be converted, and to the appropriate factor for handling rates of growth and discounting into present values from *now*, the date of reform, till *then*, the date when both the tax rate and its temporary increment can be abolished. The gain has exactly the same form, though now the first element in the proportion will be the (abolished!) tax rate rather than the temporary change, the present "utils" into which the dollars of the gain are to be converted will show that dollars that are more plentiful have a diminished worth, and the interval from *now* to *then* will have become the interval from *then* to *eternity*. In the circumstances of 1974, Feldstein judged the gain would exceed the loss enormously, and that accumulation should proceed. Here would have been a surplus for the taking of about two and one-half *trillion* 1974 United States dollars,[38] and a goodly sum only a few hundred billion better or worse in these capitalized units even if the skeptic narrowly varies the parameters.

In its essentials Feldstein's formula is
$$G = T\,u_2\,F_2 - dT\,u_1\,F_1$$
where G is the net gain in multiples of the initial wage bill (the ratio between the calculated $2.5 trillion and the given $621 billion), where T is the original rate of tax on payrolls and dT is the calculated optimum increment imposed until T and dT are both removed (about 0.10 and 0.13 in the leading illustration, with an accumulation period of about five years); where u_2 and u_1 are (present) utility measures for the post-tax period and the period of accumulation respectively, and F_2 and F_1 are the factors that reflect rates

of growth and discount for these same two periods. The utility measures require brief comment and the F_2 and F_1 somewhat extended comment, for they contain (or hide!) the residuals of all the arithmetic.

Feldstein uses the representative man for his model of a real world, a man economically identical to all others alive and all those yet to live, and indistinguishable even during life except that for middle age work is possible and in (an irrelevant) youth and old age it is not. Representative man has a known, unchanging utility function in which the marginal dollar of income just before reform is normalized at one util. His schedule for present incomes allows the low marginal utility for the post-tax period to be observed and so too the high marginal utility for the period of accumulation. Feldstein's u_2 is a working approximation that averages the low marginal utility and the original unity, and his u_1 is a corresponding approximation that averages the high marginal utility and the original unity. An observer, whether Feldstein, the state, you or I, is well on his way in a social welfare function with a representative man's utility schedule: the "observer" will weight (discounted) utilities and add them. Incidentally, although the primary text contains many nuances about the representative man's attitude to labour, the arithmetic and the facts are barely touched by setting all the labour elasticities to zero.[39] Employment at any date is unique and complete.

There are now F_2 and F_1 to look at, the multipliers that convert Tu_2 into the gross gain and dTu_1 into the offsetting loss. The system grows steadily under two forces, that of population and that of productivity, combined, say, in a parameter g. Against this expansion is the contraction that Feldstein applies to the valuation of future dollars. As productivity increases, so do real wages and individual incomes, and as a result ever smaller utilities are associated with marginal dollars. To this notion of, say, Menger, Feldstein adds the Austrian possibility of pure time preference. Far-away utilities are discounted by the observer because of his values, or because of his estimate of the values of the representative man, or even – it appears – because of the values of the representative man now perceived as immortal.[40] These offsets to the growth parameter can be combined, say, in a parameter p. The basis of the multipliers, then, is the net magnitude $e^{(g-p)t}$.

If the date at which taxes are abolished is written as t^*, then

$$F_2 = \int_{t^*}^{\infty} e^{(g-p)t}dt \text{ and } F_1 = \int_{t_o}^{t^*} e^{(g-p)t}dt$$

and with p larger than g, the condensed formula becomes the more informative

$$G = [Tu_2 e^{(g-p)t^*} - dTu_1 (1 - e^{(g-p)t^*})] /(p-g).$$

Feldstein proposes to approximate p by $-c_1 + v$ where c_1 is the rate of growth of productivity and personal income, α is a constant-elasticity summary of the utility schedule, and v is whatever "pure" time preference represents. In the principal numerical illustration g is set at 4%, p at 6%, c_1 at 2%, α at –1%, v at 4%, and c_2 (the growth of population) at 2% – not all independently of course.

Two further points of an arithmetic kind should be made. The increase in the tax rate (that is, dT) fixes the interval to the abolition of the taxes (the interval of t*). Feldstein naturally will search for that dT (or equivalently, that t*) which gives the largest G. The rate of return on the fund must show up *somewhere*, so the linkage between dT and t* and the accompanying maximization should probably be recited. At t* a sum will have been accumulated of which the immediate earnings will be precisely exhausted in two purposes, paying the benefits due at t* and increasing the fund in proportion to the growth of benefits so that these two purposes can be discharged in perpetuity. If A(t) and B(t) are the fund and benefits at t, then

$$rA(t^*) = B(t^*) + gA(t^*),$$

which leads at once to

$$(r - g)\, A(t^*) = B(o)\, e^{gt^*} = B(o)\, (dTT/T)(e^{rt^*} - e^{gt^*}),$$

for in the period of funding earnings are already being earmarked for growth from "o" to t*. The desired explicit relationship between t* and dT can thus be written as say,

$$t^* = \ln\,(T/dT + 1)(r - g).$$

The leading illustration uses a rate of return of 15% (real, social, pretax, but perhaps astonishingly high): for accumulation to make any sense r must certainly exceed g, which here it does handily!

It is a temptation, to which one shall briefly succumb, to take note of the numbers that come from the formulae and how they rise or fall. Throughout I have skipped the nuances, but I can report to the cautious that Feldstein's complete arithmetic gives a net gain of $2.428 trillion in 1974 prereform utils against $2.182 trillion in the condensed form (neither number perhaps having fully anticipated the oil crisis). The net gain of $2.182 trillion contains only a small loss against the gross gain ($443 billion set against the $2.625 trillion in which posterity will revel). From the political point of view the numbers appear troublingly sensitive to parameters difficult to observe or not yet experienced. All else being the same to change α from –1 to –2 (i.e., to make marginal utility more sensitive to income) reduces the net gain from $2.182 trillion to $639 billion,[41] while to change it to –½ increases the net to $5.275 trillion.

All else being the same, as would surely be expected, the value of "pure" time preference shows enormous effects. Raise it from 4% to 6% and net gain falls to $761 billion, but lower it to 2.5% and the net increases to $10.885 trillion (en route to infinity as every successor of ours is given minute but finite weight). Something over 70% of the $10.885 billion, either Stalin or a saint would be fascinated to notice, will belong to the years that begin a century hence! Net gains seem not much affected, incidentally, in any of these cases by hunting for the maximizing T over a considerable range. Low rates of return (even in areas where r and p exceed g as they are supposed to do) extend t* for a given T, and so both extend the period in which losses are experienced and increase the extent of a negligible net gain or an actual loss (avoidable by scuttling the entire project).

Feldstein's 15% is much higher, by the way, than rates reported for Canada (1947–76) in their study for the Economic Council by A. Tarasofsky et al., where for the nonfarm, nonfinancial sector only twice in this long period does the ex post rate exceed 10%. A technical difference seems to be that the Canadian study incorporates working capital in the denominators of its rates, but even with this considered the Canadian rates are, say, two-thirds of Feldstein's rate and are very erratic. The lesson here, I think, is that Feldstein's assumptions do not seem to allow computations that have a sound factual basis in Canadian experience (quite apart from the worth-lessness of the computations even if successfully made).

On this side of things, then, there are problems so serious with the application of Feldstein's scheme that one may be diverted from the question of whether the scheme in principle has merit. Rates of growth are certainly not constant and give no reason for summaries of the future than can be condensed into constants. Arithmetic results extend over vast ranges all within the boundaries of the possible and perhaps the probable. Large portions of surplus will only be enjoyed more than a century hence. Favoured tax rates are outside of political reality and would shake the business community as much as the union movement. A payroll tax of 25% for five or six years, differentially punitive from service to higher technology industries, is not a program on which a congressman would run twice.

Feldstein is aware of the political perils, for he supplements his basic computation by a quite different test. Thus, [he calls for] a plebiscite in which the yet-to-be-born will have been disenfranchised, in which each voter casts a "yes" or "no" with a unit weight in the ballot regardless of the magnitude of personal gain or loss, in which social rates of discount will be discarded in favour of the after-tax interest rate that individuals see, and in which (for the standard illustration) the "yes" vote easily triumphs. With a growing population and a long working life, the presumption is inescapable that the young who will be net gainers will outnumber the certain losers among the older workers, although the losses forced on the older workers might seem an unexpected initiation of pension reform.

One notices other oddities. The democratic if voracious young would be guided by personal advantage alone, and yet they would be guided under a sadly limited vision. They surely could do much better by simple expropriation of everything the old possess. While they are at it, they might notice too the democratic legitimacy that would sanction the expropriation of all the wealth, say, of Harvard professors (who, even fecund as they are, could surely not out-vote their expropriators).

The democratic confirmation pretty clearly weakens the computation it is supposed to complement. Here the population, by ballot, comes to the same conclusion as the observer who does the grand arithmetic. There is no particular reason, though, why it would pick the maximum amongst alternative choices of funding as the observer is required to do. One rule says do this, the other rule says do that. It may even be that a plebiscite would confirm a calculation that to the observer showed a net loss. Further, although the fortunes of the yet-to-be-borns convey a comic touch, Feldstein would only need to allow proxy votes to be cast for those clones, to win all his plebiscites. Their disenfranchisement is vital else almost *any* accumulation that has a terminal date is good policy, however distant the date and even if bliss in Ramsey's sense had long since been attained.[42]

These lines of criticism, however, still confine the debate to Feldstein's specifications. The reform proposed for the United States is no reform at all because it exchanges precisely the position that a savings policy and a pension policy have in relation to economic theory. Feldstein seeks to establish a positive theory of savings within which an arbitrary pension policy can be placed. To give a foundation to such a theory requires not only that computations of immense difficulty be performed, that magnitudes very subtle even to identify be measured, but that an inherently unknown, unknowable future be treated as though it were known. In a sense it is a minor matter to approximate the unknowable with evenly flowing growth for it would be no improvement to approximate it with any speculative decorations that come to mind: the unknowable is not thereby better known. Feldstein does not deal with contingent policy, though even that would merely erase a positive theory of savings rather than create a theory out of nothing. The observer who, for example, imposes such and such rates of growth, and especially such and such a rate of time preference – Feldstein himself, or his government – is acting according to spurious theoretical considerations, and so in the end will produce accidental results that are unlikely to be satisfactory from any standpoint. The public pensions this observer views as arbitrary will presumably be interfered with or sacrificed for the error in public choice.

To repeat a point made before, I am not for a moment downgrading the normative significance of redistributive policy or policy about savings. In a positive sense, though, these policies are arbitrary, and their normative significance is sacrificed if one subjects them to faulty theory. Let me indeed go one stage further: it will be remembered that for Adam Smith there *was* a positive theory (not very convincing) of savings, namely the high rate that natural liberty would determine. It will also be remembered that for Karl Marx there was also a positive theory (received with mixed reviews), namely, that enforced rate that competitive capitalists had attached to their surpluses. These perhaps by now are both remote ideas, but in principle they were theories and not normative wishes. I have denied a theory exists. It might have been even better to say, no theory of communal savings exists on the same footing as the rest of *contemporary* theory.

NOTES AND REFERENCES

1 Remarks at a November 1981 conference sponsored by the Lateran University and the University of Lublin (Poland).

2 The lines of argument in this paper have their origins in shared property, ideas found in work by A. Asimakopulos and myself. There are two joint papers, first, "On the Theory of Government Pension Plans," *Canadian Journal of Economics* (1968): 697–717 and second "On Private Plans in Theory of Pensions," *Canadian Journal of Economics* (1970): 223–87. Later work has always reflected the original approach. More recent items are "The Nature of Public Pension Plans: Inter-generational equity, Funding and Saving," by Asimakopulos, published by the Economic Council of Canada in 1980, and my paper "On the Theory of Intergenerational Transfer," *Canadian Journal of Economics* (1976): 559–79. For a piece by Asimakopulos written at almost the same time this paper has been prepared, see his mimeographed "The Nature of Public Pensions and the Federal Budget," Department of Economics, McGill University, 1982.

3 For example, the work of the Task Force on Retirement Income Policy, Ottawa, Canadian Government Publishing Centre, 1979. In Ascah's work, perhaps see first "Government and Private Pensions in Canada," Ph.D. diss., McGill University. These items lead in *their* references to much else that documents the *ex-post* facts of retirement income.

4 I emphasize, but will not bother at every stage to repeat the emphasis, that the distinction between income and consumption is particularly important in retirement. In the private economy one eventually dissaves to support consumption until savings have vanished.

5 Since the savings are earmarked for retirement, their preferred status for taxes contains a transfer.

6 There is not space to go into the intricacies. The public that supports the university also has provided quite handsome transfers to be added to savings, though expropriation has long been underway. Little of this has been calculated, for little of this has been understood (at any stage).

7 Even in the simplest money-purchased plans of small, competitive firms, the fact of preferential tax treatment produces an element of transfer income.

8 If one says that in somewhat idealized situations there is a complete economic theory of the individual considered apart from society, one may nonetheless say there is a partial theory of the individual connected with the whole of the real society (certainly not a complete theory, certainly not null).

9 One should not throw away a positive theory if one can find one. I do not imply that social significance is ranked by the existence of positie theory. Stalin's view of savings was doubtlessly more consequential to his collegial state than his view of pensions.

10 This is *not* moral admonition. It is a matter of self-interest. Clearly "satisfactory" has to gain definition from the law.

11 Canadian Labour Congress, "The CLC Proposal for Pension Reform," Canadian Labour Congress, 1982, 165 pp.

12 See Martin Feldstein's "The Optimal Financing of Social Security," discussion paper no. 388. (Cambridge, Mass.: Institute of Economic Research, Harvard University, 1974).

13 Canadian Labour Congress, "CLC Proposal for Pension Reform," 155.

14 Ibid., 156.

15 Ibid., 156 ff. It is striking, as will be stressed again, that the ceiling of average industrial wages is retained. The Congress perhaps believes that half a ghetto is better than a full ghetto, but in doing so give support all the same to the idea of the ghetto.

16 Ibid.

17 Ibid., p. 160.

18 Canadian Labour Congress, "CLC Proposal for Pension Reform," 5. Here is the piety – and in the pages that follow immediately, the information. There is, as a casual but most unfortunate introduction, the statement of the "major issue": "are Canadians going to guarantee adequate retirement incomes to middle and low income earners?" (*Ibid.*, 3). The qualifications weaken both the possibility of a theory and of a program, and enter the "half ghetto" solution.

19 Ibid., 5, item 2. I think this is a critical summary of what the CLC intends should happen, and what in any case self-interest will cause to happen.

20 The extreme, of course, is to have an empty law, under which none of us can know what the *relative* situation will be before and after retirement, and in which the odds from experience of past decades suggest that poverty, rather than continuity, is the better form to describe living standards. The extreme, I suggest, would be virtually unanimously rejected even in a community of the maniacally selfish on which our best theory builds.

21 The promised continuity is always relative – there is no question of absolute continuity – and in a changing environment requires the double comparison. One belongs to a social group (as the society distinguishes groups), and one shares the fortunes of the group as history unfolds.

22 For an extended and thoughtful discussion see D. Bellemare's "La securité du revenu au Canada : une analyse économique de l'événement de l'État-providence," Ph.D. diss. McGill University, 1981. The *evolutionary* aspects of the society-as-it-is are especially interesting documentation.

23 K. Wicksell's "A New Principle of Just Taxation," 1896. Until recently this had seemed to me a curiosity in the literature, a dangerous judgement in relation to almost any economic idea Wicksell thought important.

24 See K.J. Arrow's original well-known five conditions of a satisfactory social welfare function. If all prefer A to B it is odd if the community prefers B to A.

25 Canadian Labour Congress, "CLC Proposal for Pension Reform," 2, item 2.

26 See again Note 1 for the source. There is Asimakopulos' view and his evocation of Bryden's texts.

27 Asimakopulos, "The Nature of Public Pensions and the Federal Budget."

28 Notice that if "pensions and charity" persist on a substantial scale, or are revived as a major explanation, the positive theory fails. Even after the first draft of this text was written, the importance of contemporary events as a test has been repeatedly illustrated in journalism from Ottawa.

29 See the budget of 28 June 1982. I have so far been unable – by telephone to the Montreal offices – to obtain clarification of inherently ambiguous passages in the official texts. The present value of the expropriation is in any case a sum of which the *floor* is a billion dollars, and the ceiling a number perhaps much higher.

30 Federal budget, 28 June 1982. Here, of course, is where the second bite may exist. What happens to the new supplement two years from now is difficult to discover.

31 Asimakopulos, "The Nature of Public Pensions and the Federal Budget," 4.

32 In economics, little that has a theoretical basis moves smoothly according to the hoped for. Disturbances are bound to happen. Which message will the events of the budget eventually tell?

33 Martin Feldstein, "The Optimal Financing of Social Security," discussion paper 388. (Cambridge, Mass.: Institute of Economic Research, Harvard University, 1974), 20 ff.

34 Ibid.

35 Ibid.

36 Canadian Labour Congress, "CLC Proposal for Pension Reform."

37 For those who care, the essential formula was translated into an almost unintelligible appendix (of mine – not Feldstein's); see Canadian Centre for Policy Alternatives, Conference Proceedings, series 1, 195. Working with a word processor is a task for retirement. Here I have decided to abandon all the items (non-zero labour elasticities, for example) that add nothing but meaningless billions to computations that (if meaningful at all) would be arbitrary over a range of trillions. Feldstein, naturally, is there to be consulted directly.

38 There are the magnitudes from the formula directly *à la* Feldstein. Notice that for u_1 and u_2 the underlying approximation is the $u=$ (Real Personal Income, 1974 dollars), $u_1 = \{[0.7/(0.7 - dT)(-d)] + 1\}/2$ and $u_2 = [(0.7/5)(-d) + 1]/2$, where the *numbers* are those of the 1974 tax system.

39 This is the principal route to getting rid of phantom accuracy.

40 How anyone can push ahead with eternal calculations, simple or complex, in a century that has seen, *inter al* two World Wars, one Great Depression, one oil crisis, and a contemporary scene of tragi-comedy – how anyone can push ahead with such arithmetic – bemuses this observer totally.

41 These search out maxima for each particular case. The numbers are not sensitive to the search.

42 Ramsey poses two difficulties for the state: how to decide on terminal capital, and how to handle the infinite bliss of short term pain for eternal gain.

CHAPTER TWELVE

Preface to
The Challenge of Full Employment

Half a century after Keynes published his *General Theory*, the great issue of policy he raised is still at the centre of political economy. In this volume, Diane Bellemare and Lise Poulin Simon reaffirm that full employment is a sharply defined idea, that programs of full employment can be realized in societies like our own, and that the advantage to well-being from implementing such programs is vast. Their investigation would have little foundation without a determined effort to clarify an inherited theory that is incomplete and badly confused: they have made the effort and, I think, with considerable success. Their investigation would have little purpose without a determined effort to deal with experience, to report on the world's use of Keynesian policies these fifty years and to infer from this history what Keynesian policy should consist of for our own society in the years ahead.

Like many economists who have debated social policy in the past decade, Bellemare and Poulin Simon have repeatedly found they must return to first principles. Ideas that were supposedly well established in the early postwar years have turned out to be half defined, ideas too much supported by rhetoric and not enough by science. Facts from those years that seemed representative those few decades back were more recently augmented by facts of a quite different pattern, uncomfortable facts that did not at all fit preconceptions. Argument that had a solid basis in reality, in economic laws inspired by common sense, has proved to be vulnerable to artificial schemes that are deliberately formal and deliberately precise. One might have found these schemes counterintuitive but could not ignore them or pretend common sense by itself was enough.

There are formidable difficulties, it turns out, in making the "great issue of policy" clear and operational. Bellemare and Poulin Simon (and others

In Diane Bellemare et Lise Poulin Simon, *Le défi de plein emploi* (Montréal: Éditions Saint-Martin, 1986), 1–12. This is the English original version.

in their camp) carry a burden of proof, for their opponents would be just as content with an issue that vanishes as with an issue that is rejected. In either case society would be directed to a "null policy." "Neoconservatism," as the authors name the ideology with which they dispute, does not (to my mind) have an independent intellectual existence. It is simply the complement of interventionist economics in the democratic state, and flourishes or retreats according to the failures and successes of intervention in theory and practice. In the academic world it is endogenous to political events, unoriginal, usually trivial, and basically tautological. This means the battle over intervention needs be fought only once, *not* twice, but also means it most certainly must be fought.

By 1944, by the time of the Normandy invasion, a powerful and talented bureaucracy (here, but elsewhere as well) had decided by way of Keynes, by way of the Great Depression, by way of the war itself, that full employment could be elevated from a pious promise to a hard political commitment. The population was not very demanding about the nuances of the commitment. Everyone had the fearful experience of the 1930s in mind and was ready to accept programs that simply said "never again." Classical economics had understood business cycles and was well aware of full employment and unemployment. True, *but* the employment was of fixed capital and not of workers. Now, as the war ended, the notion of assuring jobs to everyone would seem a feasible, an all-important remedy, but it would be identified only as a consequence of the disease rather than as an independent concept. One thing missed was that, radical as the new policies might seem, they pointed to concepts and interventions more radical still. As authority drained away from wartime governments, fuzziness about what the projected policies entailed would undermine their credibility.

Keynes *had* indicated where an independent concept could be found. There will be people in essentially similar circumstances, many of whom want paid jobs and can find them and some of whom want paid jobs and cannot find them, at least in some brief, inconsequential interval of time. Those "in essentially similar circumstances" have much the same training and skills, and have had much the same relation to where jobs are located. There exist people who by the details of this test are involuntarily unemployed, all those who according to the details cannot find paid jobs. *A commitment to full employment is then a commitment to treat involuntary unemployment as socially intolerable, and as requiring intervention by the State so that jobs will almost always be available.* The assurance of "equal" jobs would then be so near absolute that the occasional failure would entail compensation to the extent of the failure. In applying such a rule to real events there plainly would be much that was judgmental or arbitrary; but any version faithful to the Keynesian abstraction would be operational and "more radical still" *because* it was operational.

In deciding that full employment must be sharply defined, Bellemare and Poulin Simon have occupied a very strong theoretical position. Whether it can be remedied or not, all involuntary unemployment is a failure of capitalistic markets, a contradiction of the *law of one price*. Nothing could be more basic, for if some can sell their labour then, in principle, with properly functioning markets, all must be able to sell their labour. But the use of markets has been socially decided, so that the failure of markets is a social responsibility. Efficiency and equity require intervention, in general to supply missing jobs, at times to provide compensation where jobs are impossible to supply.

Here the authors are developing ideas they have introduced in other works and to which they now give a central role. From its very nature involuntary unemployment is a social responsibility because reliance on markets is a social choice. It is only collectively that we can and do choose that production be based on paid labour: no individual can make that election. Employment and involuntary unemployment take us from the domain of private goods to the domain of public goods (and of public "bads"!).

Just as *reliance* on labour markets is a public institution, so then is success in providing jobs a *public good*, a public good of immense importance. This is the central fact that determines the worth of full employment. If extra jobs are treated as private goods, their value to society will be calculated as the sum of what each of the newly hired workers produces, as the sum of private benefits. If, however, the jobs are treated as public goods then their value will be extended to include whatever benefits the rest of society receives from each new hiring. What the authors emphasize and reemphasize is that the public benefits are not some minor improvement on the conventional, "private" measure, but that they are the principal part of the total, correct measure. It is hardly exaggeration to say that even the algebraic sign of the "private" measure is secondary compared to public effects.

This is a very different viewpoint from that too casually taken when the Keynesian years began. Again it had been assumed that the evil of unemployment was so immediate an experience that exact analysis was unnecessary. Estimate the real national product with and without intervention. That would show billions lost to involuntary unemployment and must be more than enough to confirm common sense.

Alas, it has proved much *less* than enough, for as the years passed, costs were discovered that could be set against these private gains (and ironically, costs that were in the main social costs). There were inflationary effects probably generated by expansion, balance of payments difficulties, ideological disputes about intervention, and claims upon administrative skills not easily supplied in peacetime Canada. It is only when the social costs of involuntary unemployment are counted on the loss side that the goals of Bellemare and Poulin Simon are once again surely conformed to commonsense. The Keynesian case may be doubtful when social consequences are excluded. It carries all before it when they are not. Oversimplification at the beginning had wasted much of the Keynesian case.

Writer after writer in the classical tradition had pointed out what every editorialist declares instinctively. Years of economic prosperity are ranked not by a few percentage points one way or the other in real output, but by whether there is *general* prosperity and *shared* prosperity. Social well-being is affected more, a good deal more, by the relativities of incomes than their levels. Columnists mention every week how well things went for most of the 1950s and how badly they have gone these past ten years – yet in the postwar years real incomes per head have much more than doubled! One does not have to be as nostalgic as the columnists to give weight to other people's employment (obviously employment of relatives, of friends, of acquaintances, but crucially, employment anywhere in the society). And if one chooses, one can be quite as unsentimental about the business as Milton Friedman. I no doubt should rejoice about your good fortune when you find a job, but whether I do or not I shall find my own welfare increased. Vulgar as the ethics of the invisible hand may be, the invisible hand must grasp public goods!

Without full employment even the employed are at risk as they consider the future. Without full employment, the youth who are jobless for years first become aliens and then hostile aliens in their own society. They, like other groups of the jobless, lose the skills they had and then lose their capacity to acquire new skills. Ghettos are created in the cities and small wastelands amongst company towns. The mobility so vital to the logic of markets is reduced, and it is reduced for everyone wherever some are threatened by unemployment. Innovation, technical advance, improvements in productivity would be welcomed in a world of full employment (and, of course, are fundamental to the logic of markets), but they are resisted and even prevented whenever unemployment is extensive. *With* unemployment they are resisted and even prevented by precisely that same logic of markets. The ideologues too easily forget that logic. Let the assumption of virtual full employment be changed to the assumption of substantial unemployment and Adam Smith's conclusions must be precisely reversed!

Suppose it *were* true (to glance at today's panacea) that some kind of continental free trade would immensely improve the level and growth of Canada's real national product. (I think the project would be absurd if it were not impossible, but I would agree that there are many ventures in international trade – import substitution, for example – that could benefit "real national product".) We see every day, but no more here than in the United States, that skepticism about promises of full employment causes the project to be (rightly!) condemned by every particular interest it threatens and, what is more, to be condemned even more by enterprises that are vigorous than by those that unemployment has displaced. What world of fantasy do those economists inhabit who can look calmly on the loss of several hundred thousand actual jobs as a modest price for their leap of faith? But the point is not that *this* policy would be folly, but that without full employment good policies are as prohibited as bad, and the use of democratic government by a society is greatly curtailed (administration "yes," policy "no").

Bellemare and Poulin Simon turn to the empirical and prescriptive side of their work. They are well aware of how dangerous the charge could be that their analysis is well intentioned but Utopian. Challenges on technical issues are to be expected and no doubt will be the more formidable and lively the better this text is. But this is *political* economy: challenges at the political level will look for every chance to say *this* is not reality but idealistic dreaming.

No one could pretend, for example, that a complete commitment to full employment would erase (or compensate for) every degree of involuntary unemployment. In improving on the earlier Keynesian policies, a vital creation would be the sharply defined model of what the policies are about. It remains true that when the badly needed model is supplied, it can only approximate institutional facts, facts of geography, peculiarities of market structure, non-economic social forces. What is achieved would result from a strict logic and the excellent quality of the approximation. Experience has shown Keynesians of the 1980s that their proposals will work. The case for intervention today is not nearly as speculative as it was for early Keynesians. Now there is a wealth of statistical evidence from greatly varied sources.

In much the same way it is plain today that the postwar circumstances were so special as to suggest policy could be marvelously simple. Macroeconomic remedies would by themselves be almost enough. Microeconomic intervention would seem enormously complicated, but would not really be needed. (Keynes had advised that a somewhat comprehensive socialization of investment would be needed, but he advised so smoothly that few noticed how far this would take governments from the handful of society-wide instruments.) At the end of the war, though, governments owned strong bureaucracies and the political authority to use them. And also at the end of the war, aggregate demand was undiscriminating, supported by unfilled backlogs that justified almost any manipulation of its total. For a few years, but only for those particular few years, macroeconomic intervention would be sufficient to get the microeconomics right.

Under the scientific method, as everyone knows, there is one and only one correct method for choosing amongst competing theories. One looks to what the theories predict and compares the predictions with the facts. Some theories compare badly and should vanish. Other theories do well and become the best ideas we have – they can never have a final form or be certainly correct – of how things happen. Bellemare and Poulin Simon have subjected their own theory to this scientific canon in a most admirable way. For several years, they have studied employment policies as they have been actually implemented, for many countries and over considerable slices of history. They have been very diligent in hunting out the written record of these facts but have supplemented this use of documents with visits and conversations. They have been able to experience directly the institutions, the personalities, the day-to-day political forces, of which the written record is a result. Even readers who in the end are not persuaded by the text as a whole, will, I suspect, use and quietly applaud these chapters on "the facts."

There is a summary finding that could hardly be overemphasised. The record *might* have shown that full employment in a strict sense had never have been obtained in modern, market societies. Instead, the theory that continuing full employment is impossible has plainly been contradicted by the facts. For long periods of time and in several countries (Austria, Norway, and Sweden are the best examples) full employment in the strict sense *has* been experienced, and has been accompanied by the public benefits interventionist theory predicts. It is economists like Bellemare and Poulin Simon who are in step with the facts, and it is the most doctrinaire of their opponents who are contradicted by reality.

But the appeal to the scientific method carries the argument much further. There is a close correlation between the achievement of full employment and explicit political commitments, commitments to full employment as the prior goal of economic policy. Societies that treat full employment as the precondition of economic welfare, societies that then adopt interventionist policies to assure the goal is reached, those societies contain almost all the examples of full employment actually achieved. Societies (like Canada!) that have abandoned the goal or never sought it hardly ever show the goal being attained by chance. So-called natural rates of unemployment are much higher than rates assisted by policy. The historical record cannot, of course, guarantee causation but it is consistent with the interventionist theses under very demanding conditions.

A prior commitment to full employment, acceptance of interventionist policies, these appear as necessary conditions of success. Something more is needed to have sufficient conditions. (*Laissez-faire* is a single policy, intervention is a multitude of policies.) Bellemare and Poulin Simon have to sift the record to find the interventions that have been consistent with full employment and those that have not. Here they approach the particular clauses of a full-employment policy for our own society. There is a negative finding. In peacetime circumstances macroeconomic intervention – by itself – cannot provide full employment. If too much is asked of it, the result may even be worse than doing nothing. But after this important negative, there are the fascinating positive findings, all of which must be connected with the requirement for microeconomic intervention.

By the logic of things, intervention is never initiated from the private sector. The public sector, however, is not a homogeneous entity called "government," but a set of collective agencies of many kinds. One discovery is that interventionist policy draws upon the economic powers of the collective agencies as a whole. And here is another correlation: success with full employment is the greater the more of the agencies that are used (trade unions, cooperatives, local governments, federations of employers, and so on). But the public sector seen in this light can be very different from country to country. Austria may be as committed to full employment as Sweden is, but Austrian institutions are quite different from Swedish ones. It is inevitable that effective intervention will have one form in Austria, another in Sweden.

Our own history has created a "public sector" with a character quite unlike the public sector of the European examples (and for that matter, quite unlike either the public sector of the United States or the public sector of postwar Canada). Bellemare and Poulin Simon point to the switch in power from federal to provincial authorities, to the much-increased responsibilities and capacity of Quebec governments, to the network of local governments and local agencies, and to the agencies representing labour, business, women, the elderly. Interventionist policy will require coordination and so will depend on strong political commitments from Ottawa, from Quebec, and from the other provinces. Interventionist policy will require that tasks be proportioned to economic power within the agencies of the public sector, and so would replicate the large responsibilities for actual programs that belong to Quebec and the provinces. In this society as in the others, Keynesian programs do not require that new Keynesian institutions be invented, but that vigorous use be made of the institutions that history has created.

It is in these sections that the authors will encounter the practical people who will want to see whether full employment can actually be implemented (people elected and people who wish to be, assistant deputy ministers, officials of popular organizations – the pragmatists who care little about ideology but a great deal about feasibility). One might conclude the program the authors propose would frighten the pragmatists because of *complexity*. I think not. Bellemare and Poulin Simon are indeed suggesting a simplification of policy, for at every level of intervention they want as much delegation as possible to smaller and more local bodies. This is much in the spirit of participatory democracy, and both draws upon the European models just considered and would appeal to the instincts and experience of most of the pragmatists.

What *will* worry the pragmatists is whether *political will* exists in the public sector (or can be brought into existence). I think the authors show that the basic question about full employment is not whether a theory or a technically feasible program exists, but whether the Canadian political system can put a feasible program into operation. Do our institutions, does our history, allow our democratic state to intervene on the scale full employment would require? The European models cannot decide the question. Again, institutions and circumstance give political will a different domain from one country to another. One has little difficulty with the program advocated in this book, little doubt about whether it is technically possible. Just as the case is with the authors, though, one can only hope rather than predict that this society has a political will that can be harnessed for economic welfare. But if everything finally turns upon political will, what role could such a book as this have in practical affairs? The authors can hope to persuade us of exactly this: that with political will our society can be greatly enriched. The stock of political will may not be easily varied, but neither is it a given of nature. As this work is studied by the pragmatists, to the extent that they are convinced, they will help generate political will. And with respect to full employment, though Bellemare and Poulin Simon cannot accomplish more, what political economist would wish to attempt less? These two authors, it seems to me, have offered a considerable contribution to our welfare.